2001 GAMES

(and counting)

Book Design & Production:
Columbus Publishing Lab
www.ColumbusPublishingLab.com

Copyright © 2022 by
Steve Basford
LCCN: 2022913062

Paperback ISBN: 978-1-63337-648-9
E-Book ISBN: 978-1-63337-652-6

Printed in the United States of America
1 3 5 7 9 10 8 6 4 2

2001 GAMES

(and counting)

A SPORTS ODYSSEY

Steve Basford

proving
press

TABLE OF CONTENTS

FOREWORD

by Randy Rhinehart

TRYING TO PAINT A PICTURE of Steve Basford in one paragraph is like condensing *Gone With The Wind* into a 30 second movie trailer. I've known Steve Basford for half of my 65 years, and I'll never understand him. I mean that in the most complimentary way possible. As a statistician, Steve is the closest thing to a human computer that you'll ever meet. He anticipates trends before the first event in the chain ever happens. Then after being as analytic as any artificial intelligence form could be, he can turn on his people skills and impress you as a sports diplomat. Most importantly, Steve fluidly adjusts to sports and broadcast partners like nobody else I've ever met. Preparation is never a question with Steve. If you can use all the information he supplies in one broadcast, that's the main issue. He's there when you need him, whether it's at work or something in your personal life. Steve is there without question. You search a lifetime for a Steve Basford. I'm one of the lucky ones that he found. His stories are worth the read. Thanks, Steve, for always being there, and there, and there …

Randy Rhinehart is a veteran sportscaster in Central Ohio.

FOREWORD

by Steve Geiger

I HAVE HAD THE PLEASURE of broadcasting athletic events with my good friend Steve Basford for 13 years. He does the play-by-play, and I provide the color. We have worked together at Ohio Wesleyan University broadcasting football, men's basketball, and women's basketball for the past nine years. Steve is a true professional, and he has taught me how to plan, prepare, and perform a live broadcast. We do not have a stat team, so Steve does all the research. Steve always does an excellent job calling a game, he is smooth and steady. He always gives me plenty of time and space to provide my analysis. Steve and I have a great time broadcasting together. It is fun, but always professional. I always try to stump him on the air, but he is always prepared. One of Steve's most impressive traits is how he can precisely recall important details of who and how the games were won and lost from previous seasons. Steve has an outstanding resume of high school and college games that he has called over the past several decades. I look forward to reading his books, because I know that they will be entertaining, insightful, and full of great stories and impressive statistics.

Steve Geiger is a former Ohio Wesleyan basketball player and a color analyst for Ohio Wesleyan basketball and football.

INTRODUCTION

ON FEBRUARY 8, 1975, I worked the stats and did some color commentary for the Upper Arlington vs. Marietta high school boys' basketball game broadcast on Time Warner cable TV in Columbus, Ohio. I know this date for a fact, because I logged it on a sheet of notebook paper. By logging it, I must have somehow known that I would be working on more games in the future.

On February 15, I noted a second game, Upper Arlington vs. Westerville–the only high school in Westerville at the time, as opposed to three now–also on Time Warner cable TV. That game was so significant that a full story on it appeared on the second page of the *Columbus Dispatch* sports section the next day. A player on the Westerville team was Ed Calo, and the *Dispatch* shows that he had 13 points in the game and averaged 14.5 points per game in the 12 conference games. Ed went on to be the highly-successful coach at his alma mater, which would be re-named Westerville South when Westerville North opened. He won the 2016 Division I state championship with a team that featured future Ohio State players Kaleb and Andre Wesson. The new court at South was named in Calo's honor when the gym opened in the fall of 2020. I would do the play-by-play for a few games where he was coaching. To give you an idea of how long I have been doing these gigs: in recent years, I have also done the play-by-play for games where Ed's son Anthony was coaching the Olentangy Orange High School team.

In those two games, Rob Hardy of Upper Arlington, who would play at Duke, had 18 and 19 points. And, I was a good-luck charm for my alma mater, with Upper Arlington winning both games.

For my color commentary in that first game, I am not bragging about it. I recall that for a few of my first games where I did color commentary, I mostly talked about a player's scoring average and highest scoring game, though I was able to share what I knew about the teams' and coaches' histories fairly well. I had done my research for the scoring by saving all the high school box scores from the local newspapers--the *Columbus Dispatch* and the *Columbus Citizen-Journal*. These days, box scores no longer appear in the *Dispatch*--the lone remaining Columbus newspaper--and are rarely found online.

I soon learned the meaning of the word "mundane", when Red Jamison, a Warner QUBE cable TV play-by-play sportscaster, used that word in his office in giving me feedback. He did say that he liked the background information that I was able to provide–"You've got that stuff coming out of your ears." On another occasion, I asked a friend to watch a replay of one of my first games with me. When it was over, he said "Well, you projected well", which sent a message to me, loud and clear.

As the years went by, I continued to handwrite my games on my log. Up through 1993 (game #337), I also noted who the broadcasters were, a practice that I wished I had continued. In recent years, I started to note the score, to remind myself of monumental games, another practice that I wish that I had done from the beginning for every game. It's interesting to see how my handwriting has changed over the years, from a finer to a broader style. I wish that I had kept more extensive notes, since by looking at my log, I do not recall the details of events such as the Clark Kellogg 3-on-3 basketball tournament in August 2000 or the Colorado State vs. Louisville women's basketball game in 2001. By doing a web search for that Colorado State vs. Louisville game, I learned that it was the championship game of the two-day Women's Sports Foundation Classic tournament, played at Ohio State's Jerome Schottenstein Center. It was the day after I did the play-by-play for the Oregon Clay at Findlay High School boys basketball game, televised on Time Warner Cable in northwest Ohio; that game is the last time that I have appeared on camera (no wisecracks, please).

On May 1, 2021, I worked my 2,001st game, which includes roles as play-by-play broadcaster, color broadcaster, statistician, game reporter, scorekeeper, two games as a public address announcer, four games as a timeout coordinator, and one game as a parabolic microphone operator. I was once offered a gig to work bull riding for $275--I have no idea what my role would have been--but had to pass, since it was on the same day as an Ohio State football game.

The number "2001" has a nice ring to it, since that was the year that Jim Tressel became the Ohio State football head coach, producing a win over Michigan in Ann Arbor that year and leading to a national championship in 2002, Ohio State's first national championship accomplished on the playing field since 1968.

I wrestled (no pun intended) with whether to keep "2001" in the title of this book, having surpassed 2,100 games a year later. Naturally, "2100 Games A Sports Odyssey" doesn't have the same recognition factor. The word "counting" is pertinent, in that I have always loved numbers and counting items in a list. Jerry Lucas, the basketball star and mental genius, said that as a kid, he would count the number of painted center stripes per mile on a road as his family took a drive, as mentioned in the October 8, 1973 *Sports Illustrated*. On one of my Psychology class exams in college, one of the questions had a list of about a dozen behaviors in the left column and a set of interpretations, listed randomly, in the right column, and we students were to match them up. For something like "continuously counting the number of steps in a stairway", I matched it with "this is normal behavior", when the correct answer was "obsessive/compulsive". That shows you where my head is!

I learned recently that I am in good company regarding my handwritten log of games. In the book on the legendary Duke University basketball coach, *Coach K: The Rise and Reign of Mike Krzyzewski*, the author Ian O'Connor wrote: "Emily [Mike's mother] kept a handwritten journal of every game her son coached over twenty-one seasons at Army and Duke, including the name of every opponent and every score, the date of the game, and a *W* or an *L* to signify a win or a loss." Coincidentally, both Mrs. Krzyzewski and I started our record keeping in 1975.

The sports that I have worked include NBA basketball, college basketball, high school basketball, men's semi-pro football, college football, high school football, women's semi-pro football, arena football, major league baseball, minor league baseball, college baseball, high school baseball, college softball, high school softball, college volleyball, high school volleyball, Major League Soccer, college lacrosse, high school lacrosse, high school wrestling, college ice hockey, high school ice hockey, and high school field hockey. I was also hired to work stats for boxing matches, and I did perform the duty somewhat, only by relaying Mark "Munch" Bishop's scoring decisions to the graphics staff in the production truck.

The 2013-2014 school year was especially memorable. I started a new gig of Columbus Academy High School football play-by-play for the Gameday Broadcasting Sports Network, started a new gig of Ohio Wesleyan University football and men's and women's basketball play-by-play (which included calling a historic women's basketball win over DePauw), worked the stats for the boys high school basketball championship game where my alma mater Upper Arlington lost in overtime, and started a new gig of calling Gahanna Lincoln High School baseball, which took me to Huntington Park--the home of the Columbus Clippers--for the semifinal championship game.

In the fall, a typical weekend for many years had me working the stats on a televised Thursday night high school football game, calling a high school football game on Friday night, and either working on the official stats crew for Ohio State football or calling an Ohio Wesleyan football game on Saturday. On Sunday, I was all footballed-out.

I have called games, worked the stats, or done reports for these media:

- Television: ESPN, NBC, the Big Ten Network, Columbus Sports Network, Ohio News Network, Sports Channel, Coaxial Communications, Insight Communications, Metrosports (based in Rockville, Maryland); Warner QUBE, Spectrum Cable, WCMH-TV and low-power Channel 8 (W08BV) in Columbus; the CW Columbus (WWHO-TV, Channel 53), WXIX-TV in Cincinnati, and WVIZ-TV in Cleveland
- Radio: WMNI-AM, WTVN-AM, and St. Gabriel Catholic Radio (820 AM) in Columbus; WCVO-FM in Gahanna; WBBY-FM in Westerville; WMOA-AM in Marietta; WUCO-FM in Marysville; and WFCO-FM and WLOH-AM in Lancaster
- Internet stream: the Gameday Broadcasting Sports Network, Mega Sports News, Upper Arlington Radio, Ohio Wesleyan University, and Capital University

In 1975, if someone had told me that I would go on to interact at games or interviews with these below, I would have said *Yeah, right!*

- The only two-time winner of the Heisman Trophy
- The all-time winningest coach in women's college basketball, who also has three national championships

- Other basketball coaches who had won championships at the high school, college, and professional level
- A basketball coach who was the interim coach at Duke when Mike Krzyzewski had a health issue
- A basketball player who be a long-time San Antonio Spurs assistant coach and had been a ball boy for John Wooden's 1975 NCAA Championship UCLA team
- The Ohio State basketball player who made the winning three-point shot against Illinois–ranked #1 with a 29-0 record at the time–in 2005 to give the Illini their only regular season loss
- A member of a college Division III national championship basketball team
- The all-time scoring leader in Ohio high school basketball, at the time
- A future college basketball scout for the Golden State Warriors
- Former major league baseball players–one of whom was a relief pitcher in the majors and hit a home run on the first pitch that he saw in the big leagues, as a pinch hitter; another who pitched in a World Series; and another who was a member of a World Series championship team
- A future NBA player
- Former NFL players, including first round draft picks and a receiver who led the NFL in receiving touchdowns twice
- A coach who coached in three NFL championship games
- An NFL official who worked in three Super Bowls
- An Arena Football League Most Valuable Player who was also a two-time ArenaBowl Most Valuable Player

- A quarterback of a national championship college football team, a backup quarterback of another national championship college football team, and a winning quarterback of a Rose Bowl
- The only Ohio State quarterback to date to pass for at least 2,000 yards in three straight seasons
- A three-time college football all-American as a punter
- A kicker who holds a share of the record for the most field goals in a Rose Bowl
- The only coach to win the Rose Bowl for a Big Ten team and for a Pac-12 team
- A former assistant coach under Earle Bruce at Ohio State
- A volleyball coach who won three national championships
- A future ESPN broadcaster
- Major league baseball broadcasters, who would also appear in movies
- Several members of a Hall of Fame
- Two Olympians
- Several book authors
- A distance runner who was featured in *Sports Illustrated*
- Marathon winners
- A triathlon winner
- The man who created the Whiteout at Penn State football games

In 1975, if someone had told me that I would go on to broadcast or do the stats for high school games that would feature these below, I would have said *No way!*

- The 1986 Baseball America National Player of the Year, later the agent for baseball stars Derek Jeter, Freddie

Freeman, Paul Goldschmidt, Zack Greinke, Clayton Kershaw, and Ryan Howard
- A total of eight points scored in three football games, in the span of six seasons
- A football game that needed five overtimes
- Future NFL players, including one who was the number one player selected in an NFL draft and who was also the runner-up for the Heisman Trophy, another who was a future Heisman Trophy winning quarterback, another who was a future winner of the Butkus Award, and another who was a future winner of the Rotary Lombardi Award
- Two football players in the same game who would go on to score a touchdown in a Rose Bowl, two years apart
- Future major league baseball players, including one who also managed a World Series team
- The all-time scoring leader in Ohio high school basketball
- A future owner of a Major League Soccer team

This book is a recap of experiences from my broadcasting, stats work, and other duties as assigned; highs and lows; hits and misses; and adventures. Obviously, my total number of games worked is a drop in the bucket compared to those of Vin Scully, who called baseball games for 67 seasons for the Brooklyn and Los Angeles Dodgers, but he and I are at opposite ends of the spectrum; I am at the Walter Mitty end.

Some of the memorable times over the years are:

- In 1982, I worked the stats for the Ohio State football win over Michigan for WOSU-TV, then took off to Dayton with WOSU's color analyst Jeff Logan to work the stats for a televised high school football playoff game that night.

- On one Saturday in 2018, I called both the Ohio Wesleyan men's and women's basketball games, which ended around 5:00, then sped the 18 miles from Delaware to Dublin in time to set up and call the Dublin Jerome boys' basketball game at 6:00.

- On another occasion, I called an Ohio Wesleyan baseball game at 3:00 and was scheduled to call a Dublin Jerome High School basketball game at 7:00 at Jonathan Alder High School in Plain City, a 35 minute drive away. I jokingly asked the umpires to make sure that the game ended no later than 6:00, and they assured me that it would. However, the baseball game ended at 6:20. Luckily, I had arranged for Chris Intihar to set up and call the basketball game with Jim Sanders if I were to be late, which turned out to be the case. Chris compared my two-sports-in-one-day situation to the time in 1992 that Deion Sanders tried to play two sports in one day; he played in an NFL game for the Atlanta Falcons and flew to join the Atlanta Braves for a baseball playoff game, but did not get into that game.

- From January 14 through February 23 of 2019, seven of my 19 basketball games went into overtime--three Ohio Wesleyan men's games, three Dublin Jerome boys games, and one Ohio Wesleyan women's game. This included a group of three out of five games in the span of nine days.

- In the span of 13 days between March 11 and March 23 of 2021, I called eight games in five different Ohio Wesleyan sports--men's basketball, women's basketball, football, baseball, and softball. The football game in a non-traditional month was a result of the 2020-2021 pandemic; Ohio Wesleyan had no games in the fall, but arranged three games in March.

CHAPTER 1

Getting Started

THE BEST ADVICE THAT MY DAD ever gave me was in the "When I was your age ..." category. When I was nine years old, I was reading the Freddy the Pig books; Freddy and his other animal friends who could talk lived on a farm in rural upstate New York. My dad took me aside and said "When I was your age, I read Ivanhoe." I didn't switch to books like Ivanhoe, but I did switch to biographies of past presidents (please, no wisecracks about the low number of them!) and sports figures. The Upper Arlington Public Library had several baseball biographies written by Milton J. Shapiro--titles such as The Warren Spahn Story, The Willie Mays Story, and The Hank Aaron Story. I had no idea who the player Billy Martin was, but since a book had a baseball player on the cover and was titled The Billy Martin Story, I read it, too. These books served as a crash course on baseball history for me and would become valuable years later.

While most kids were idolizing athletes, I was also locking in on sportscasters. I grew up listening to Jimmy Crum call televised Ohio State basketball games on Channel 4 in the 1960s. When Jimmy Crum opened with, "Live from Saint John Arena...", I would get goose bumps. The word *Saint* made me think that this was a holy shrine. I have his book,

"How About That!", which bears his autograph and Ohio State's coach Fred Taylor's autograph.

When I heard that Jerry Lucas was 6'8" tall, I thought that he must be the tallest person in the world, only to learn that every team had a player that tall. My grandfather lived with us, and I asked him if Mel Nowell's name was pronounced "No-well" with two syllables, and he misled me by saying that it was.

To imitate football broadcasters, I took my pillow that had vertical stripes, which conjured up an image of a football field for me, and I would use it for play-by-play: "He's at the 40 ... the 30 ... the 20 ..."

The equivalent of a smartphone in the 1960s as the must-have gadget for kids was a transistor radio, mainly to tune in to the rock-and-roll stations—for me and my friends, it was WCOL, 1230 AM. I would ride my bicycle to a record store in the Lane Avenue Shopping Center each week to get the WCOL top 40 survey, which was on a piece of paper that was the size of a regular envelope. On occasion, I would see Woody Hayes's wife, Anne, at the Super Duper in the same shopping center, which was near their house. I earned my radio as my commission for selling personalized Christmas cards; if you sold a specified number of cards, you received a transistor radio. I don't recall if there were other prizes, but they would not have interested me. I was a door-to-door salesman, trying to sell the cards to families in our neighborhood. The radio that arrived in the mail did not look like the one in the brochure, go figure, but I didn't care.

It also opened the world of sports fandom and sportscasters to this youngster. I would use it to listen to Cincinnati Royals NBA games under the covers when I should have been sleeping. A few years ago, I had a chat with former Royals player Arlen Bockhorn—I had caught the tail end of his Royals career in the 1960s—while working the stats at a televised Dayton Flyers game that he was broadcasting for their radio network. I had obtained Oscar Robertson's autograph when he appeared at the downtown Lazarus department store in the 1960s. I still have a program from the 1st Annual Youth Charities Benefit Pro-Am game in 1974, played in St. John Arena, which bears the autograph of Jack Twyman, a former Royals star.

I was hooked on the Cincinnati Royals when Ohio State's Jerry Lucas joined the team in the 1963-1964 season. My dad and I would listen to their games, broadcast by Ed Kennedy on WLW radio in Cincinnati. My mother was supportive of my interest. One morning, when she woke me up, she said "Lucas scored nine points in the first quarter last night, but he was injured and missed the rest of the game." Having a doubt about her facts, I picked up the Sports section of the newspaper and read "In the Royals game last night, Jerry Lucas scored nine points in the first quarter, but he was injured and missed the rest of the game." My grade school class took a field trip to see the Ohio State team--which had Lucas, John Havlicek, Mel Nowell, Larry Siegfried, and Bob Knight--practice in St. John Arena. I had one of Lucas's many books, *The Memory Book*, co-authored by Harry Lorayne, but I don't know where it is [Insert joke here]; I know that I loaned it to a co-worker, but he says that he can't find it. One of Lucas's many mental exercises was to rearrange the letters in a word or phrase into alphabetical order; his example was that his name evolved into *Ejrry Aclsu*. In a college programming class, I tried to write a program that would do that, but was unsuccessful. He was on the Tonight Show once and challenged Johnny Carson to rearrange the letters of "floor", which Johnny fell for.

In the 1964-1965 NBA season, I kept a log of Jerry Lucas's scoring stats for every game, calculating his average through each completed game. While I no longer have it, a web search confirms my recollection that he had 12 field goals and one free throw for 25 points in the 1965 All-Star Game in St. Louis, where he was named the Most Valuable Player and won a motorcycle. My dad was at that game, and I still have his ticket.

I would listen to Jim Martin call the Columbus Jets minor league baseball games–the Jets were the AAA affiliate of the Pittsburgh Pirates and supplied the bulk of the stars on the Pirates' 1971 World Series championship team–on WMNI-AM (1965-1967) and WTVN-AM (1968-1969). In 1970, Jim teamed up with Joe Hill. *Note: Thanks to Joe Santry, the Historian, Media Director, and Director of Communications for the Columbus Clippers minor league team for supplying these details.* One of Jim's sayings was to call the outfielders the "sky patrol". Another, to describe a double play, was "You put them on, and you take them off."

In 1974--coinciding with Marty Brennaman's first year calling Cincinnati Reds games on WLW Radio--I kept score for over 70 Reds games either in person at Riverfront Stadium or by listening to the entire game on the radio. If you score that many games in a year, you are bound to learn a lot about baseball and sportscasting.

In those days, it was common for teams to produce a long-playing record album with their radio highlights from a memorable year. I had such albums from the 1972 and 1973 Cincinnati Reds seasons, with Al Michaels and Joe Nuxhall calling the games, and from the 1972 Los Angeles Lakers' 33-game winning streak, becoming a fan of the Lakers' play-by-play announcer Chick Hearn. I was a huge Lakers fan, having attended three games at the Fabulous Forum while on Rose Bowl trips. I had ordered the Lakers album, yearbook, program from their 1972 championship, and keychain from a Lakers catalog; it was a bad omen when the keychain broke as the Lakers were losing to the New York Knicks in the 1973 finals. I have stolen some of Chick's sayings to use in my broadcasts, but have tried to avoid his original, colorful ones. Of course, I have read the books "You Can't Make This Up" by Al Michaels, "Chick: His Unpublished Memoirs and the Memories of Those Who Knew Him" by Chick Hearn, and "So You Want To Be A Sportscaster" by Ken Coleman, among many other books on sportscasters.

Starting in the 1970s, when I went to Ohio State basketball games in St. John Arena, I would buy the program. For many years, it was 6 inches by 9 inches, costing 10 cents–I had a friend who sold them, and he made

4

a few cents for each one that he sold–and had eight pages, with a grid with the players and numbers so that you could keep score for each player, which I did. The programs for the 1973-1974 season expanded to a size of 8 ½ by 11 inches, at a cost of 25 cents. I bound the programs–from the 1970-1971 season through the 1982-1983 season–and some box scores from newspapers, and some handwritten game scoring sheets in a notebook, which I still have. I was surprised to see that Coach Taylor typically used only a few reserves in the 1970-1971 season, even in a comfortable win. In the 91-75 win over Indiana to clinch the Big Ten championship, he used only two.

The oldest program that I have is from the February 15, 1964 game against Wisconsin; all five of us in my family went to this game in which Gary Bradds of Ohio State scored 40 points, the last of his six straight games with at least 40 points. Late in the game, he went to the free throw line to shoot two free throws, having scored 38 points to that point and with his replacement at the scorer's table, ready to come in, and he made them both. Interestingly, that 1964 program shows the conference as the Western Conference instead of the Big Ten, and lists the 18-member freshman team, which included future MLB pitcher Steve Arlin. When I was in high school, Gary conducted a basketball camp one summer at my Tremont Elementary School; I remember the defensive drills and that he complimented me on my rebounding. My family took a vacation to Michigan during the camp sessions, and when I got back, he said that I looked rusty.

At first when keeping score, I would circle the digits as the player recorded a field goal, free throw, or foul, and use a vertical line to separate the first half from the second half. I changed my system later by marking an X on the digits for the second half and drawing a rectangle around the digits for overtime. I would also track turnovers, using hash marks. While watching games on TV, I would often keep player scoring and fouls stats, and occasionally a running score, using a two-character code for the player, the first two letters of his last name. At first, I would use only a hash mark to record each field goal, free throw, and foul, separating the first and second half counts, and later implemented the circles-and-X's system.

My prized programs of the 1977-1978 and 1978-1979 seasons are from the games against Michigan State. Despite the blizzard of January 1978, there was no way that I was going to miss seeing the Spartans' player listed in the program as Earvin Johnson, more commonly known as Magic Johnson. After the game, I saw people walking across the Olentangy River … literally, walking on the frozen river instead of on the bridge.

One of my favorite programs illustrates that I had the foresight to bring both a black-ink pen and a red-ink pen, the red one to be used for overtime. This particular scoresheet is filled with black and red markings. Whenever the subject of the best home OSU basketball games comes up-- the two-overtime Indiana game in 1991? Illinois 2005? Wisconsin 2007?-- my list includes the three-overtime, 93-92 win over Purdue in 1981. There wasn't much riding on it--the Buckeyes had a 12-13 record at the time and were on a five-game losing streak--but for sheer drama, it belongs. The Buckeyes committed 40 fouls, with six players fouling out, and they were down to five players, with one playing with four fouls. Ed Major had scored one point through the previous 25 games but scored eight, including the winning shot with six seconds remaining. Purdue's Kevin Stallings—he would become a college coach at Illinois State, Vanderbilt, and Pittsburgh—had a last shot that was off the mark.

Stallings was not the only future coach to appear in St. John Arena that season; Isiah Thomas of Indiana would go on to coach the Indiana Pacers and New York Knicks, Randy Wittman of Indiana would go on to coach the Cleveland Cavaliers, Minnesota Timberwolves, and Washington Wizards, and David Blatt of Princeton would go on to coach the Cleveland Cavaliers to the 2015 NBA finals, losing to Golden State. The schedule in the programs that season had "All Home Games Begin at 8:10", though the Indiana game was indicated with "Time to be Announced".

If you are wondering how someone can go crazy cheering his team on and keeping score at the same time? As Benjamin Franklin said, "Energy and persistence conquer all things."

I still have my two programs from the 1970 NCAA Mideast Regional Tournament, played in St. John Arena. They contain 19 autographs, including those of future NBA players Austin Carr of Notre Dame, Jim Cleamons and Dave Sorenson of Ohio State, and Artis Gilmore (he gave me a glare when I asked him) of Jacksonville; sportscaster Curt Gowdy; Jacksonville's coach Joe Williams; and Fred Taylor. I tried to get Notre Dame's coach Johnny Dee's autograph when he walked up to chat with Curt Gowdy after the consolation game, but he declined. I kept score of all four of the games, of course, which includes Austin Carr scoring 52 and 45 points in his two Notre Dame games. Part of a page of one of the programs is missing, because I cut out the application for tickets for the 1971 Final Four, to be played in the Houston Astrodome. I did win the tickets, but I had to put them on sale in an ad in the *Columbus Dispatch*, since I had blown my travel budget that year on the trip to the 1971 Rose Bowl.

When watching the Buckeyes football team on TV when they played UCLA in the Los Angeles Coliseum in 1975, I tracked each player's stats on my own, and my stats were very close to the official stats. Three years later, I would be working the OSU stats in a paid capacity for Warner QUBE, at the Indiana football game in Bloomington in 1978.

When I applied for jobs at Ohio State University in 1976, a question on the application form was the type of job that I was interested in. I filled in "statistician for the basketball team", since that was a dream job and since I had a friend who had been a manager for the team. After submitting the form, I was told that under the Classified Civil Service rules, I could not apply for a specific position in a specific department. So, I "settled" for a position in the Office of Personnel Services--later re-named to the Office of Human Resources--which turned out fairly well for me, as I stayed there for 45 years. Ironically, in less than three years of stating that I wanted to be a statistician for the basketball team, I would work the stats for that 1978 football game at Indiana for Warner QUBE.

All kids write a fan letter to their favorite athlete, right? Not me, I wrote one to Alan Roth, whose name came up as a statistician every time that Curt Gowdy called a baseball game on NBC. Mr. Roth passed away in 1992, and shortly after his death, his executor found my letter and returned it to me, and we had a chat on the phone.

I sent letters to several organizations In the 1970s and 1980s, asking if they could use my services, and I have kept the letters of responses from:

- The Director of Security (interesting!) of the Office of the Commissioner of Major League Baseball. They sent me the list of the mailing addresses for every major league team, the American League Office, the National League Office, and the National Association of Professional Baseball Leagues, in case I wanted to contact any of them for jobs.
- Bob Howsam, President of the Cincinnati Reds
- The University of Cincinnati Department of Athletics–I had sent a general inquiry about jobs and received a reply that the position of Assistant Sports Information Director had been filled. I guess that my interest had sparked a belief that I may have been qualified for that!
- The Cincinnati Stingers of the World Hockey Association, before they started their first season
- SportsVision in Chicago, whose slogan on their letterhead was "Chicago's Winners on Cable"
- WTTV in Indianapolis
- WVIZ-TV in Cleveland–ironically, 19 years later, I would work the stats for a few high school football playoff games for them.

Fast-forward over the years: I give myself credit for taking the initiative several times to seek out broadcast opportunities. As the Roman philosopher Seneca said, "Luck Is what happens when preparation meets opportunity." My four years of taking Latin in high school must have had some value.

For many years, I would go to the boys' high school basketball tournament games at the Coliseum on the Ohio State Fairgrounds as a basketball junkie, seeing three or more games in a day. In 1975, I saw a banner for WBBY-FM (103.9 FM) hanging from the Coliseum's press box. I had no idea what WBBY was all about, nor did I care. In an article in the *Agenda, Ann Arbor's Alternative Newsmonthly* in February of 1988, Linda Yohn–the former music director of WEMU, the NPR/Jazz station at Eastern Michigan University–describes her WBBY experience as in "... a brick shack off the side of a cow pasture in Sunbury, Ohio". In documents, WBBY was associated with the city of Westerville.

The *Broadcasting Yearbook 1976* for WBBY has "Format: Old gold, rock". One Ohio State men's basketball program in the 1978-1979 season has an ad for "104FM WBBY The Jazz Pocket", and another has, under the heading BUCKEYE BASKETBALL BOOSTERS: "WBBY - FM - 104 ... 24 HOUR JAZZ ... Sunbury, Ohio". According to the April 15, 1978 edition of the *Radio World* publication, "Jazz is now being programmed 24 hours a day ... WBBY-FM, serving Columbus, has dropped its daytime top 40 programming and replaced it with jazz."

Prior to the 1975-1976 season, I sent a letter to WBBY, asking if they would consider using me for their broadcasts. At that point, I had a total of two games experience, with minimal color commentary. Incredibly, I received a phone call from WBBY-FM early one February morning to offer me the opportunity to do the color commentary for a game. I was still living with my parents at the time, and my mother woke me up to tell me that I had a call from the station founder, William "Wild Bill" Bates. If my mother were alive today, she would confirm that after the call, where

I naturally said yes, I was trembling with nerves and excitement at the breakfast table, even though the game was a few days away. Since I had been half-asleep when I took the call, I called the station later to confirm what I understood--that the game was Sunbury Big Walnut vs. North Union, to be played at a neutral site, Hayes High School in Delaware.

On game day, since I was unfamiliar with the city of Delaware and had no idea where Delaware Hayes High School was, I stopped at Ohio Wesleyan University to get directions. Ironically, Delaware would eventually be my home away from home starting 37 years later, when I became the play-by-play broadcaster for Ohio Wesleyan football, baseball, softball, and men's and women's basketball. I would also make several trips to Delaware Hayes High School to call football and basketball games for WINF-FM in 2010-2011 and in the 2010s for the Gameday Broadcasting Sports Network, an Internet streaming company. I always looked forward to football and basketball games at Delaware Hayes, since their popcorn at the concession stands was the best.

Bill Bates had founded the station in 1969 and was known for, among other things, hosting a weekly radio program called "Wild Bill's Disco". One famous person who was a disc jockey for WBBY-FM was Diane Townsley at age 19, who has since written the book " 'Twas the Night Before 'Christ' mas" and in 2011 became the host of "The Date With Diane Show" (thedatewithdianeshow.com), which was syndicated and heard around the world. She was documented in *TV Radio Mirror Magazine* with "... the only girl disc jockey in Central Ohio and am on the air for a total of 33 hours a week, which is a record for a personality in our area.", and on the cover of *TV Picture Life magazine* with "Personality of the Month/In Columbus, the Sweetest Sound Around is Diane Townsley/ WBBY-FM Radio".

Several other notable personalities worked for WBBY. Michael Perkins wrote the book about the Leveque Tower in Columbus, "Leveque: The First Complete Story of Columbus' Greatest Skyscraper".

His biography in it describes him as "a programmer, producer, talk show host, journalist, photographer, and illustrator for WBBY, WTVN, and other regional media companies." In the book, he talks about John Fraim, who was best known as the morning radio personality on WTVN radio in the 1960's and 1970's; John had an apartment on the 44th floor of the tower and was able in July of 1986 "... to provide WBBY listeners with details on a giant sinkhole that had opened up along Broad Street, swallowing up an entire Mercedes in the process." Bill Moss was a politician who "had unsuccessful runs for mayor of Columbus and for seats in the US as well as the Ohio House of Representatives", as mentioned in an NPR.org item. He was also an author and a member of the board of education for the Columbus City School District. His photos and accounts of his community activities appear in the "Columbus Radio" book. Terri Blair later worked at Channel 6 and married the famous music composer, Marvin Hamlish.

The *Popular Communications* publication for April 1991 has "... the sad news of the loss of WBBY, 103.9MHz. This was one of the few stations in the nation that played jazz, full time ... WBBY's last day was December 31st, 1990."

My second take-the-initiative experience was in 1981, when I saw in the *Columbus Dispatch* "Sports On The Air" section that WCVO-FM (104.9 FM, though "105 FM" would appear often in print) was broadcasting the New Albany at Grandview Heights high school basketball game. Like a salesperson making a "cold call", I showed up at the game and asked the broadcast crew if they wanted someone to keep stats for the game. I had a resume in hand, with 28 games experience to that point, and I was hired on the spot! The producer was Paul Gierman, who lived in Grandview Heights and was a founding board member and volunteer at WCVO-FM for many years, and he also invited me to ride with him to the following week's game at Gahanna Lincoln High School. At that game against Groveport Madison, he had me do two quarters of play-by-play and two of color. So, after a three year break from being on the air, I was back in the saddle as a sportscaster. This started a gig that would last for ten years for WCVO-FM, doing both play-by-play and color for basketball and football.

I recently found a couple dozen cassette tapes containing football and basketball games that I had called in the 1980s for WCVO-FM. At the time, I had a radio with an integrated tape recorder, and when you pressed the right buttons, it would record whatever you tuned the radio to. I would have my mother do that for me for some of my games. For other games, our Sports Director/my broadcast partner Stu Mason would make a copy of his tape for me.

A co-worker once reminded me of the saying "when one door closes, another one opens". That definitely applies to my third take-the-initiative experience, in 2008. When Columbus Sports Network--I did the stats for several of their televised games–went out of business, this meant that I was unemployed for working high school games in some capacity after about 27 years ... but for only one game, missing out on the first game of the season. During the week leading up to the second game of the year, I checked the newspaper listings of games being broadcast and found that WINF-FM (101.9 FM, now 98.5 FM) was carrying games in Delaware County. I gave them a call offering to do the stats, and Jason Whitt, the play-by-play broadcaster called me back. He said "sure ... but how much do you want to be paid?" Like the Godfather, I made him an offer that he couldn't refuse; I said that I would do it for free. I did the stats gig for two years, for their football and basketball games, and did get compensated ... a $10.00 Pizza Hut coupon for each game.

A couple of times, Jason had to pass on calling a game and had me take his place. I had to shake off about 18 years of rust from not calling games. One of the games was Dublin Jerome vs. Olentangy Liberty in basketball, so I went to Jerome for an earlier game to scout them. In the early 2000s, when it was announced that Jerome would be built in Union

12

County, instead of Franklin County, where the first two Dublin high schools are located, I found it hard to believe. For scouting that game, I was not familiar with where Dublin Jerome was, which was ironic in that nine years later, I would start calling their football and basketball games. Another irony was that their coach was Chris Carlisle, whom I would connect with years later in his role as Jerome's assistant athletic director. At the end of the 2009-2010 basketball season, Jason wanted to stop calling the games; in his words, he was passing the microphone to me for the next football and basketball seasons.

Thanks to that door closing in 2008, the door that I opened set off a chain of dominos that led me to become the play-by-play voice of Ohio Wesleyan football, baseball, softball, and men's and women's basketball. I will describe that later.

In 1983, I had worked the stats for an all-star basketball game on Warner QUBE where Chuck Underwood was the play-by-play broadcaster, and later asked him if he could use me when he called the Ohio State vs. Maryland basketball game at the Brendan Byrne Arena in the New Jersey Meadowlands for WTVN-AM the following season, since I was making the trip anyway. Luckily for me, he said yes.

A lesson learned for you aspiring broadcasters ... Ask! Show Up! Volunteer! If a student would even offer to carry my heavy equipment, that could lead to bigger things, such as giving a report at halftime to give me a break. I once had a chat with a school sports staff member who said that he had trouble finding students who would work at a game for the pay that was offered. I told him that in college, I would have given my right arm—OK, that would have been contradictory—to do it for free!

I wasn't always successful with cold-calls, or in one case, a cold-walk-up-offer. After an Ohio State women's basketball game, I saw broadcaster Terry Smith walking up the ramp from the court to the mezzanine at St. John Arena, walked up to him, and said something like "Hi Terry, I notice that you called the game alone. I have done some broadcasting.

Any chance that I could be your broadcast partner?" I can only imagine what he must have been thinking. When I worked at a Mid-American Conference men's basketball tournament game in 1993 to get a post-game interview with Ohio's Gary Trent, Dan Patrick called the game for ESPN, and I gave him my resume, but nothing resulted from it (*surprise!*).

I was fortunate that I got my start doing stats in the 1970s, a time long before broadcasters had access to a monitor that showed the official stats, which is always present now at the college and professional levels. Furthermore, to this day, you will typically not find access to official stats for high school games, unless it is a significant game such as a state tournament semifinal or final game. Broadcasters and production staff had to rely on people like me for their stats. If my stats turned out to be significantly different from those published in the newspapers the next day, my credibility would be at risk.

I was also fortunate to be part of a few start-ups: Warner QUBE cable television kicked off on December 1, 1977, and Columbus Sports Network (WCSN-TV, low power Channel 32) launched in March of 2007. I still have the *Columbus Dispatch* article on Columbus Sports Network from April 27, 2007. The photo shows president and general manager John Ertmann and broadcasters Randy Rhinehart and Greg Frey in the broadcast booth at the Bill Davis Stadium for an Ohio State baseball game. The article lists these teams that Columbus Sports Network would cover: Columbus Clippers minor league baseball, Columbus Crew soccer, Columbus Destroyers arena football; Ohio State baseball, softball, volleyball, tennis, and lacrosse; Capital University, Denison University, Kenyon College, Ohio Wesleyan University, Wittenberg University; and Ohio High School Athletic Association events. I have another *Columbus Dispatch* article that mentions that the network covered 159 events in 14 different sports in its first year. I also still have the *Columbus Monthly* article on Columbus Sports Network from August of 2007, which includes a photo of John Ertmann. When it ceased operation in June of 2008, it had just been nominated for six regional Emmy awards. The tag line for Columbus Sports Network was "Local. Sports. Now.", which sportscaster Randy Rhinehart would emphasize on every broadcast. I have a polo shirt that has the CSN logo and "Local. Sports. Now." on it.

I also still have a resume that I prepared in 1996; I have to laugh when I see that I labeled my email address as "Internet address".

CHAPTER 2

Stats Work

PROFESSIONAL BASKETBALL

THIS WILL BE ONE OF MY SHORTER SUMMARIES, since it entails only a handful of games. Both of the Cleveland Cavaliers games in December of 1977 were memorable. During the 2020-2021 pandemic, broadcasters called games remotely, either at a studio or from their home. My first Cavaliers game had that setup 43 years earlier, in the Warner QUBE studio on Olentangy River Road. Red Jamison and Fred Taylor were scheduled to call the Cavaliers vs. Portland Trailblazers game for QUBE on December 6 from the Richfield Coliseum, but could not make it to the game due to weather issues–a web search for the Cleveland area shows that the low was 7 degrees with 7.8 inches of snow–so the producers quickly summoned John Gordon and Jim Thurman to call the game by watching the feed in the studio, with me doing the stats. Trying to impress John and Jim (I think that it worked), I passed them notes during the game informing that the Trailblazers' Larry Steele had led the NBA in steals (how appropriate!) in 1973-74 and that the Trailblazers' Dave Twardzik had been an all-star while playing for the Virginia Squires in the American Basketball Association. For Portland, Bill Walton had a triple-double in the game with 22 points, 10 rebounds, and 10 assists.

The second Cavaliers game was an in-person trip to see the Golden State Warriors on December 18 at the Richfield Coliseum, the game where the Cavaliers honored the career of Nate Thurmond, whose last season in the NBA had been the season before. There was a section of the court out of bounds near the scorer's table that was covered before halftime, and the Cavaliers representative removed the covering in the halftime ceremony to show Thurmond's number 42. Before the game, I saw the legendary Cavaliers broadcaster Joe Tait in the media room. Red Jamison of Warner QUBE and former Ohio State Coach Fred Taylor called the game, and I must have sent Coach Taylor a letter afterwards, because he sent me a reply--which I still have--17 days later, thanking me with "you really made things easy for us and I appreciated your thorough preparation."

In 1993, I worked the stats for three televised Columbus Horizon--they were in the Continental Basketball Association--basketball games, played at the Greater Columbus Convention Center. The games were against Rapid City, Yakima, and Rockford, and they won two of those three games--perhaps a good luck charm?--but won only 18 of 56 games that season. The 1993-1994 season would turn out to be the Horizon's last, as Cazzie Russell and Gary Youmans split the coaching duties.

In 1996, I worked the game between the Columbus Quest and the Richmond Rage of the women's American Basketball League for Sports Channel. The game featured two Quest players who would become members of the Women's Basketball Hall of Fame--Ohio State's Katie Smith and Valerie Still, the all-time leader for the University of Kentucky (men or women) for career scoring and rebounding, and a three-time consensus All-American. Jackie Joyner-Kersee--the Olympic track star and *Sports Illustrated for Women*'s top female athlete of the 20th century--played four minutes and scored three points for Richmond. The Quest won the

American Basketball League championship that season. The Quest coach was Brian Agler, whom I would interview 14 years later at a high school basketball game.

SEMI-PRO FOOTBALL

On July 12, 1980, Warner QUBE televised the season-opening game between the Columbus Metros of the Mid-Atlantic Football League and the Racine Gladiators of the Northern States Football League at Franklin County Stadium, the home of the Columbus Clippers minor league baseball team. One broadcaster, who will remain nameless, accidentally called the Racine team the "Racine Radiators" during the game.

It was designed as a "Your Call" game. Quoting from THE COFFIN CORNER: Vol. 4 (1982), THE COLUMBUS METROS: FORCED TO PUNT By Kevin B. McCray (http://profootballresearchers.com/archives/Website_Files/Coffin_Corner/04-An-124.pdf), "... the Metros entered into an off-season agreement with a Columbus cable television system, Warner-AmEx QUBE, to play a televised game for $2,500 and a $2,500 winner-take-all purse against the Racine, Wisconsin Gladiators ... The unique element would be that QUBE's home viewers, using the cable system's interactive television push-button consoles, would direct the Metros' offense and defense against the Racine coaching staff. The home viewers, given several options designed in respect to field position and game situation, would push their play selection, with the plurality's choice then being relayed to the players on the field ... [it] turned to disaster as a severe thunderstorm washed away Franklin County Stadium's synthetic surface's markings and much of the stadium crowd."

The *Columbus Dispatch* had the headline "Rain, Lights, Racine Wreck Metros", and Tim Krumlauf wrote that the start was delayed 40 minutes–the front page of the *Dispatch* had "Severe Storm Lashes Central Ohio"--and that "the game dragged on and on with one-minute intervals between plays as a concession to the Warner Qube TV play-calling experiment". The Associated Press story of the game had the headline "Qube Experiment 'Excites' Viewers" and had "Before the plays began, five options were listed on the television screen and viewers pushed a button listing their preferences." It mentions that the coaching staff could overrule the viewers, but generally did not. At one point, the TV production staff arranged for Metros Coach Hal Dyer to speak on-camera to the fans, and he suggested what strategy would work better.

I also still have a magazine article written by Sandy Schwartz, a *Columbus Citizen-Journal* sports reporter, describing the experience. He wrote that the options on defense were straight defense, blitz, or team's choice, and the options on offense were run up the middle, run wide, screen pass, play-action pass, and bomb. The viewers had about five seconds to decide.

Scott Kurnit, the program director for QUBE, was quoted in www.digitalriptide.org/person/scott-kurnit: "My favorite show I've ever produced in my life probably was 'Your Call Football.' The game took four hours. The stadium got hit by lightning as a coincidence. I'd say that could never happen except in the last Super Bowl where the power went out, but the power went out. So for our little semi pro event, we got something, believe it or not, like a 60 rating across our 25,000 subscribers. It was huge because it was really interesting. When you put the power of calling the plays in the viewers' hands, they did crazy things. It's fourth and one and they throw a bomb. A coach wouldn't do that, but the viewers did."

I remember that I committed a blunder in summarizing the first-half stats; I wrote that the Metros had something like 40 rushing plays, when it should have been 40 rushing yards. Former Ohio State quarterback Cornelius Greene scored the Metros' only touchdown on an 11-yard endaround in the 10-7 loss. The next year, I would reunite with him when he was the analyst for WOSU-TV Ohio State broadcasts.

COLLEGE FOOTBALL

Working the stats for Ohio State football is my pride and joy, so I have devoted an entire chapter to it.

My other experiences include televised games at Ohio University and Akron in 2013 for Spectrum Cable, and games on radio with Randy Rhinehart for Capital University in 2012 and 2013, and for Ohio Dominican University in 2004 with Randy. It was the first year for the Ohio Dominican program in 2004, and the team finished with an 0-10 record, but it was a fun experience, especially the road trip to Upland, Indiana, for the game against Taylor University. Their running backs coach was Pepe Pearson, who led Ohio State in rushing in 1996 and 1997. Ohio Dominican's venue is very scenic, surrounded by trees, and it reminds me of a New England setting.

In 1994, I worked the Central State vs. Knoxville game at Ohio Stadium, an event that included a parade taking place in downtown Columbus. In 2021, I worked the stats for the Central State vs. Kentucky State at Ohio Stadium, the HBCU Classic for Columbus.

COLLEGE BASKETBALL

In 1981, I worked a men's and a women's game at Ohio Wesleyan University for Warner QUBE. I have a photo of John Gordon, Fred Taylor, and myself from one of the games.

Let the record show that both of my two Ohio State games in St. John Arena doing the stats for NBC were Buckeye wins. Both, with Bob Costas doing the play-by-play and Fred Taylor as the color announcer, are memorable. The first was the 59-57 win over Northwestern in 1982 (game #50 in my log), a game that took two overtimes and had OSU's Granville Waiters (a Columbus icon for playing on the 1979 Columbus East state championship team, his NBA career, and for his community work) hitting the game-winning shot at the final buzzer. This inspired a song "Give the Ball to Granville". I still have my handwritten player stats on yellow legal paper; they show that Clark Kellogg–he played 49 of the 50 minutes and had a double-double in points and rebounds–had both OSU field goals in the first overtime, and that Waiters was playing with four fouls. I also have a photocopy of the check for $20.00 for working the game. It shows "NBC/TVS" as a comment; TVS was the TVS Television Network, founded by Eddie Einhorn. Northwestern was coming off a one-point loss to Iowa and would win only five games that season, but two of them were against teams that had won a national championship in the last three years–Michigan State and Indiana.

That game was on January 23, and Bob Hunter's report on it filled about one-third of the first page of the *Columbus Dispatch* Sports section the next day. The remaining two-thirds had articles by Tim May and Dick Fenlon on the Super Bowl, to be played that day by the Cincinnati Bengals and the San Francisco 49ers. The *Dispatch* also had a story on Indiana's win over Purdue, which included a technical foul on Indiana's … no, not the coach, but the cheerleaders, for staying on the court too long after a timeout.

The second collaboration was the 76-65 win over Purdue in 1983. Purdue had a player named Ricky Hall, and late in the game, Bob apparently wanted me to inform him of Hall's point total. The box score shows that Hall fouled out, so that was probably the occasion. I wasn't paying attention, until I heard Bob say "Hall?", in the same way that Ben Stein said "Bueller?" in the movie *Ferris Bueller's Day Off*. Later, on Facebook, I posted a photo of Bob, Coach Taylor, and myself at one of the two games, with the caption that two of the three of us are in a Hall of Fame. I had Coach Taylor and Bob autograph my *Buckeye Basketball Ohio State University* book, written by Bob Hunter. Bob's autograph has "To Steve - a Great Stat Man".

Jeff Elliott of the Big Ten office was part of the TV production. He appears in the "Tiebreaker" documentary on the Ohio State-Michigan football game of 1973, which ended in a 10-10 tie and entailed a vote by the athletic directors that resulted in sending Ohio State to the Rose Bowl. That Rose Bowl is the only one that the Buckeyes won in my three trips to Pasadena.

In March of 1983, I worked the stats for Chuck Underwood for a high school basketball all-star game. This later led me to ask if he could use me for the stats for WTVN-AM's broadcast of the Ohio State-Maryland game on December 1, played at the Meadowlands in New Jersey, and he said yes. My brother Mark and I took the People's Express airline (which did not have advance tickets; you paid the $19 one-way fare after the flight took off, and if you did not pay, you were informed that you would meet with an authority upon landing) into Newark. When I picked up my pass at the game, I heard a gentleman asking for his pass under the last name of Branch. I asked him "Adrian Branch?", and he was surprised, but said yes, he was the father of the Maryland star. I recall that one of the notes that I passed to Chuck was that the teams had four sequences of alternating scoring runs of 10 or more points; Bob Hunter's *Columbus Dispatch* report mentions Maryland having a 14-0 scoring run and the Buckeyes having a 14-2 run. This was before college basketball had a shot clock rule. The Buckeyes beat the 6th-ranked Terrapins, 72-68, making 14 of 17 field goals in the second half. Tony Campbell, playing in his home state, led the Buckeyes with 23 points, and the late Len Bias as a sophomore had 16 for the Terrapins.

Thirty-eight years later, I would interview Chuck on his sportscasting experiences and his current venture. Let the record show that all three Ohio State games where I did the stats, including the two for NBC, were Buckeye wins.

On that trip, Mark and I had a chat with sportswriter Bill Estep of the *Columbus Citizen-Journal*, who was staying at our New Jersey motel. Mark asked the motel desk clerk if we could catch a bus into the city, and the front desk agent said "You mean New York City"? (*Umm, yes.*) While sightseeing in Manhattan, we saw the actor Jeff Daniels–who had recently become famous for starring in the movie "Terms of Endearment"--walking on the sidewalk. I recognized him from the movie but did not know his name. We passed by a movie theater that had a poster for the movie, and by eliminating Jack Nicholson from the cast list, concluded that his name must be Jeff Daniels. I bought a pretzel from a street vendor, and it was the best pretzel that I ever had. With Christmas about three weeks away, two of the hot items at that time were the Cabbage Patch Kids doll and the Coleco Adam personal computer, which included a letter-quality printer and whose packaging was described as the size of a phone booth. Returning from New York that night, we realized that we were on the wrong bus. Mark asked a gentleman on the bus, "Excuse me, I think we're lost", to which he replied in his east-coast accent, "You're in Secaucus." Amazingly, we found our way to our motel.

The day before the Ohio State game, we went to the New York Knicks vs. New Jersey Nets game at the Meadowlands, which the Knicks won, 113-104. Former Buckeye Kelvin Ransey had five points for the Nets. It was entertaining to see opposing fans trash-talking at each other. Assuming that I was in Pretzel Heaven, I bought a pretzel at the game, which turned out to be the worst pretzel that I ever had.

When the Ohio State vs. Maryland game was over, it meant that in the span of 27 days, I had worked the stats for an Ohio State football game in Bloomington, Indiana, and for another in Ohio Stadium, and for another in Ann Arbor, Michigan; for a high school football championship game in Ohio Stadium; and for a college basketball game in New Jersey; and had broadcast a high school basketball game.

In December of 2007, I worked the stats for the Capital University vs. Ohio Wesleyan men's and the Capital University vs. Muskingum women's game for Columbus Sports Network. In that men's game, Capital won 70-68 on a tip-in by Steve Kyser with two seconds remaining. Dustin Rudegeair led Ohio Wesleyan with 22 points; he would achieve Fourth Team All-America honors from D3hoops.com and go on to be inducted into the Ohio Wesleyan Athletics Hall of Fame. A few years later, I asked him if he could fill in as the analyst for an OWU game, but he had to decline. He would later become the Assistant Director of Athletics for Facilities and Intramurals at Capital University.

For several years in the 2010s, I did the stats for Randy Rhinehart's broadcasts of Capital University men's and women's basketball. We had a chuckle when the men's team had Michael Sommer and Kelly Winter, who went on to be the Ohio Dominican University coach.

In the 2015-2016, 2016-2017, and 2017-2018 school years, I did the stats for televised games on Spectrum Sports, which had me traveling to the University of Dayton, Wright State University, Ohio University, Kent State University, Cleveland State University, Miami University, and Northern Kentucky University. At the Dayton Flyers games, I was able to catch a glimpse of the Flyers' Kostas Antetokounmpo, brother of Giannis. Chuck Murr, the graphics operator who has been an official scorer for Major League Baseball among his many sports production activities, would ask me to give him a heads up if a shot was a three point attempt the moment that the player took it, so that he could update the score accordingly if the shot was good. Referring to the Wright State Raiders' three point shooting, Chuck called it the "Raiders of the lost arc", which I plagiarized a few years later when calling a Mount Union Purple Raiders game. *Thank you, Chuck!* One of my duties was to bring the printout of the first half statistics to the graphics staff member in the TV production truck. On a cold winter night, even a short jaunt outside the arena would make me regret not wearing my jacket.

A few times, I would show up at the media parking checkpoint of an arena and learn that the parking pass was in the production truck. I must have an honest face, since in each case, the parking employee trusted me to enter the lot and get a pass to display.

On a related note, on several instances, I was able to enter an arena through an unattended entrance, though I did have a credential. If anyone reading this book has a position that entails this security function, please note.

I once worked a basketball game for a broadcaster who instructed me to signal how many points a player had by using my fingers. The example that he gave was that for 20 points, show two fingers on my left hand and a closed fist on my right, indicating a zero. I didn't ask him to illustrate what to do for 19 points. My customary practice was to jot down a player's points on an index card or sticky-note. Randy Rhinehart had the best method--write down the numbers 1 through 40 in advance on an 8 ½ by 11 inch piece of paper (1 through 10 on the top row, 11 through 20 on the next row, etc.) and point to the number.

COLLEGE BASEBALL

When I work the stats for a broadcast, besides tracking the batters in my scorebook, I record the number of balls and strikes for each pitcher/batter in the order that each pitch is made, which allows me to inform the broadcasters of the total number of pitches, the pattern of the number of pitches by inning, the number of first-pitch strikes, and the number of pitches to a batter, which can be significant if he fouls off a high number of pitches. This also allows me to see if a given batter has a pattern of facing a high or low number of pitches.

In 2007, Columbus Sports Network broadcast a game at Ohio Wesleyan, a 10-8 loss to Otterbein. This was before Ohio Wesleyan had a press box, so the broadcasters and I worked the game on top of a scissors lift. That same year, we broadcast a game in the Great Lakes Summer Collegiate League between the Delaware Cows and the Licking County Settlers, played in Newark.

I worked several Ohio State games from 1999 through 2003 for television. The highlights included seeing Buckeyes players:

- Nick Swisher, who had a 12-year career in the major leagues with the Oakland A's, Chicago White Sox, New York Yankees, Cleveland Indians, and Atlanta Braves.
- Josh Newman, who played for the Colorado Rockies and Kansas City Royals
- Scott Lewis, who played for the Cleveland Indians

In June 1999, the Buckeyes hosted a three-game series in the NCAA Super Regionals against Cal State Fullerton, a team that seemed to have every player hitting at least .400. Ohio State won the first game, but lost the last two, with the three games having 17, 16, and 15 runs scored. In the first game, Chad Ehrnsberger of the Buckeyes hit a grand slam in the bottom of the eighth inning off of Kirk Saarloos, who would pitch in the major leagues for the Houston Astros, Oakland A's, and the Cincinnati Reds. The *Los Angeles Times* story that I found for this game referred to him as "the Titans' highly regarded closer, Kirk Saarloos". The centerfielder for Cal State Fullerton was Reed Johnson, who had a 13-year career in the major leagues with the Toronto Blue Jays, Chicago Cubs, Los Angeles Dodgers, Atlanta Braves, Miami Marlins, and Washington Nationals; he went 6-for-14 in the series, with a home run. This was the first year of the new Bill Davis Stadium, and the *Times* story said that the game had "a boisterous sellout crowd".

HIGH SCHOOL FOOTBALL

When I work the stats for a broadcast game, I keep track of each player's rush attempts and yards; pass attempts, yards, and interceptions; receptions and receiving yards; punt returns and yards; kick returns and yards;

and punt yardage. I also keep track of first downs, rushing and passing yards, turnovers, and penalties for each team, and I keep a play-by-play so that I can relay scoring drives (number of plays, yards, and time of the drive) to the graphics operator and the broadcasters. I also write all of the scoring drives on a single index card–showing the number of plays, the length of the drive, the time of possession, the scoring play, the quarter, and the score. This allows me to highlight a column containing the number of plays or time of possession, for example, if they are consistently high or low. Before one game, the graphics operator asked me before the game: "Can you keep track of tackles, too?" I said "No way". Honesty is the best policy, right?

When doing high school stats, where I am the only set of eyes in determining yardage gained, when an interception takes place, I lock in on the yard line of the interception in order to calculate the return yardage. Kickoff and punt return spots are much easier, because the returner is usually planted on a yard line for a second when he catches the ball.

When West Jefferson (6-0 at the time) beat Columbus Academy (5-0 at the time), 41-23, in a Warner QUBE televised game in 1982, I had West Jefferson running back Mike Mast with 298 rushing yards. Jeff Logan, a running back in his Ohio State days, said on the air "Oh, come on, give him 300! Steve doesn't like running backs." West Jefferson's coach John Sines later said that his stats crew had Mast with 303 yards; the *Columbus Dispatch* article shows Mast with 298 yards, but it's possible that the reporter used my number. I have a DVD that has a brief part of the game, and our play-by-play broadcaster Pat Hughes said that "the key block was thrown by the back judge!" on Mast's 77-yard touchdown run; he would have two other scoring runs of 47 and 46 yards. The 23 points allowed were the Roughriders' most all season; they recorded six shutouts, including a 6-0 win over Archbold to cap a 13-0 season and the Division IV state championship.

I worked the stats for WXIX-TV, based in Cincinnati, for the 1982 Division I state championship game between Massillon Washington and

Cincinnati Moeller at Ohio Stadium, won by Massillon 35-14 in front of a crowd that the Ohio High School Athletic Association reported as 31,409, as part of the doubleheader with the Division III championship game between Akron St. Vincent-St. Mary and Ironton. This was the first time that I saw Chris Spielman, who never left the field for Massillon. Our play-by-play broadcaster Red Pitcher at one point said, "so help me, folks, the Massillon Tigers do have other players on defense, it's just that Spielman is making all the tackles!" Spielman had 23 tackles, caught five passes for 60 yards, threw two passes, and carried the ball five times. The massillontigers.com website mentions that Spielman led the Tigers that year in scoring, yards rushing, punt returns, recovered fumbles, pass interceptions, and tackles--both solo and assist. When Spielman, as a Massillon player, had his photo on the box of Wheaties, I bought four of them, thinking that they would be valuable should he become a star, and I still have them. He would win the Rotary Lombardi Award in 1987, his senior year at Ohio State.

In the 1983 Upper Arlington vs. Gahanna Lincoln game, played in rain, Gahanna had a 20-play drive that ended on the one-yard line without scoring. The *Columbus Dispatch* story referred to "ankle-deep mud", and reported that Gahanna had a first-and-goal from the six-yard line and was stopped on fourth down at the one. Upper Arlington won, 7-0, scoring on a 52-yard touchdown on the first play from scrimmage by Mike Sabo. In 1983, I worked the stats again for WXIX-TV, for the Division I state championship game, where Cincinnati Princeton beat Akron Garfield, 24-6; that game was played on a Sunday.

On November 3, 1990, Randy Rhinehart arranged for me to work the stats for him for the Grove City vs. Piqua playoff game broadcast on WMNI-AM. That was a night game, and I had worked the stats at the Ohio State vs. Northwestern game for WOSU-TV that afternoon. Grove City had a 10-0 record entering the game, but lost 3-0. Their coach was Brian Cross, the same Brian Cross who was the coach at Eastmoor when I called his 3-0 overtime loss to Gahanna Lincoln in 1985. To the best of my knowledge, these are the only two games that I have worked that had a 3-0 score. This also meant that in the span of five years, I had worked at games with the scores of 2-0, 3-0, and 3-0.

The next year, Randy asked me if I would consider giving up my WCVO-FM play-by-play gigs to join him as a statistician for his high school football games broadcast on Coaxial Communications cable TV. Debating on *What, and Give Up Show Business?*, I agreed, thus starting a collaboration of over 30 years with him. I still have the Coaxial memo showing the schedule for 1991, which shows the playback times as Friday at 11:00 p.m. and Sunday at 11:00 a.m., also shown on All-American Cable. I quickly learned Randy's gestures for what he needed from me during a game. When he stretched out his hands, it meant "What was the gain on that play?" When he did the "Let your fingers do the walking" gesture, it meant "Who carried the ball on that play?"

At first, I needed to write my halftime stats on an index card and carry it to the graphics staff in the production truck, but after a while, I was given a headset in order to read them off to the operator and to supply up-to-the minute stats during the games.

One year, Randy and I carpooled to a game in Mount Vernon, and after the game, Randy filled up on gasoline before we headed home. To show how much we think alike and like the same movies--in this case, *The Blues Brothers*--we looked at each other and said in unison "We're 40 miles from Columbus, we've got a full tank of gas, half a pack of cigarettes, it's dark, and we're wearing sunglasses ... hit it!"

In the 1991 game between St. Francis DeSales and Beechcroft, Luke Fickell of DeSales–who would go on to be an Ohio State star as a defensive lineman, the interim Ohio State head coach in 2011, and the University of Cincinnati head coach–caught a 16-yard touchdown pass in their 27-15 loss to the Cougars.

In 1996, I worked the stats for a televised high school football game at Dayton Welcome Stadium between Dayton Colonel White and

Springfield North. I figured that since this was a televised Thursday game in a big stadium, there must be a huge crowd in attendance. Well, I think that our crew outnumbered the fans. This was the first of many games where I worked with Ed Warren doing the graphics. Ed is a master on the graphics; he also keeps some stats on his own, which allows us to compare numbers before he displays them on the screen. Other stats/graphics gurus with whom I have worked include Dave Ashbrock, Tom Bochenek, Chuck Murr, Karl Kronenberger, Mark Phillips, and Matt Jurewicz.

For a game at Newark, I brought my ticket stub that I had saved from a trip to see Upper Arlington play at Newark in the 1970s–displaying the admission price of $2.00–and the production staff placed it on the turf and showed it in the pre-game show.

At a game at Johnstown-Monroe High School, our broadcast location was out in the open--luckily, no weather issues--and the stadium is unique in that the players enter the field by walking down the steps in the middle of the home stands.

One year, we had Westerville North at Grove City, two high-powered offenses. It must have been the 1992 game, where Grove City won, 35-28, in overtime. Grove City was ahead 21-7, but Westerville North flew down the field and scored, got the ball back and flew down the field and scored again. Then Grove City scored, but Westerville North flew down the field and scored again. After each touchdown, the Westerville North band played the theme from the movie *Superman*.

Randy Rhinehart and Jeff Logan have called the televised games for over 20 years. Jeff's daughter Katie--I remember when she was born, during the time that I did the stats for Jeff on Ohio State football games for WOSU-TV--was the sideline reporter for several years. At one game at Watkins Memorial, she interviewed Jeff's former Ohio State teammate Ken Kuhn, a Watkins Memorial assistant coach. One memorable game had her ankle-deep in the mud. Randy has persevered to call games despite foot injuries, once driving a golf cart up a ramp to our booth at Mapfre Stadium–the home of the Columbus Crew soccer team at the time–another time trudging up and down the many rows at the stadium in Parma for a playoff game. The field at Mapfre Stadium had a unique feature for football games; it did not have the crown that football fields do.

In 1996, 1997, and 1998, I joined Randy for a few high school play-off games broadcast by WVIZ-TV in Cleveland and played in Lakewood, Parma, Baldwin-Wallace University in Berea, and Euclid. Gerald McNeil, who was a receiver, punt returner, and kick returner for the Cleveland Browns and the Houston Oilers, and whose nickname was "Ice Cube", was our sideline announcer for some of the games. After one game, it started to snow like crazy, so we decided to find a motel rather than drive back that night, having luck on our second try in the Middleburg Heights area. Up to then, I would always find it amusing to see a motel vending machine that had a toothbrush and toothpaste kit, but never again, since I purchased one that night.

In 1999, we had the Brookhaven-Olentangy playoff game on Friday and another the next day, both to be shown on a delay. During the Saturday game, Randy Rhinehart gave a tease on the air to entice viewers to watch the replay of the Brookhaven-Olentangy game. He said something like "Not to spoil the surprise, but the Butler did it", the reference being that a key play was a 54-yard touchdown pass from Bryce Culver to Bryan Butler.

In 2000, I worked the Marysville vs. Piqua playoff game in Dayton's Welcome Stadium. Marysville had a 13-0 record coming into the game, but lost 18-7. It was memorable for the rainy weather and for the fact that I received my only speeding ticket, for driving 52 miles per hour in a 35 zone on the way. I must have been a good luck charm for Piqua in playoff games, since I had worked their 3-0 win over Grove City in 1990.

The next day, I worked the stats for the Ohio News Network for the Upper Arlington 10-7 win over Cincinnati Colerain (coached by future

Ohio State assistant Kerry Coombs) that advanced my alma mater Upper Arlington to the state championship game, which they won to finish the season with a 15-0 record. Colerain had a 13-0 record coming into the game, which meant that three of the four teams in those two days had a 13-0 record at the time. Upper Arlington had lineman Simon Fraser, who starred on Ohio State's 2002 national championship team, and running back/defensive back Jeff Backes, who was the Ohio Division I Player of the Year, set a state record with 3,354 yards rushing, and had 44 touchdowns as a senior. Backes also started at safety at Upper Arlington, recording seven interceptions in 2000. He played both as a receiver and a defensive back at Northwestern.

The Ohio North-South All-Star Football Classic at Crew Stadium in 2001 featured future NFL players Simon Fraser (Ohio State signee and defensive MVP), Chase Blackburn (Akron), and Mike Nugent (Ohio State; he had a 48-yard field goal); and future Ohio State players Angelo Chattams (game MVP) and Maurice Hall.

In 2002, Pickerington--there was only one Pickerington high school at the time, as opposed to two now--beat Dublin Coffman, 28-14, in a game matching Pickerington's A.J. Trapasso (113 yards rushing) and Coffman's quarterback Brady Quinn. Three years later, I would see them on opposing teams again, when Trapasso was the Ohio State punter and Quinn was the Notre Dame quarterback in the Buckeyes' 34-20 win in the Fiesta Bowl.

At a playoff game at Grove City High School in 2002, the Ohio State vs. Illinois game was ending just as the high school game that I was working was starting. It was weird to be in an empty stadium near kickoff time for such an important game. Walking to the stadium, I could see fans in their cars, obviously listening to the Buckeyes game, and then saw them scurrying into the stadium after the Buckeyes pulled out another of their many nail-biting wins, 23-16 in overtime, in the season that produced a 14-0 record and a national championship.

In 2008, since Columbus Sports Network went out of business, I was left with the prospect of not working a high school football game for the first time since 1981. In the first week, I sneaked into the press box at Upper Arlington and asked a *Columbus Dispatch* sports writer if they needed someone to cover games, but had no luck on that. The next week is when I reached out to WINF-FM and was able to do their stats for two years, before taking over the play-by-play in 2010. That first game in 2008 was Delaware Hayes at Olentangy, and as game time drew near, the broadcasters--Jason Whitt and Mike Carsey--were nowhere to be seen, making me wonder if I had understood which game would be broadcast. All turned out well, with the bonus being that I met a gentleman doing the engineering--Aaron Cassady, the owner of the Gameday Broadcasting Sports Network; he would eventually kick-start my return to play-by-play opportunities a few years later.

For the game at Big Walnut in 2008, Jason told me that there wouldn't be room for me in their small press box, so perhaps I could ask Aaron if I could do the stats for his broadcast of another game? I turned it down, wanting to go to the Alabama at Kentucky game in order to continue my goal of seeing every Football Bowl Subdivision team in person; I had already seen Kentucky a few times, but it would be the first time to see Alabama. If I had not turned it down, I could have begun my collaboration with Aaron a few years sooner than I eventually did. The Olentangy school district now has three additional high schools that opened after 2000--Orange, Liberty, and Berlin--and whenever we had an Olentangy game, Jason referred to the school as "Olentangy Original Recipe".

I worked the official stats for the state championships several years in the 2000s; some games were in Ohio Stadium, others in Canton. For the Canton games, the arrangement was that the six championship games alternated between Canton and Massillon in the two days--the first game was in Canton, the next in Massillon, then back to Canton, etc. The team that I was on worked the games in Canton and would drive to Massillon in case help was needed. In the 2014 Division III game, Toledo Central Catholic beat The Plains Athens, 56-52. Future Heisman Trophy winner Joe Burrow of The Plains Athens–playing in Ohio Stadium, his future home turf for a few years–passed for 446 yards and six touchdowns in a losing cause. The two teams combined for 1,217 yards of total offense and 12 lead changes.

During a game in Canton, I heard someone say, "Steve Basford?" It was Jack Kramer, whom I had not seen in over ten years. He was there to broadcast games for teams in western Ohio, and we reminisced about the WOSU-TV days. I said, "Those were the days," and that they were the ten best years of my life, based on working the stats for the home games, taking a few plane trips to work at road games, and working the stats in eight of the ten conference press boxes.

In 2009, 2010, and 2011, there were two days of doubleheaders played in Ohio Stadium and televised on ESPNU on Labor Day week-end--called at various times the Kirk Herbstreit Varsity Football Series and the Kirk Herbstreit National Kickoff Classic--and our Ohio State stats crew would do the official stats. We saw visiting teams from Florida, Georgia, Indiana, California, and Virginia matched up against Ohio teams. The 2009 event had the legendary St. Thomas Aquinas team from Fort Lauderdale, Florida, and had quarterback Jake Rudock, who would play at Iowa and Michigan. The Cleveland Glenville vs. Dwyer (Florida) game in 2010 featured future college and NFL quarterbacks Cardale Jones and Jacoby Brissett, and had a controversial ending in the 26-22 Glenville win, where Brissett was ruled down on quarterback sneak attempts just short of the end zone on the game's final two plays. The 2010 event also had Steve Miller of Canton McKinley; Miller and Cardale Jones would each have a hand in a touchdown in the win over Alabama four years later in the College Football Playoff semifinal game.

In 2011 and 2012, I joined Randy Rhinehart to do the stats for the Central Catholic League games on 820 AM. With Bishop Hartley,

St. Francis DeSales, and Bishop Watterson being traditional powers, this would add several playoff games to my log, with games in Mansfield, Piqua, Ashland, Clayton, and Zanesville.

One year, a team had an offensive lineman who was also their place-kicker. Every time that his team scored a touchdown, it took him a while to change into his kicking shoe for the extra-point attempt. The team never tried to avoid the delay-of-game penalty, taking the five-yard walk-off every time. Another year, a team had a late addition as a placekicker, from the soccer team. The coaches and players had trouble pronouncing his name, so they just called him "Kicker".

In 2012, the CW Columbus began televising games on Thursday nights. Since we had a five-minute pre-game segment, kickoff was to be at 7:05 instead of 7:00. This was a novelty in our first game, with the two kickoff squads on the field and ready to go at 7:00, and the officials holding them back for another five minutes. These games were streamed online, so that anyone with Internet access could watch them. Randy Rhinehart and Jeff Logan called the games, and whenever we had a game at Canal Winchester, Randy would jokingly remind Jeff that Canal Winchester is in fact in Franklin County, although in the far southeast corner, a commute from the extreme opposite corner of the county for Jeff. One of my duties was, at halftime, to guard the door leading to our broadcast booth; Randy and Jeff are on camera recapping the first half highlights and statistics, and we obviously don't want press box person-nel walking through during the live shot. I was almost that intruder in 2021, as I was calling the Dublin Jerome vs. Olentangy Berlin game for the Gameday Broadcasting Sports Network, and the CW was televising the same game.

On one occasion, for a game at Westland High School, the video production truck, which made the trip from Kent State University to cen-tral Ohio each week, had mechanical problems along the way, but made it in time to get the game on the air.

In 2014, I flew back from Atlanta, where I had seen Georgia State play Abilene Christian in the Georgia Dome, and drove to Reynoldsburg that night to work the stats for the televised first game of the year between the Reynoldsburg Raiders and the New Albany Eagles, a game that New Albany won 36-35 in two overtimes. Reynoldsburg failed to score after returning an interception to near the goal line late in regulation, and each team missed a PAT kick in the first overtime that would have won it. Aaron Cassady was calling the game for New Albany on the Gameday Broadcasting Sports Network, and he and I looked at each other several times and just shook our heads in disbelief.

There must have been something in the water at Reynoldsburg High School. In 2016, the Olentangy 52-51 win over Reynoldsburg was on September 8 ... and on September 9. Our Thursday night broadcast carried over past midnight due to delays when lightning was spotted in the area. Olentangy rallied from a 51-24 deficit to get the win.

One year, we had a strange game: a team dominated the first half with over 400 yards of total offense, then eased up--they had negative yardage in the second half!

In a 2020 Thursday night game, Worthington Kilbourne had four different players--three quarterbacks and a running back--complete a pass. It was similar to what I saw when I went to the 1991 Ohio State vs. Northwestern game as a fan, played in the old Cleveland stadium, where four Buckeyes--including punter Tim Williams on a busted punt play-- did the same.

The camera operators are obviously vital to the telecasts. For outdoor sports, they work in all kinds of weather, some of them on the roof of the press box. Many of them travel around the country for gigs, and it's fun to eavesdrop on their conversations before a game: "I worked at a golf tournament in North Carolina last week, how about you?", with the response: "I have a golf tournament in Hawaii this week."

The TV station always provided the crew with a pre-game feast that included at times pizza, subs, salad, chicken fingers, and French Fries.

While working at high school football games, I have seen these players who went on to play at Ohio State: Chris Spielman of Massillon Washington, Alex Higdon of Cincinnati Princeton, Maurice Hall of Columbus Brookhaven, future head coach of the Cincinnati Bearcats and interim head coach at Ohio State Luke Fickell of Columbus St. Francis DeSales, Karl Coles and Jonathon Cooper of Gahanna Lincoln, Jake Stoneburner and Mike Adams of Dublin Coffman, Jay Richardson and Nick Goings of Dublin Scioto, Rodney Bailey of Lakewood St. Edward, Kenny Peterson and Tyler Everett of Canton McKinley, Joe Burrow of The Plains Athens (who transferred to Louisiana State and won the Heisman Trophy there in 2019), Dimitrious Stanley and Hayden Humphrey of Worthington, Brandon Joe, Jalen Gill, and Andy Katzenmoyer (who doubled as a running back and would win the Butkus Award as the top college linebacker for the Buckeyes) of Westerville South, Ben Buchanan of Westerville Central, Jack Sawyer of Pickerington North (also in basketball, where he did it all--score, shoot three-pointers, rebound, bring the ball upcourt), Simon Fraser, Tim Schafer, Jesse Kline, and Mark Pfister of Upper Arlington, Derek Combs of Grove City, Matt Finkes and Quinn Pitcock of Piqua, Braxton Miller of Huber Heights Wayne, Tim Cheatwood and Jerome Baker of Cleveland Benedictine, Darron Lee of New Albany, Joshua Perry of Olentangy, Cardale Jones of Cleveland Glenville, Jacoby Boren and A.J. Trapasso of Pickerington Central, Marlon Kerner of Brookhaven, Eric Starks of Bishop Ready, Denzel Ward of Macedonia Nordonia, Mike Nugent of Centerville, Angelo Chattams of Dayton Chaminade-Julienne, Alex Boone of Cleveland St. Ignatius, Robby Schoenhoft of Cincinnati St. Xavier, Andre Amos of Middletown, and Drue Chrisman of Cincinnati LaSalle.

I have worked games that had these players who went on to other Football Bowl Subdivision college teams on a scholarship: Ki-Jana Carter of Westerville South (Penn State and the number one player selected in the 1995 NFL draft), Chase Blackburn of Marysville (Akron), Ray Ball of Westerville South (Wisconsin), Jack Tomlinson of Westerville South (Ball State), Sean Clifford of Cincinnati St. Xavier (Penn State), Jeremy Ebert of Hilliard Darby (Northwestern), Jeff Backes of Upper Arlington (Northwestern--breaking Buckeyes fans' hearts with his play in the overtime upset in 2004), Michael Taylor of Cincinnati Princeton (Michigan), Mario Manningham of Warren Harding (Michigan), Tyrell Sutton of Akron Hoban (Northwestern), Harlon Barnett of Cincinnati Princeton (Michigan State), Hassan Bailey of Gahanna Lincoln (Kansas), Jon Bowsher of Gahanna Lincoln (Toledo), Joe Foley of Gahanna Lincoln (Bowling Green), Matt Smith of Gahanna Lincoln (West Virginia), Andy Billman of Gahanna Lincoln (Miami of Ohio), Deric Phouthavong of Hamilton Township (Bowling Green), Trevor Stover of Big Walnut (Bowling Green), Jacob Matuska of Bishop Hartley (Notre Dame), Hiawatha Francisco and D'Juan Francisco of Cincinnati Moeller (Notre Dame), Shane Bullough of Cincinnati Moeller (Michigan State), John Shaffer of Cincinnati Moeller (Penn State), Jeremy Larkin of Cincinnati LaSalle (Northwestern), Nick O'Leary of Dwyer High School in Palm Beach Gardens, Florida (Florida State University), Jacoby Brissett of Dwyer High School (Florida State University and North Carolina State University), Brady Quinn of Dublin Coffman (Notre Dame), Cole Stoudt of Dublin Coffman (Clemson), Eilar Hardy of Pickerington Central (Notre Dame and Bowling Green), Bob Niemet of Beechcroft (Bowling Green), Shane Wynn of Cleveland Glenville (Indiana), Joe Kleinsmith of Lakewood St. Edward (Indiana), Dante Love of Cincinnati Withrow (Ball State), Brian DeWitz of Massillon Washington (Indiana), Benny Snell of Westerville Central (Kentucky), Godwin Igwebuike of Pickerington North (Northwestern), Dominick Goodman of Cincinnati Colerain (University of Cincinnati), Mike Warren of Toledo Central Catholic (University of Cincinnati), Chazz Anderson of Pickerington Central

(University of Cincinnati), Sam Crosa of Dublin Scioto (University of Cincinnati), Lorenzo Styles Jr. of Pickerington Central (Notre Dame), Mershawn Rice of Reynoldsburg (Purdue), Charles Gladman of Akron Garfield (Pittsburgh), Monte Cozzens and Pat Brown of Westerville North (Kansas), Brian Kennedy of Bishop Watterson (Southern Methodist), Messiah deWeaver of Huber Heights Wayne (Old Dominion), DeWight Pickens of Worthington (Ohio University), Cam Craig of Dublin Jerome (Purdue), Dominic Nardone of Dublin Jerome (Miami, Ohio), Joe Huber of Dublin Jerome (University of Cincinnati), Quinta Funderburk of Oscar F. Smith in Virginia (Syracuse), Jake Rudock of St. Thomas Aquinas in Fort Lauderdale, Florida (Iowa and Michigan), Brandon Linder of St. Thomas Aquinas (Miami of Florida), and Lamarcus Joyner of St. Thomas Aquinas (Florida State).

HIGH SCHOOL BASKETBALL

When I work the stats for a game, I keep track of shots attempted and made by each player--including three-point field goals, free throws attempted and made--individual fouls, and team rebounds and turnovers. My notebook paper has a row for each player, and I record in the top of the row a number with a circle around it for each made shot--a 1 with a circle around it for the first one, a 2 with a circle around it for the second, etc. If the made shot is a 3-pointer, I put an asterisk next to it. In the bottom of the same row, I record 1, 2, 3, etc. for each missed shot. If the missed shot is a 3-point attempt, I put a slash through the number. This way, I can easily see the number of made and total shots for a player.

At practically every televised game where I have worked the statistics, I would have a headset to communicate with the television graphics staff. I give the team stats to the broadcasters and graphics staff after each quarter or half. I also keep a play-by-play showing what each team did on each possession--a field goal made (with an asterisk for a three-pointer), free throws attempted and made, with the number of the player for these, whether there was a turnover, a T to denote a turnover, and an X to denote an empty possession (a shot attempt that was rebounded by the other team). If points are scored, I jot down the score at the time and the time remaining in the period, so that I can inform the broadcasters of scoring runs or how long a scoring drought has been, if significant. I can also determine scoring patterns after a team calls a time out, and a comparison of various metrics for a team by half or by quarter. One risk of having a stats monitor is the slight chance that the stats do not get refreshed quickly, which I would know but may not be apparent to the broadcasters watching the monitor.

In 1979, I worked the stats for Warner QUBE's coverage of the Worthington Sertoma Classic doubleheader at the Ohio State Fairgrounds. Eric Kellogg, Clark's brother, had 15 points as Cleveland St. Joseph beat Staten Island McKee, 51-44. The *Columbus Dispatch* reported that coaches Digger Phelps of Notre Dame and Eldon Miller of Ohio State were in attendance.

For several years, I was able to work the stats for the boys and girls state basketball championships, either for television or for the official stats. In 1983, I started a streak of four straight years doing the stats for the television productions--two years for WXIX-TV of Cincinnati and two years for WCMH-TV of Columbus.

The very first game in 1983 had the Shelby girls team, with their star Jodi Roth, who set a big-school finals record with 34 in the win over Barberton and had a combined 61 points in the two games in St. John Arena, would play for Ohio State, and was a 2019 inductee into the Ohio Basketball Hall of Fame. The WXIX-TV graphics operator in the production truck was Dave Ashbrock, and whenever I communicated with him through my headset with a stat to display, he would compose it and yell to the director "font's good!" Jimmy Crum was the play-by-play announcer for some of those games, and his method for me was to record players' made field goals and free throws in the scorebook as a string of 2's and 1's; this is the common practice for a scorer who does not need to know a player's total at a given time. If a player had 10 points, you would hear Jimmy on the air say "He has 2, 4, 6, 8, 10 points", as he counted up the 2's.

I had gone to the championship games since 1972 and kept the souvenir programs. The program always shows the photos and names of the coach, principal, and athletic director of each school. In 1981, for Kalida, all three of those positions were held by the same person–Dick Kortokrax, who would finish as the all-time winningest high school coach in Ohio with 890 wins. I would broadcast a Bishop Hartley game in 2021 where his son Randy was the coach.

Oddly, in my first year of 1983, the boys' tournament would have three players whom I would connect with about thirty years later–John Betz, Pat Delaney, and Frank Stams. The six teams in the three championship games had a combined three losses, by a combined seven points.

On the boys' side in 1983, the Bexley team won the Class AA state championship, 77-58 over Oak Harbor. Their star was all-Ohio guard Steve Willard, who scored 27 points and would play for Wittenberg. I can still see the smile on his face after the game; his photo in the *Columbus Dispatch* the next day matches my memory. Another member was John Betz, who would become the athletic director at Olentangy Berlin High School during my years of broadcasting Dublin Jerome games. John pointed out their high scoring games, before the three-point shot was implemented; they scored 108 points in a regular season game and 113 in their first tournament game. Bexley finished with a 26-1 record on a 26-game winning streak, and Oak Harbor had a 26-0 record entering the game. In Bexley's semifinal win, their opponent Akron St. Vincent-St. Mary had Frank Stams, who is more noted for his football career; I would work the stats for Mid-American Conference football games televised by Spectrum Sports where Frank was the analyst.

Also in that *Dispatch* photo was Rich Gatterdam, who scored 21 points in the two games combined. Rich writes:

"Probably the biggest memory of the semifinal was that after we were down 15 points early to Akron St. Vincent-St. Mary there was no panic in our team, maybe coaches, but after we settled down and some shots fell. We cut the lead to 9 at halftime [Rich hit a 20-foot shot at the buzzer] and had all the momentum after some great halftime adjustments by the coaches with box and 1 [Rich was the chaser on St. Vincent-St. Mary's Class AA Player of the Year, Curtis Wilson], which had them rattled. With our leading scorer, Steve Willard, having an off night scoring, David Elliott and Steve Calhoun [Associated Press second team all-Ohio the next year] picked up the offense. Reflecting back, this showed the depth of our team and that we were probably better than we gave ourselves credit for. As the game progressed so did our confidence.

"After that game, I realized we were a pretty special team with some great talent, great coaches and our confidence was sky high. Knowing we matched up perfect against Oak Harbor, I had no doubt we would win. Steve Willard showed everyone what a great shooter he was, because he might have hit his first 10 shots [he finished 11 for 14], Elliott & Calhoun stayed hot offensively, and we quickly jumped out to a 20-point lead. Looking back, we had a very solid team with Steve Willard (1st Team All State) leading with 20 pts, David Elliott 6'5, Steve Calhoun 6'5, Bob Bohn 6'6, myself, and a bench with Patrick Bellamy 6'3 and John Betz, [who would be a third team all-state in 1985].

"... the best memory ... We were not only great teammates, but we were best of friends and still are today. Maybe the last basketball team

*who grew up together in the same neighborhood and won a state
championship. Today they are my dearest friends!"*

In the 1983 Class AAA championship game, Toledo St. Francis DeSales
beat Akron Central-Hower, who had future Georgetown and Ohio State
player Grady Mateen. DeSales had beaten Middletown, which had future
Ohio State football stars Cris Carter and Sonny Gordon, in the semifinal
game. DeSales had Pat Delaney, who would play football at Toledo and be
the Defensive Coordinator for the Ohio Wesleyan football team during
the seasons that I have done their play-by-play. DeSales also had Todd
Mitchell, who would score 1,699 career points at Purdue and would play
for the Miami Heat and the San Antonio Spurs in the NBA. Pat Delaney
writes: "What I remember about the game was that we were down most
of the 1st half, but ramped up the pressure and got it close before half and
we all knew we had them then. Todd dominated their big guy Mateen,
and they were not prepared to handle our defensive toughness. That was
a fun year."

For those tournament games played in St. John Arena in 1983, Stu
Mason had me phone in a report to him after every game, to play on the
air for WCVO-FM. Since this was years before cell phones came into
being, I called Stu from my office at Ohio State, a stone's throw from the
arena. After the first game, I assumed that I could wing it without preparing any notes--big mistake, it was a disaster. I called him back to re-do it
with a prepared report, and I took the time to prepare my summary for
the rest of the games.

In the 1984 Class AA girls championship game, Lisa Cline, who
would star at Ohio State, scored 24 of Millersburg West Holmes's 36
points in the 36-35 overtime win over Orville. West Holmes finished
with a 28-0 record. Lisa was a 2007 inductee into the Ohio Basketball
Hall of Fame. Bruce Gerber, an Orrville graduate who has broadcast Ohio
Wesleyan men's and women's basketball games with me, writes: "That was

a great game. I was there as that was my senior year. We were in the same league at the time and West Holmes beat us both times in the regular season. The championship game went into overtime and Lisa Cline made the game-winning shot to beat us."

In the 1984 Class AAA boys championship game, Canton McKinley beat Dayton Dunbar, 79-75 in overtime. The leading scorers were Gary Grant of McKinley, who would play for Michigan, with 25 points, and Michael McCray of Dunbar, who would play football for Ohio State, with 27 points.

In the 1985 Class A boys championship game between Jackson Center and Graysville Skyvue, Jeff Teeters hit the winning shot to give Jackson Center the state championship, 63-61. The box score shows him with the one field goal attempt and an assist in his two minutes of play. Teeters had played one minute in the semifinal win over previously undefeated Wehrle but did not score in that game, so his only two points that weekend were the winning points for the championship. His surprise performance was similar to what Ed Major of Ohio State did four years previously on the same court against Purdue. A *Dayton Daily News* story has:

Late in the game, Jackson Center not only was trailing, but it had lost both of its starting guards — Keith Doseck and then Tony Meyer — to fouls. When Meyer fouled out, Tigers coach Jerry Harmon stunned everyone when he put junior Jeff Teeters into the game. "Quite frankly, he hadn't really played one quality minute at the varsity level the whole season," remembered Meyer. Dave Ross called the game for WMVR in Sidney that night. Tuesday, he found the transcript of his radio broadcast. Jackson Center had managed to tie the game, but with 11 seconds left Skyvue was fouled. Their player missed the front end of a 1-and-1 and this was Ross's take: "Rebound (Brian) Scoggin at 10 seconds. Up to Teeters. Teeters to (Shawn) Lenhart with six. Lenhart to Teeters ... He'll take the shot. ... IT'S GOOD! ... IT'S

GOOD!. ...WE WIN! ...WE WIN! ... JACKSON CENTER WINS
THE STATE CHAMPIONSHIP."

In the 1985 Class AA girls championship game, Millersburg West Holmes beat New Lexington 54-29, with Lisa Cline of West Holmes outscoring New Lexington by herself with 30 points. In another game on the boys side, Cincinnati Purcell Marian, which had future Ohio State football player Jay Koch on its team, beat Mansfield Senior for the Class AAA championship.

In 1986, instead of playing the semifinals and championship games in St. John Arena in Columbus, the girls' games were in Akron's James A. Rhodes Arena--I was treated to an overnight stay by WCMH-TV the night before--and the boys' games were in the University of Dayton Arena. In each case, I saw a Columbus team win a state championship--South on the girls' side and Wehrle on the boys' side. For the next year's girls' basketball finals souvenir program, the cover photo shows me at work on the stats, with a headset on and wearing a sport coat and tie.

In the 1986 Class A girls championship game, Tipp City Bethel beat Richmond Dale Southeastern, 80-71, with both Kelly Lyons of Bethel–a 2020 inductee into the Ohio Basketball Hall of Fame–and Kelly Downs of Southeastern scoring 37 points on 17 field goals and three free throws.

In March of 1991, I went to St. John Arena a few hours before the state basketball championship games were to start, to see if I could contact someone on the TV production staff about offering my services. Randy Rhinehart was there, and he pointed me to a production member to talk to. I handed him my resume and stretched the truth a bit; I said that I had worked games for Randy, when in fact, it had been one game. Little did I know that the guy I was talking to was Drexel Yokoyama, who had worked with Randy for several years. I can still remember the look on his face, as if to say *So, if you had worked on all these games, how come I never saw you at them?* Though I did not land that gig, I would start a long run of games with Randy and Drexel in the fall.

In January of 1995, 1996, and 1997, I worked the stats for the Coaxial National Hoops Classic, televised boys games in Battelle Hall at the Greater Columbus Convention Center. In 1995, it had a team from Freeport, Bahamas, one from Logansport, Indiana, and one from Penn Hills of Pittsburgh. In 1996, it had Las Vegas Durango–which would win the Nevada state championship with Ra'oof Sadat, who would play at the University of San Francisco–and Paterson Catholic in New Jersey–which had Tim Thomas, who would play for Villanova and for 13 years in the NBA with the Milwaukee Bucks, Los Angeles Clippers, New York Knicks, Philadelphia 76ers, Chicago Bulls, and Dallas Mavericks. Tim Thomas, Donald Hand (who would play for Virginia), and Kevin Freeman (who would play for Connecticut) combined for 75 points in the 83-66 win over Cincinnati Withrow. In 1997, it had the legendary programs of DeMatha Catholic High School in Hyattsville, Maryland, and Oak Hill Academy in Mouth of Wilson, Virginia, with their legendary coaches, DeMatha's Morgan Wootten and Oak Hill Academy's coach Steve Smith, each of whom won over 1,200 games. Zanesville surprised Oak Hill Academy, 54-48 with an 18-0 run in the third quarter, and DeMatha squeaked by Westland, 67-66. DeMatha had sophomore Keith Bogans–he had 22 points and 10 rebounds–who would play for Kentucky and in the NBA for the Orlando Magic, Charlotte Bobcats. Chicago Bulls, New Jersey/Brooklyn Nets, San Antonio Spurs, Houston Rockets, Milwaukee Bucks, and Boston Celtics.

In 2004, I began another streak of several years of doing the stats for the boys and girls basketball state championships, with three days of four games each on two consecutive weekends--a quick way to add 24 games to my log each year. An extra bonus was the sumptuous meals provided to the media workers at the Jerome Schottenstein Center.

I saw Jon Diebler's Upper Sandusky team–his brother Jake, a future assistant coach at Ohio State was also on the team–win the Division II state championship with a 27-0 record when he was a sophomore in 2005 and lose in the championship game when he was a senior in 2007. Jon is the all-time scoring leader in Ohio high school history and would go on to a stellar career at Ohio State. In 2005, Diebler had 29 points in the semifinal game, and future Buckeye Daequan Cook of Dayton Dunbar had 26. In the 2005 championship game, Diebler scored 32 and added 14 rebounds. In the 2007 semifinal game, Diebler had 24 points, and in that 2007 loss in the championship game, a rematch against Dayton Dunbar, he had a nose injury, played at times with a mask or cotton in his nose, and still had 48 points, 10 rebounds, seven steals, and three blocks. He made 15 free throws in that game, compared to 11 as a team for Dayton Dunbar.

In a 2005 tournament game, I saw a girls' team--Xenia Christian High School--that had 6' 3" triplets Megan, Moriah, and Molly Frazee combine for 39 of their 41 points in the semifinal loss. All three would play for Liberty University, and Megan would go on to play for San Antonio in the WNBA. I saw another girls tournament game where a team made a tying three-point field goal late in the game, a split second after the coach had called a timeout, negating the score in an eventual loss.

On March 17, 2007, while finishing the stats for a girls' championship game in the Jerome Schottenstein Center, I heard a thunderous cheer coming from the suites and the concourse. It was from fans reacting to Ohio State's Ron Lewis hitting a deep three-point shot at the end of regulation to force overtime in the Buckeyes' second round tournament game against Xavier, a game that they won and led them to the national championship game against Florida.

Since my location for working the stats at the state championship games was close to a team's bench, photos in the *Columbus Dispatch* would sometimes capture me, including one that caught me scratching the top of my head.

On December 21, 2007, Columbus Sports Network had the Upper Arlington at Grove City boys game. Randy Rhinehart arranged for me to get on camera to salute me for having passed 1,000 in games worked. I had a hunch that might happen, so I held up a piece of paper with "1,000" on it--prompting Randy to compare it to the iconic photo of Wilt Chamberlain after his 100-point game in 1962. It had taken 32 years to reach #1,000, and it would take 14 years for my next 1,000.

For the 2008-2009 and 2009-2010 school years, I did the stats for WINF-FM. By far, the loudest venue was in Delaware Christian's tiny gym for a boys game when they played Northside Christian. Through an extreme stroke of luck, Jason Whitt arranged for former basketball coach Steve Geiger to join him for a few games as an analyst, which has led Steve and me to a long collaboration of calling football and basketball games.

In 2018, I supplied a few stats for the streamed broadcast on the NetCast Sports Network of the Loudoun Valley (Purcellville, Virginia) vs. St. Paul's (Brooklandville, Maryland) game, played in a December tournament in Greensboro, North Carolina. The broadcasters were Desmond Johnson, owner of Tobacco Road Sports Radio, and James Wilhelmi, a former men's basketball coach at Winston-Salem State University.

While working at boys games, I have seen these players who went on to play at Ohio State: Jared Sullinger, J.D. Weatherspoon, and Seth Towns of Columbus Northland, David Lighty of Cleveland St. Joseph-Villa Angela, Jon Diebler of Upper Sandusky, Daequan Cook of Dayton Dunbar, Jordan Sibert of Cincinnati Princeton, B.J. Mullens of Canal Winchester, Aaron Craft of Findlay Liberty-Benton, Kosta Koufos of Canton GlenOak, Cliff Kirchner of Euclid, Henry Grace of Groveport Madison, Danny Hummer of Upper Arlington, Grady Mateen of Akron Central-Hower, and Jerry Francis and Eli Brewster of Columbus Wehrle.

I worked games that had these players who went on to play at other Division I colleges: Trey Burke of Columbus Northland (Michigan), Devon Moore of Columbus Northland (James Madison), Eric Kellogg of Cleveland St. Joseph (Brigham Young), Doug Davis of Westland (Michigan State and Miami of Ohio), Gary Grant of Canton McKinley (Michigan),

Raymar Morgan of Canton McKinley (Michigan State), Anthony Robinson of Canton McKinley (Bowling Green), Trey Jackson of Westerville South (Wisconsin), Khalil Iverson of Delaware Hayes (Wisconsin), Todd Mitchell of Toledo St. Francis DeSales (Purdue), Shawn Reid of Toledo St. Francis DeSales (Furman), Roy Ware of Toledo St. Francis DeSales (Wyoming and Kent State), Dapries Owens of Mansfield (Nebraska), O.J. Mayo of Cincinnati North College Hill (University of Southern California), Bill Walker of Cincinnati North College Hill (Kansas State), Jamelle Cornley of Columbus Brookhaven (Penn State), Matt Kramer of Gahanna Lincoln (Miami, Ohio), Rob Hardy of Upper Arlington (Duke), Steve Taylor of Gahanna Lincoln (Ohio University), Jermaine Guice of Westerville South (Butler), Jake Diebler of Upper Sandusky (Valparaiso), Troy McCracken of Enon Greenon (University of Dayton), Adreian Payne of Dayton Jefferson (Michigan State), Ray Gaffney of Dayton Dunbar (Minnesota), Aaron Pogue of Dayton Dunbar (Cleveland State), Kevin Vannatta of Upper Arlington (University of North Carolina-Asheville), Reggie Rankin of Columbus Linden McKinley (Ohio University), Eric and Tim Pollitz of Ottawa-Glandorf (Miami, Ohio), Alex Kellogg of Columbus St. Francis DeSales (Providence), Nick Kellogg of Columbus St. Francis DeSales (Ohio University), Desmond Watson of Columbus St. Francis DeSales (Davidson), Nick Aldridge of South Webster (Western Carolina), Jalen Sullinger of Thomas Worthington (Kent State), DJ Moore of Worthington Christian (Liberty), Greg Cave of Lancaster (University of North Carolina Wilmington), Kipper Nichols of Lakewood St. Edward (Illinois), Kevin Haddock of Wehrle (Evansville and Youngstown State), Dave Minor of Cincinnati Purcell Marian (Indiana), Matt Bingaya of Delaware Hayes (Southern Mississippi), Matt Allocco of Hilliard Bradley (Princeton), Matt Sobolewski of Worthington (Air Force Academy), Troy Hitchcock of Columbus Mifflin and Columbus Wehrle (Georgia), Dominiq Penn of Dublin Coffman (Washington), Don Christie of Oak Harbor (Ohio University), Dan Christie of Oak Harbor (Dayton), Tony Lucas of Bishop

Hartley (Youngstown State), Travis Young of Zanesville (Marshall), Jordan Potts of Columbus Northland (UNC Greensboro), Ra'oof Sadat of Las Vegas Durango (University of San Francisco), Tim Thomas of Paterson Catholic in New Jersey (Villanova), Donald Hand of Paterson Catholic in New Jersey (Virginia), Kevin Freeman of Paterson Catholic in New Jersey (Connecticut), Keith Bogans of Hyattsville, Maryland DeMatha (Kentucky), and Eric Roberson of Pittsburgh Penn Hills (Bradley).

While working at girls games, I have seen these players who went on to play at Ohio State: Nicole Sanchez of Pickerington, Lisa Cline of Millersburg West Holmes, Gennifer Johnson of Canton McKinley, Jodi Roth of Shelby, Cait Craft of Findlay Liberty-Benton, Joni Mazzola of Bishop Watterson, and Savitha Jayaraman of Olentangy Liberty. I have seen these players who went on to play at other Division I colleges on a scholarship: Taylor Agler of Olentangy Orange (Indiana and Ohio University), Yamonie Jenkins of Reynoldsburg (Ohio University), Shiloh Murphy of Reynoldsburg (Morehead State), Lauren Prochaska of Jonathan Alder (Bowling Green), Kelly Lyons of Bethel (Old Dominion), Kelly Downs of Richmond Dale Southeastern (Morehead State), Frannie Frazier of Thomas Worthington (Ball State), Jane Phend of Chagrin Falls (University of Cincinnati), and triplets Megan, Moriah, and Molly Frazee of Xenia Christian (Liberty).

HIGH SCHOOL BASEBALL

I was hired to work the stats for several state championship games. In 2004, I was at the Thurman Munson Memorial Stadium in Canton, where the games for three of the four divisions were held. In other years, the games were in Huntington Park in Columbus and at the minor league Dragons' ballpark in Dayton. The Reynoldsburg team in 2004 had Eric Fryer, who would be a catcher for Ohio State and in the majors for the Pittsburgh Pirates, Minnesota Twins, and St. Louis Cardinals. In the semifinal 2-1 loss to Mentor in 10 innings, Fryer pitched the first nine innings, giving up one run and striking out 10.

One year, I kept each pitcher's pitch count on paper and compared it periodically to what my supervisor had in the software. I had a different supervisor during the weekend. One supervisor was very laid-back; if we were off by two pitches, he'd say "Oh, that's all right". The other was the opposite; he'd say "Oh no, let's compare every batter sequence and find the difference!"

One tournament game had an unusual ending--on an appeal play when a runner was ruled to have tagged up on a fly out to the outfield but left second base before the catch.

In 2007, Columbus Sports Network had the Columbus City League high school baseball championship game between Columbus Centennial and Columbus West, played on West's diamond that overlapped the football field and did not have an outfield fence, which meant that inside the park home runs were more likely than anywhere else. Tied at the end of seven innings, the game went into extra innings ... as in 13 innings. That game, like one at Ohio Wesleyan, had us located in a scissors lift booth behind home plate.

In 2010, I worked the stats for Upper Arlington games that Randy Rhinehart broadcast on an Upper Arlington Internet stream network.

ARENA FOOTBALL

I worked the stats for the Columbus Thunderbolts games in 1991 for WMNI-AM (Randy Rhinehart did the play-by-play, and Jim Karsatos was the analyst), played at the Coliseum on the Ohio State Fairgrounds, and for the Columbus Destroyers, played in Nationwide Arena, for two different gigs from 2004 through 2008--one for televised games on Columbus Sports Network and the other for the official stats, working for Paul Hummel, the stats leader.

For the Thunderbolts vs. Detroit Drive game in 1991–a 56-20 win for Detroit, with the help of eight Thunderbolt turnovers–the Detroit quarterback was Art Schlichter of Ohio State, which was ironic in that he was playing for a team in Michigan, he had lost both of his home OSU games to the Wolverines, and he had won both of his OSU games in Ann Arbor. He completed only nine of 27 passes, but ran for a touchdown.

The Destroyers' coach in 2004 was Earle Bruce, the former Ohio State coach, and Ohio State legend Chris Spielman was the coach in 2005. Their quarterback in 2005 was Matt D'Orazio, for whom I would eventually work the stats for televised high school games, and the quarterback in 2007 and 2008 was Matt Nagy, the eventual Chicago Bears head coach.

COLUMBUS CLIPPERS BASEBALL

I worked the stats for several televised Clippers games in the 1980s, 1990s, and 2000s. For a while, I worked in the production truck, before getting promoted to the press box. I communicated stats to one young lady who created the graphics, and she thought that every time there was a stolen base attempt, it was time for a new batter, and she would ask me for his stats! For many years before he became the radio voice of the Los Angeles Angels, Terry Smith would occupy the booth to our right, calling the games for radio. I still have a listing of the credits on paper for the June 3, 1983 game televised by Warner QUBE, and it includes my brother as "Executive Producer MARK BASFORD".

In 1987, I worked the stats for a Clippers game for broadcasters Paul Cox and Mark Bishop of low-power Channel 8. Paul and Mark's pre-game segments were creative. On one of their high school basketball games that involved a school where some students had pulled a prank by putting glue on doorknobs, Paul and Mark continued the theme by pretending that their stick microphones were stuck to their hands with glue.

My first gig for the Coaxial Communications cable TV company was a Clippers vs. Denver doubleheader in 1991. I still have a *Columbus Dispatch* article about Coaxial productions from October 22, 1996; the photos show Drexel Yokoyama in the studio, and President Joel Rudich and Vice President Bob Lay at the production truck at Cooper Stadium, home of the Clippers. The article lists events scheduled in a three month period of 1996 as Columbus Quest women's basketball, high school football, Ohio State women's volleyball, Ohio State women's basketball, girls high school basketball, and boys high school basketball. Some of the games were sold to SportsChannel, to be shown on their network. During the MLB players strike in April of 1995, fans could still get their baseball fix by tuning in to a televised Clippers game on Coaxial Communications. In the 2000's, some of our televised games were carried on the New York Yankees' YES Network.

For a while, I tried using the spreadsheet program in my Handspring Visor personal digital assistant--already a dinosaur, given what tablets and smartphones can do now--to update batting averages after every player's at-bat, but it was slower than molasses, so I switched to using a calculator.

A highlight in many years was when the Ottawa Lynx would play in Columbus, and we would have their radio broadcaster call an inning in French. The only words that I would understand were "une, deux, trois". At one game, Randy Rhinehart was joined by Yankees' owner George Steinbrenner in our booth for a chat. In one year, we saw Darryl Strawberry playing for the Clippers on a rehabilitation assignment and were wowed by his sweet swing, launching hits out of sight in batting practice.

On August 19, 2002, the Clippers beat Louisville, 10-9 in 17 innings to snap a six-game losing streak, a game that took five hours and seventeen minutes. Comparing it to the infamous 33-inning game between Pawtucket and Rochester in 1981, I guess that I can't complain about the duration. Each team scored in the 13th, 15th, 16th, and 17th innings. Columbus's designated hitter Billy McMillon homered in the 15th inning and gave the Clippers a walk-off win with a two-run homer in the 17th. Those were two of his eight home runs for the season. Our TV production staff had saved its best for last, as it was our final broadcast of the season. It was also the final "Dime A Dog Night" of the season; the crowd of 11,497 ate 32,050 hot dogs, as reported by Joe Arnold of the *Columbus Dispatch*.

During the 2007 season, I worked several televised games that included Brandon Watson's International League-record 43-game hitting streak. On July 31, 2007, we saw Curt Schilling pitch seven scoreless innings in a rehabilitation assignment for Pawtucket.

I often take a chance at injecting some humor during a game. In a game in 1997, the Clippers second baseman Homer Bush–who would play seven years for the New York Yankees, Toronto Blue Jays, and Florida Marlins–chased a ball hit into foul territory but ran out of room and tumbled over the fence. I handed Randy a note: "That last play was a Homer over the fence." In another game, we had a matchup between a pitcher and batter whose last names were Reed and Malloy. Referring to an old TV show, I handed Randy a note: "Adam-12 … Reed and Malloy".

SOFTBALL

In 2007, I was a good-luck charm for the Ohio State softball team, as I worked the stats for their first-ever Big Ten softball tournament championship, a 2-1 win over Northwestern, televised on ESPN.

In 2015, I worked the stats for two New Albany High School softball tournament games for the Gameday Broadcasting Sports Network, a 1-0 win over Olentangy Orange, played at Pickerington Central High School, and a 2-1 loss to Teays Valley, played at Ohio State's Buckeye Field.

In July 2021, I was a scorekeeper for 15 Girls Fastpitch Softball games in three days, including eight in one day, at the Ohio Stingrays College Showcase, seeing teams from Indiana, Michigan, New York, Pennsylvania, and Ohio. Several college coaches were in attendance, and the Mission Statement for the event read "The competitive purpose of this Junior Olympic softball event is to provide a quality playing venue with like teams so that the softball athlete can state her case for why she should be playing at the collegiate level."

OTHER GIGS:

- In 2007, I worked the stats for the women's football game between the Columbus Comets and the Kentucky Karma--their league was the Women's Football Alliance--played at Dublin Coffman High School. From the press box, it was like watching any football game where the teams' play looked very crisp and organized.
- Ohio State women's volleyball matches
- In 2007, I worked the stats for ESPN at the NCAA men's volleyball national championship in St. John Arena, won by UC-Irvine over Indiana University Purdue University Fort Wayne.
- Girls high school state championship volleyball matches in the Nutter Center at Wright State University
- Ohio State hockey
- High school hockey, on the practice rink at Nationwide Arena and at the OhioHealth Chiller North in Lewis Center
- High school wrestling
- High school lacrosse
- Columbus Crew vs. Houston Dynamo MLS soccer in 2009

For volleyball, we would have stat monitors that gave the broadcasters just about everything they needed, so I added to that by supplying scoring runs, the number of kills by a player after he or she had one (since the stat monitor takes a while to refresh), and the number of kills by a player in the game, since the stat monitors had only cumulative stats.

CHAPTER 3

OHIO STATE FOOTBALL STATS
In a Class by Itself

AS FAR AS WORKING THE STATS, nothing compares to Ohio State football. I have extracted much of this section from my first book, *BUCKEYE MEMORIES FROM THE COUCH, THE STANDS, AND THE PRESS BOX ... and a few Fun Facts.*

In 1978, I got it in my head that perhaps visiting radio stations would want someone to keep statistics for their broadcasts and feed them information, so I wrote (snail mail, of course) to OSU Sports Information Director Marv Homan to ask if he had contact information for each station. He graciously sent me a typed response that I still have, though I didn't follow through on it.

For one game in 1978, and starting in 1979, and except for 1991, 1992, and the 2020 pandemic year, I have worked in a press box as a statistician--the 1979 and 1980 home games for Warner QUBE telecasts, from 1981 through 1990 for the WOSU-TV delayed telecasts, and since 1993 as part of the athletics department's official statistics crew for home games. In 1991 and 1992, I sat in the stands for the games, which means that the last tie game in Ohio Stadium, the 13-13 game against Michigan, would occur in the last time that I sat in the stands.

The team has had good fortune during my first year of each of my four gigs:

- 1978: in my only game, it was Woody Hayes's last win, at Indiana.
- 1979: the team had an 11-0 record in the regular season.
- 1981: the team beat Michigan and won the bowl game in the same season for the first time since 1968.
- 1993: the team had a 10-1-1 record, ending a streak of 13 straight seasons with at least three losses.

After working that 1978 game, little would I know that I would be working the stats for a last memorable game of the last six former Ohio State coaches: Woody Hayes's last win, which was on the road; Earle Bruce's last win, also on the road; John Cooper's last home win; Jim Tressel's last home win; Luke Fickell's last win; and Urban Meyer's last home win. Three of the six games were wins over Michigan.

Warner QUBE was able to carry Ohio State games for my 1978 through 1980 gigs, as documented in the July 28, 1978 *New York Times*: "ABC-TV and the Warner Cable Corporation have reached an agreement out of court to permit the cable company to offer five Ohio State University games on its pay-television system in Columbus, Ohio, next fall. ABC has described the agreement as a two-year experiment to measure the impact of live cable coverage on attendance at the football stadium."

I still have the July 19, 1979 news release for QUBE's pay-per-view Ohio State football broadcast package, priced at $19.95 for all five games, or $5.00 for individual games, a significant reduction from the 1978 rates. Steve Bornstein, QUBE's OSU football producer, would go on to be the president/CEO of ESPN and the first-ever president of NFL Network. Before the first game against Syracuse, our broadcasters John Gordon and Jeff Logan were given instructions to emphasize what was new this year—the new coach, a new offense, and a new turf that replaced the one that was so slippery the year before.

After working the stats for Warner QUBE in 1979, they were not sure if they would carry the games in 1980. I reached out to ESPN to offer my services, and they used me for the opener against Syracuse. I still have a handwritten note from Jim Huie of ESPN after the game, saying that he had recommended that I work the stats for the game two weeks later. However, I returned to Warner QUBE for the rest of the season.

In 1981, Warner QUBE stopped televising the games, as described in the book "Play-by-Play: Radio, Television, and Big-Time College Sport" by Ronald A. Smith: "... when the Warner-QUBE two-year agreement allowing telecasting in Columbus of Ohio State games came to a close in 1980, ABC and the NCAA both decided not to allow QUBE to cablecast games that were not otherwise televised by ABC unless QUBE purchased all remaining tickets of all college games within its cablecasting area." I guess that was an offer that QUBE could refuse!

I wrote a letter to WOSU-TV–which showed the games on a delay on Saturday night and Sunday morning on more than twenty PBS stations throughout Ohio–asking if they could use me for the stats. Through a stroke of luck, they were making significant changes that year, with Marv Homan and Kaye Kessler no longer the broadcasters. So, I got the job and held it for the last ten years that they produced the games, ending in 1990. I have called those ten years the ten best years of my life.

My WOSU contact told me on the phone that the broadcasters would be Jack Kramer (I assumed that it was spelled Cramer) and Cornelius Greene. Jack is a graduate of Indiana University, as is John Gordon. Jeff Logan would replace Cornelius midway in the 1981 season and return in 1982, and Paul Warfield would be Jack's broadcast partner from 1983 to 1990.

When the game was also on the USA Network in 1981, Jack and Paul would record the pre-game stand-up and do it a second time, with the USA Network logo on their stick microphones. Near the end of the first game, Jack asked me to jot down my name, so that he could give me credit on the air. I must have been destined to be a doctor; he read it as "Steve Barford."

In the beginning, I would pass my notes to Jack on an index card. Broadcasters are getting information from several sources, such as their broadcast partner and the director. Over the years, I noticed that my index cards often got lost among other cards that the broadcasters had, so I switched to yellow Post-It notes, for a color that would stand out and as a way for the broadcasters to mount it on a surface at more eye-level. After a few games, the producers supplied me with a headset so that I could communicate with a staff member located in the studio in the Fawcett Center to arrange the stats on graphics.

Jack had a huge cork board about an inch thick for his spotting charts. He had the OSU offensive alignment and opponent defensive alignment on one side, and the reverse on the opposite, two deep at each position. He had pushpins to be placed next to the name of each player in the game at the time, and our spotter Jim Henderson's job, among others, would be to watch for each substitution to adjust the pushpin to the new player's name. For a tackle, he would point to the player/pushpin on the chart, and for a block, he would point to the player with one hand and put his other arm at a 90 degree angle to signify the block.

Tom Keys, a *Columbus Citizen-Journal* sportswriter, and OSU tennis coach John Daly would help out on occasion, too. Since these games were on commercial-free TV, the broadcasters often would not get a break and would need to keep on talking throughout the timeouts. Thirty years after meeting Jack, he asked me to take over the maintenance of his website for his broadcasts of high school sports in western Ohio.

After the first few games, Ed Clay, the longtime station manager of WOSU-TV, said to me at a game: "I didn't know that you were an OSU employee!" He had submitted paperwork for me to get paid, which turned out to be the incorrect method to pay OSU employees; this was ironic in that I worked in the Payroll office.

I still have a spiral-bound notebook that contains my handwritten play-by-play, passers' running totals, receivers' running totals, and various other statistics for every game that I worked between 1985 (starting with the Pittsburgh game where Jim Karsatos threw the winning touchdown pass to Cris Carter on fourth down on the two-yard line), and 1990 (ending with Michigan's game-winning field goal). For penalties, I crammed multiple plays onto one line, so that my number of official plays does not change, a practice that I no longer do; now, I count the plays instead of subtracting Play #X from Play #Y. Most of the writing has a very fine (thin) style.

From the play-by-play, I can easily recall and visualize the key plays of those games from over 30 years ago, from Chris Spielman's fourth-down stop on Ronnie Harmon in the 1985 Iowa game in the rain, to David Brown's 100-yard interception return in a night game in 1986 at Purdue, to Carlos Snow's 70-yard catch-and-run in Earle Bruce's last game in 1987 against Michigan, to Bobby Olive's 20-yard diving touchdown catch with 38 seconds remaining against LSU in 1988, to Jeff Graham's 50-yard punt return in the 1990 opener against Texas Tech for the winning score. On the minus side, there was the late missed field goal against Michigan in 1986, the 28-yard touchdown pass by Iowa on 4th-and-23 in 1987 with six seconds remaining, and the Michigan 41-yard touchdown pass with 1:37 remaining in 1988.

Before the stadium was renovated in 2000, I could leave the press box after the game through a door that opened onto B Deck and walk down the steps in the stands to the track. With each step, the view of the field became more amazing. With the renovation, our stats crew location was now in a private room, with the visiting assistant coaches to our left. With a window separating them from us, the coaches would paper the windows with newspaper so that we could not see in. One year, I was able to peek through a tiny seam between the papers and catch a glimpse of Joe Paterno.

One of the perks in the press box in my early years was enjoying the sumptuous pre-game meals, a different one every game, ranging from the omelets to the full Thanksgiving dinners for the Michigan game. Over the years, while enjoying the meal in the press box, I was able to chat with several noted former coaches.

- Larry Catuzzi, who had been an Ohio State assistant coach from 1965 through 1967 and was instrumental in recruiting the "Super Sophomores" of the 1968 National Championship team.
- Bill Peterson had been the Florida State coach from 1960 through 1969 and the head coach of the Houston Oilers. I chatted with him during one of the games against Florida State in 1981 or 1982, both wins by the Seminoles. At the time, I had no idea that he was a native of Toronto, Ohio, had earned a degree from Ohio Northern University, and been the head coach at Mansfield High School. I had recalled the 1967 Gator Bowl 17-17 tie against Penn State, the game where Penn State led 17-0 at halftime, and Florida State kicked a field goal with 15 seconds left. I asked him to recap the key play of the game where Penn State, up 17-0, failed on a fourth-down play at its 15-yard line in the third quarter.
- Floyd Stahl, the Ohio State basketball coach from 1950 through 1958 and an assistant football coach from 1933 through 1938. The subject of the football team's trip to play Southern California in 1937 came up; he said that taking the flight to California was a novelty.

In a big game, it is common to see a VIP in the press box, such as former Texas coach Darrell Royal when the Longhorns visited in 2005, and LeBron James on another occasion. At one game, Calvin Hill, who had played for the Cleveland Browns and been a consultant for the Browns, dropped by our booth to say Hi to Paul Warfield. Another time, I did not recognize a broadcaster who dropped in, wearing glasses and looking very scholarly in his dress shirt and tie, former OSU quarterback Mike Tomczak. Before an Ohio State vs. Florida State game in the 1980s, I passed one of the booths in the press box and saw the late Tom Mees of ESPN taping his pre-game comments for a Tallahassee TV station.

In the ten years of working for WOSU-TV, I was able to fly with the crew to work a few games at Illinois, Indiana, Iowa, and Northwestern, and drive to Michigan and Michigan State to work a few others. We would fly out of Don Scott Field, the university's airport on Case Road. One flight was on an eight-seat propeller plane, and the others were on six-seat planes. On one occasion, my mother dropped me off and came into the lobby. She said, "There's Jack Kramer!", to which Jack looked up in surprise that someone had recognized him. I have photos that she took of us getting ready to leave Don Scott Field, showing me in a dress shirt and tie. Times have changed. For the 1983 flight to Iowa, all of the photos of us outside the terminal have my back turned to her; I didn't want her to see how nervous I was, after having a kidney stone the week before.

After sitting in the stands as a fan in 1991 and 1992, I received one of the best phone calls of my life on September 3, 1993. The day before the opening game against Washington, about 24 hours before kickoff, D.C. Koehl, the long-time OSU sports information staffer, called me at my OSU office to say that he needed someone to assist him keeping the official stats, and was I interested? *Yes, Captain Obvious.*

My duty on the official stats crew has been to write the yardage gained by the player on each play, pass attempts, scoring plays, punts, punt returns, kickoff returns, interception returns, fumble recoveries, and more in a spiral notebook, with forms for each. I also keep my own play-by-play notes on a page of notebook paper. One of the "other duties as assigned" is to record the start time and the end time of the game, hopefully remembering to check my phone, when mobile phones came into being. A rule in the press box is: no cheering. Thankfully, there is no rule about pumping your fist.

One play in particular that keeps me busy is a touchdown pass. I keep my own play-by-play, so a touchdown pass entails jotting down the play on my notebook paper, updating the quarterback's stats, updating the receiver's stats, writing down the scoring play, and updating the first downs, if applicable.

For several years, it was just the two of us, with D.C. keying the plays on a computer, though for a while, a third staffer would check my math on the cumulative rushing yards for each player at halftime. These were the days before the media had stat monitors, and once the game was over, reporters--Rusty Miller of the Associated Press was usually the first--would come to me to get a few stats.

Luckily, I do not need to record the tackles. As we added staff over the years to track tackles, I would hear them calling out "tackle by number 25 ... tackle by number 25 ... tackle by number 25 ... he's making all the tackles!"

In the early days, one of our biggest challenges was to calculate in our heads the length of a play when it started on one side of the 50 and ended on the other. Take a play that went from the 35 to the opposite 29. I would add the two numbers and subtract from 100: 35+29 = 64, subtract from 100 gives 36. D.C.'s method, and he would say it softly, was: "that's 15 on one side and 21 on the other, total of 36."

D.C. passed away in 2012, in his 39th year with the Department of Athletics. The ohiostatebuckeyes.com website mentions that a reference in an Ohio State basketball media guide in the 1980s stated that Koehl "has devised a system of storing historical athletic information in a computer."

One stat that the staff responsible for defensive plays determines is whether a defensive player should get credit for breaking up a pass, called a break-up. On one occasion, Scott Rex, who identifies every play, asked if a break-up took place. Our stat guy who tracks the tackles said *No, it hit the defensive player in the back.* I asked if the player should get credit for a back-up ... which produced some polite laughter from our crew.

In another situation illustrating that the crew puts up with my attempts at humor: in the WOSU-TV days, the team had Bryan Cook and Jay Koch (pronounced "Cook") on defense. I informed Jack Kramer to be prepared to say that too many cooks spoil the play.

For many years, Paul Hummel, who inputs each play into the software, would read off the individual stats from his computer screen to me at the end of the first half and the end of the game, for us to compare. This meant that, on rare occasions, we had to delay the paper distribution of the stats if we had to work out a discrepancy. In recent years, I was given an iPad that provided the live official stats, so that I could compare them to my stats whenever I had a break.

For each play in the official account, each team gets a one-letter code, typically the first letter of the college, to designate where the ball is on any play—for example, "Ball on the O20." This often invites fun on our crew when we call out the play, such as in a game with Rutgers: "Ball on the R2," would be followed by, "Insert Star Wars joke here." When we called out plays with players' numbers, we would have similar opportunities. When in future years Dwayne Haskins passed to Austin Mack, we would follow the "Pass 7-11" play code with, "He's always open."

Stadium officials are stationed at the entrances to confirm credentials, of course. One year, officials used a dog to sniff our belongings for contraband. At one game, we had to wait for the dog to arrive before we could enter.

During the 2015 season, Doral Chenoweth of the *Columbus Dispatch* recorded and uploaded a few minutes of video showing our official stats crew at work, including comments from Scott Rex, Mike Basford of the Athletics communication staff, and me.

In the pandemic year of 2020, no fans were allowed in the stadium, and we had fewer staff on the official statistics crew for home games, and so I was laid off for the season. This meant that after years of having a Thursday (high school stats), Friday (high school stats or play-by-play), and Saturday (OSU stats or Ohio Wesleyan play-by-play) routine, I had only a Thursday/Friday routine. This also meant that I had missed attending a home game for the first time since the opening game of 1970, when I had a sprained foot.

It was odd to watch games on TV at home on Saturdays, though I was able to attend other games by driving to the University of Kentucky and West Virginia University, and by flying into Atlanta to see Georgia State and into Savannah to see Georgia Southern play in Statesboro. For the 2021 season, things were back to normal at Ohio State, and I returned to the press box on the stats crew.

I have worked the stats for the Ohio State spring game at four different venues: Ohio Stadium, Paul Brown Stadium in Cincinnati, Crew Stadium (the soccer stadium later renamed to Mapfre Stadium), and the practice field that is adjacent to the Woody Hayes Athletic Center. The last two were used due to the renovation of Ohio Stadium, and the game at the practice field had very few spectators in attendance.

SOME ADVENTURES ALONG THE WAY

For the 31-28 win over Navy in the Liberty Bowl game, Jeff Logan, as the sideline reporter, was able to get me the job of statistician in the booth for the Metrosports company and my brother Mark the job as spotter. I still have a *Columbus Dispatch* article from November 24, 1981, stating that WTVN-TV in Columbus had signed an agreement with Metrosports a month beforehand to carry the Liberty Bowl, not knowing at the time who the opponents would be. The article misspelled the play-by-play broadcaster Harry Kalas's name twice–"Callas". In my ignorance, I spelled it "Callas" in my log.

To prepare for the game, I wanted to get Navy's stats on my own, so I went to the Ohio History Center near the Ohio State Fairgrounds to get their box scores from the *Columbus Dispatch* Sunday sports sections. The security clearance for this was impressive ... I had to answer several questions explaining why I wanted to look at the newspapers! I still have my handwritten accumulation of both Ohio State and Navy stats, which looks like a spreadsheet, with perfectly drawn lines for rows and columns containing game-by-game statistics at both the player and team levels. I also had stats for Navy's opponents. Not having the luxury of Excel Conditional Formatting, I circled in red the season high and low in each category.

We drove to Memphis two days before the game, eating at a KFC in Jackson, Tennessee where half of the eight customers were OSU fans. We went to the team's hotel that night and shared an elevator ride with Edward Jennings, who was in his first year as OSU President. The day before the game, we went to Graceland (Elvis Presley's home), and the Liberty Bowl stadium at night to check it out. We asked a worker there what gives with the 30 degree weather, I thought that the South was supposed to be mild in the winter? He replied succinctly, "This is not the South." The game time temperature was 34 degrees.

I was in a production meeting with the producer, Guido D'Elia, who has an extensive biography that can be found online. He was the Vice President of Location Production for TPC Communications in the Greater Pittsburgh area at the time. Among his vast experiences was his position as the Director of Branding and Communications for football at Penn State University; there, he will be forever famous for creating the Whiteout at Beaver Stadium, where the home crowd dressed in all white. The producers let us see some taped action that they had ready to use during the game, including Mike Tomczak's touchdown pass in the Northwestern game.

Harry Kalas, the Philadelphia Phillies' broadcaster from 1971 through his death in 2009, did the play-by-play, and Hall of Famer Joe Theismann was calling his first ever game as a color announcer. My gig as the statistician was contingent on the availability of another guy. In our pre-game chat, he was suffering from a cold and had to bail on doing the stats, and I was in. He worked the stats for Notre Dame telecasts and shared some of the stats that he kept for their game. I found a video of the entire game online, and my name does not appear in the credits, though the name of the guy I replaced does, since he had other duties.

The highlight during the game for us was Mark seeing Woody Hayes in the press box and asking the producer if it would be OK to ask Woody to come on to the broadcast for a while. Woody did oblige, spending several minutes early in the third quarter chatting with Harry.

I have a photo of Harry, Joe, and myself in the press box. The crew had a get-together at a hotel after the game, and I asked Joe to confirm the story that his name was actually pronounced thees-man, changed by Notre Dame staff to rhyme with "Heisman", and he did.

I still have my handwritten individual rushing stats on yellow legal paper. Compared to the official stats, I match the Navy total and am off by seven for Ohio State. For the Buckeyes, I have one more carry for Tim Spencer and one less for Jimmy Gayle.

Mark asked me how much I thought we would be paid, and I said, well, last year, I was paid $50.00 for a regular season game by ESPN, and this was a bowl game, so probably $100.00, which would cover the expenses of our trip–this was in 1981, remember. When the check came, it was for $25.00, but hey, we are not in it for the money.

Later in the 1980s, the WOSU producers asked me to create some trivia questions that Jack could read on the air, along with a graphic, to challenge our viewers. One of them was: "Who was the last Buckeye to run for a touchdown, pass for a touchdown, kick a PAT, and kick a field goal in the same season?" The answer was Bob Atha, and, interestingly, Earle started him at wide receiver at the Liberty Bowl. If Bob had caught a touchdown pass in that game, his accomplishments would have been off the charts.

Another one in a few years was this: "Which of these was the quarterback in a winning bowl game as a sophomore: Rex Kern, Cornelius Greene, Rod Gerald, Mike Tomczak?" Jack thought that it was a trick question, since the answer was all of them.

I would work the stats for 188 consecutive home games between 1993 and 2019, but I nearly missed the Northern Illinois game of 2006. I had checked myself into the emergency room of the Ohio State University Hospital with extreme exhaustion the night before. I called D.C. and informed him that I could miss the game. The doctor kept me overnight, so my main concern was whether or not I would be released in time for the game. Luckily, the game had a 3:30 start, and I walked the short distance to the stadium. The late Dave Railsback worked in our booth for many games, relaying information to the TV production staff, and he and I had a routine every game. Dave was a high school football official, and, knowing that I worked the stats for a high school game every Friday night, would ask me, "Where were you last night?" On this occasion, my answer was "University Hospital".

Highlights of each season are below, for significant games where I worked the stats.

1978
- My only game was the 21-18 win at Indiana, with Gib Shanley and Allie Sherman calling the game. During the game, I handed Gib a note that in the last three times that the Buckeyes played in Bloomington, the scores were 27-7, 37-7, and 47-7. Allie added "and all 7s."

1979

- In the 45-29 win over Washington State, the biggest play was an 86-yard catch-and-run (mostly run, the longest completion in OSU history at the time) by Calvin Murray—who added two scores on the ground—on a pass from Art Schlichter.
- The defense pitched back to back shutouts of Wisconsin (59-0) and Michigan State (42-0). The Buckeyes would duplicate the 59-0 score against Wisconsin in the 2014 Big Ten Championship game, on their way to the national championship.

1980

- I worked the stats for the opener against Syracuse for ESPN, with John Sanders (not Saunders) and Paul Maguire as the broadcasters. Somehow, I knew that Maguire--the American Football League's all-time leader in punts and punt yards--had the most punts in a season, so I ribbed him about that ... in hindsight, probably not a wise move. They used a stat that I had prepared when Mark Sullivan made a tackle--my stat was that he had had two tackles for loss in the 1980 Rose Bowl, on Charles White and Paul McDonald. After the game, my ESPN contact was so happy with my work that he doubled my pay from $25.00 to $50.00.
- Calvin Murray celebrated his birthday by rushing for 224 yards and two touchdowns in the 27-17 win over Indiana. It was the fourth highest rushing performance by a Buckeye at the time.
- The offense rolled up 603 total yards in the 48-16 win at Michigan State. Murray ran for 115 yards, and Bob

Atha had the team's longest run of the year, 63 yards for a touchdown in the fourth quarter. Gary Williams had 113 yards in receptions and two touchdowns, including one with seven seconds left in the first half where no one on defense covered him. Schlichter passed for 212, with 173 in the first half. My parents and I drove to the game, for my Warner QUBE stats gig. This was Halloween weekend, and at dinner the night before the game, we ate at a restaurant where the staff were in costumes. Our server was Harpo Marx, who took our orders without saying a word.

- Against Illinois, the Buckeyes won a wild game, 49-42. Illinois had a 659-398 edge in total offense. The Illini's Dave Wilson passed for 621 yards, with 344 in the second half, and six touchdowns to close to within seven points after trailing 35-7 at halftime. Schlichter passed for 284 and four scores. Five players in the game had over 100 yards receiving, 137 for Doug Donley and 120 for Gary Williams. Wilson's completions, yards, and touchdowns numbers remain the highest by a Buckeyes' opposing quarterback. Late in the game, our analyst Jeff Logan said on the air, "Our statistician Steve Basford is on his sixth pencil."

- The Michigan game, a 9-3 loss, was a typical low-scoring contest between the two rivals. Between 1971 and 1980, half of the 10 games had a combined score of 20 points or less. It was not an all-field goals game; Michigan's PAT attempt after their touchdown in the third quarter was no good. This marked the fourth straight Michigan game in Columbus where the Buckeyes could not score a touchdown. The two teams combined to complete 19 of 49 passes.

1981

- The season started with a bang in the 34-13 win over Duke; the very first OSU play that I tracked for WOSU-TV was Tim Spencer running 82 yards for a touchdown on the Buckeyes' first play from scrimmage. It was the second longest rushing play in OSU history at the time.

- The very next week, in a 27-13 win over Michigan State, I put my reputation on the line in my second game on the job. The Spartans' Morten Andersen kicked a 63-yard field goal. Without anything to refer to, I was 99% sure that this was a Big Ten record and that OSU's Tom Skladany had the previous record, so I scribbled a note with "Big Ten record" to Jack, who read it on the air. Luckily, it was true!

- Against Florida State in Columbus, each team had 496 total yards, a team record 458 passing yards (260 in the second half) by Art Schlichter, but the Seminoles won 36-27. Gary Williams set another Buckeyes record with 13 catches for 220 yards, and Cedric Anderson had a breakout game with 158 receiving yards. Florida State scored 17 points on a touchdown off a blocked punt, a touchdown on a fake field goal play, and a 52-yard field goal. Neither team had a turnover.

- Jimmy Gayle exploded for 186 yards in the 29-10 win over Indiana, a year after Calvin Murray had racked up 224 against the Hoosiers. Bob Atha kicked a team-record five field goals.

- The 31-28 win over Navy in the Liberty Bowl game saw each team score at least six points in each quarter and the Buckeyes recover an onside kick to seal it. Navy had a 20-17 lead midway through the third quarter before Jimmy Gayle ran for his second score and Schlichter had his second touchdown pass of the game. The clock was down to one second in the game and Navy was down by 11 points, but, as the play-by-play shows, "clock operator is resetting 12 seconds on the clock for an unknown reason." The Middies scored a touchdown and a two-point conversion on a "one-handed stab". A few plays before, "staggers forward to the 1" and "at the last minute, he tries to pass".

1982

- The largest crowd in Ohio Stadium history to that point witnessed the lowest point of the 1982 season, the 23-20 loss to Stanford. John Elway threw for 407 yards, 284 in the second half, and led the team to the winning score with 34 seconds left following a Mike Tomczak interception in the end zone, not the last time that Elway would break hearts in Ohio. The two teams combined for seven interceptions.

- The Buckeyes broke a 14-14 tie at the end of the third quarter and beat Michigan 24-14 in front of an Ohio Stadium record crowd. After the game, Jeff Logan and I took off for Dayton to work the Gahanna Lincoln vs. Cincinnati Moeller high school playoff game.

1983

- The game at Iowa was my first flight with the WOSU-TV crew. Even though the Buckeyes lost 20-14, this was my favorite flight trip, it being my first one and the only one where we stayed overnight, in the Amana Colonies. At dinner on Friday night, several kids recognized Paul Warfield and asked him for his autograph.

- Garcia Lane had two nearly identical punt returns--63 and 71 yards--for touchdowns in the third quarter as the Buckeyes beat Purdue, 33-22.
- I flew with the WOSU-TV crew to the Indiana game, a 56-17 win. The Buckeyes gave equal time to the four quarters, scoring 14 points in each. This was Sam Wyche's only year coaching the Hoosiers, and his team threw 52 passes, scoring on the final play of the game and adding a two point conversion. Keith Byars had 169 yards and four touchdowns, and the Buckeyes scored three times on fourth down plays.
- I worked the stats for the game in Ann Arbor, a 24-21 loss, with some adventure. Mark and I got there fairly late, so I jumped out the car and sprinted the last mile to the stadium. I was to pick up my pass at the production truck, only to see that it was inside the fenced-in perimeter where they took your tickets or checked your passes. I told the portal guy that my pass was in that yonder truck, and he believed me! A key play was a fumble on "Lachey Right", where the left guard Jim Lachey was to pick up the ball placed on the turf by Tomczak. Ten years later, this play, the guard-around "fumblerooski" play, would be ruled illegal.

1984
- Keith Byars did it all in the 45-26 win over Iowa--he ran for 120 yards and two touchdowns, caught a 20-yard touchdown pass, and threw a 35-yard left-handed touchdown pass to Mike Lanese, whose only carry netted another touchdown. Larry Kolic returned a Chuck Long pass 25 yards for another score, knocking over Long at

the goal line. The score was 31-26 in the third quarter after the Hawkeyes ran off 16 straight points. Iowa had a 458-335 edge in total yards, but turned it over four times, two on fumbles and two on interceptions.

- I flew to the Purdue game with the WOSU-TV crew, a game that the Buckeyes lost 28-23. With five seconds left, Tomczak threw the ball out of bounds to stop the clock, not knowing that it was fourth down. The Buckeyes had a 570-376 edge in total yards and eight more minutes of possession, but Purdue scored on a 65-yard pass and a 55-yard interception return. Byars ran for 191 yards and added 102 reception yards.

- The 45-38 win over Illinois was the game where the Buckeyes trailed 24-0 and the game where Byars lost his shoe on a 67-yard draw play in the third quarter, the team's longest run of the year. After he scored to make it 24-7, Byars looked into a camera and said, "We're coming back!" When the score was 17-0, Paul read a stat from me that said that the Buckeyes had been outscored 38-7 going back to the previous week's loss at Purdue. Byars scored five times to tie Pete Johnson's record, the winner with 36 seconds left, and broke Archie's record with 274 on the ground, 195 in the second half. When he went airborne on one of his touchdowns, Paul Warfield compared him to Superman in flight. Five hours after the game was over, Byars would celebrate his birthday. The two teams combined for 549 yards passing and 1,073 total yards.

- The Buckeyes had nearly twice as many yards as Michigan State, but they survived a missed 43-yard field goal attempt for the tie with three seconds left to win 23-20. Byars needed 40 carries for his 121 yards, and Tomczak passed for 256, with Lanese having 116 receiving yards. Byars scored once, after having 12 straight games scoring at least twice. The Spartans scored on a 75-yard pass and a 93-yard kickoff return in the fourth quarter, the longest such plays against the Buckeyes this year. I worked the stats for WOSU-TV in this game at East Lansing, and after the game, I rode the elevator down with the two governors, Dick Celeste of Ohio and James Blanchard of Michigan.

- I flew to the Northwestern game with the WOSU-TV crew, a game that the Buckeyes won 52-3, outgaining the Wildcats 562-149 and scoring all 52 after the first quarter. We flew into Palwaukee Municipal Airport--it is now known as the Chicago Executive Airport and has PWK as its airport code--north of O'Hare and about 16 miles from Evanston. The stadium is near Lake Michigan and noted for the effect of the wind, like Wrigley Field. Rich Spangler's kick for a field goal was headed right for the uprights, until the wind caused it to fall like a brick.

- Against Michigan, the lead was only 7-6 at the end of the third quarter, but Byars had two two-yard touchdown runs in the fourth quarter in the 21-6 win. A key play was a great catch by Mike Lanese on a third-and-12 play. The stadium had a new scoreboard and some renovations that year, which displaced our broadcast location to the roof, in the open but under an awning. This meant that I had no contact with the official stats. At the end of the game, I gave Jack the stat that Keith Byars had 102 yards rushing. To my horror the next day, the official stats in the newspaper had him for 93 yards. I knew that the play in question was a nine-yard loss on a handoff that was mishandled. To my relief, on Monday, the athletics department informed that the nine-yard loss should be credited to Tomczak and that Byars in fact had 102 yards.

1985

- The opening game against Pittsburgh was the first ever night game at Ohio Stadium. With Byars injured, the Buckeyes ran for only 48 yards, but Jim Karsatos passed for 246. On fourth and goal at the two-yard line with 4:19 remaining, Karsatos rolled to his right and passed to Cris Carter for the winning score. Several fans spilled onto the track to celebrate with Carter, including a man jumping up and down with a young child in one arm!

- I flew with the WOSU-TV crew to the Illinois game, a 31-28 loss where Chris White, the coach's son, kicked a 38-yard field goal on the last play, rallying from a 28-14 deficit. If the field goal had been off the mark, it would have been Coach Bruce's only tie in a Big Ten game, and the Buckeyes' first Big Ten tie since the 1973 Michigan game. The Buckeyes themselves had rallied from 14-0 down with two Carter touchdown catches in the third quarter. Carter caught seven passes for 147 yards--no other Buckeye had a catch--and freshman Vince Workman ran for 100 yards. The Farm Aid concert had been in the stadium 13 days earlier.

- The #1 Iowa Hawkeyes came to Columbus in a game that the Buckeyes won 22-13 in a monsoon, with the lights reflecting off of the puddled field. The defense picked off four of Chuck Long's passes, two by Chris Spielman. Iowa also lost a fumble, making it a total of nine Hawkeye turnovers in Columbus in the last two years. George

Cooper had a breakout game with 104 yards, and John Wooldridge had a 57-yard scoring run--the team's longest of the season--on his first carry of the game, in the second quarter. Vince Workman scored on a four-yard run, but looking at the replay, we saw his knee go down at the two-yard line. Jack gave me a wide-eyed look of surprise at the Buckeyes' good fortune, but he said nothing on the air.

- I worked the stats for WOSU-TV for the Michigan game in Ann Arbor. Carter caught a 36-yard touchdown pass on fourth down and 15 to cut the lead to 20-17 in the fourth quarter, but Jim Harbaugh connected on a 77-yard strike to John Kolesar 51 seconds later as Michigan won 27-17. Harbaugh's pass came on second and seven at his own 23 over a blitzing Sonny Gordon, and it was the longest pass play against the Buckeye defense all year.

1986

- The offense had 715 yards, a Big Ten record and nearly as many as the first three games combined, in the 64-6 demolition of Utah, with Vince Workman running for 168 yards and Jaymes Bryant—wearing #41, as had Keith Byars—giving a Byars-like performance with 145. Half of George Cooper's eight carries went for touchdowns; he would score six on the year. The running game accounted for 394 yards, and the passing game added 321. The 64 points matched the total of the previous six games. It was the 600th win for the program.
- I flew with the WOSU-TV crew to the Indiana game, a 24-22 win, as Bryant ran for 131 yards, and the defense recorded five more turnovers. Spielman was called for a late hit on IU quarterback Brian Dewitz, his high school

teammate, and celebrated his birthday with one of the team's three interceptions. Sonny Gordon had the other two. Down 24-14, Indiana had a 15-play, 85-yard drive in 6:16 for their last score with 2:12 left. On the way back, Jack said that the Hurryin' Hoosiers weren't hurryin' on their last drive.

- I flew with the WOSU-TV crew again the next week to the Purdue game, a 39-11 win. The offense had 263 yards on the ground--129 by Bryant--and 281 passing. Freshman David Brown had a 100-yard interception return, a Big Ten record. Matt Frantz had practically instant-replay field goals of 21, 22, 22, and 21 yards. On the way back, Jack said that the first night game in Ross-Ade Stadium had the feel of a high school playoff game.

- The Buckeyes led Michigan 14-3, but lost 26-24 in the game where Jim Harbaugh guaranteed a win for the Wolverines. For the second straight year, Carter brought the team within a field goal with a touchdown catch, in his seventh straight game. The Buckeyes had a chance for the win with 1:06 left, but Matt Frantz' 45-yard field goal attempt was wide left. Workman ran for 126 yards, and Spielman was credited with 29 tackles.

1987

- The defense made it 11 interceptions and three for touchdowns in the last two games--they had five interceptions and two for touchdowns in the 28-12 Cotton Cowl win to end the 1986 season--as they picked off six Mountaineer passes in the opening 24-3 win over West Virginia. The Mountaineers completed as many passes to the Buckeyes as they did to their own receivers. For

Spielman, it was his second straight game with two interceptions. The total offense edge was only 213-197 in favor of the Buckeyes, but William White returned an interception—one of three on the day for him to tie a team record--29 yards for a score in the fourth quarter and flattened a cheerleader in the process. The defense added two fumble recoveries. The Mountaineers' quarterback Major Harris would play for the Columbus Thunderbolts in the Arena Football League in 1991 when I did the stats for the radio broadcasts.

- Carlos Snow had his breakout game as a freshman with four touchdowns--three on the ground and a 45-yard catch--as the Buckeyes broke open a 14-9 halftime game and beat Minnesota 42-9. He had the most rushing yards, the most receiving yards, the longest run, the longest reception, and the longest kickoff return in the game for the Buckeyes. Five Buckeyes had an interception. Jack would often punctuate his call on a Snow breakaway touchdown run with "Adios, Carlos!"

- Coach Bruce was fired after the third straight loss, to Iowa 29-27, the three losses by a total of 10 points. Everett Ross had four catches for 123 yards and two touchdowns on plays of 24 and 60. The Hawkeyes had the winning score on a fourth-and-23 pass play from the OSU 28. They had kicked a field goal as the first half ended. A YouTube video of this game has Jack Kramer giving me credit as the statistician at the end of the game.

- The 23-20 win at Michigan was the game where Earle Bruce wore his suit and fedora in his last game as the coach and the players wore headbands with "EARLE" lettering. Tom Tupa threw two touchdown passes in the span of about four minutes--four yards to Ross with 1:36 left in the first half, and a 70-yard pass play to Snow on the Buckeyes' first play of the second half. The Buckeyes trailed 13-0 before Ross's touchdown. Matt Frantz, who missed a go-ahead field goal late in last year's game and had missed an extra point in this game--his only miss in 53 career attempts--kicked the winning 26-yard field goal with 5:18 left.

1988

- In John Cooper's first game, a 26-9 win over Syracuse, the team had no penalties and no turnovers. Pat O'Morrow tied the team record by kicking five field goals.
- The Buckeyes scored 16 points in less than four minutes to beat Louisiana State, 36-33, after the Tigers had taken a 33-20 lead with 4:29 left. LSU helped the Buckeyes by passing instead of keeping the clock running and taking an intentional safety. On the free kick, Bobby Olive had a 30-yard return, and Greg Frey connected with Olive on a crawling 20-yard touchdown catch with 38 seconds left for the winning score--Olive's first scoring reception ever. The official account has "the game ostensibly ended at 7:19 P.M. but fans stormed the field as LSU tried to call a time out; the officials gave up at 7:21 P.M."
- In the Michigan game, a 34-31 loss, the Buckeyes trailed 20-0 at halftime. Carlos Snow ran for 170 yards and scored a touchdown on the team's first possession of the second half, as he did in 1987 against Michigan. Bill Matlock ran for his only two touchdowns of the year, and Bobby Olive had a diving catch for a score; including his only other score of the year, against LSU, both of his

touchdowns were on diving catches. Michigan had a 499-469 edge in total offense.

1989

- The offense had 200 yards rushing, 133 with two touchdowns by Scottie Graham, and 220 passing in the 28-18 loss at Michigan, which I worked for WOSU-TV. It was the second straight year in this matchup that each team had at least 400 yards of total offense.

1990

- Michigan kicked a field goal on the last play to win the game, 16-13. At the time, I did not know that it would be my last game for WOSU-TV, and so the bookends of my 10 years were Tim Spencer running 82 yards for a touchdown on the very first Ohio State play that I recorded, in 1981, and the Buckeyes losing on the very last play of my ten-year gig.

1993

- The offense had 207 yards rushing and 246 passing--144 from Bobby Hoying and 102 from Bret Powers and a touchdown pass by each–in the opening 34-7 win over Rice.
- Six Buckeyes each had a touchdown in the 51-3 win over Northwestern, and the total offense edge was 428-162. Ten players had carries, and nine had catches. The defense had five interceptions that averaged 28 yards per return.
- On a snowy October 30, the Buckeyes held Penn State without a touchdown in the 24-6 win. I saw a regatta taking place on the Scioto River in the snow on the way

to the game. The field was chewed up, and not just by Raymont Harris' 151 yards. The defense picked off four Nittany Lion passes.

1994

- The total offense was 553 yards--373 in the first half--in the 52-0 win over Houston on a hot day in Columbus. Eddie George ran for 105 yards on his birthday, and ten ball careers combined for 312 yards.
- Chris Sanders led the Buckeyes in receiving touchdowns on the year, and he had two in the 48-14 win over Purdue. Joey Galloway topped him with three. Hoying had 290 yards passing and four touchdown passes in the first half as the Buckeyes led 41-0, finishing with five touchdowns and 304 yards. The five touchdowns tied the team record held by John Borton in 1952. The Buckeyes had an even 500 yards of total offense.
- The Buckeyes were outgained 271-210 in Coach Cooper's first win over Michigan, 22-6. It was the first time in 111 games that the Wolverines had failed to score a touchdown. The Buckeyes scored on a touchdown, safety, and field goal in the first half. Marlon Kerner blocked a field goal, and Luke Fickell, a defensive lineman and the least likely player to have an interception, had one in the fourth quarter.

1995

- The Buckeyes had 15 more minutes of possession in the home opening 30-20 win over Washington. Eddie George ran for 212 yards and two touchdowns. The Huskies had 10 penalties for 101 yards, the Buckeyes only one for eight yards.

- After 60 years, the Buckeyes and Notre Dame met again in Columbus, a 45-26 win. After a scoreless first quarter, the Irish led 17-7 before Dimitrious Stanley made a twisting catch in the end zone for a score with 44 seconds left in the first half. Terry Glenn gave the Buckeyes the lead with an 82-yard catch and sprint late in the third quarter. He finished with 128 receiving yards. Eddie George had his fourth career game of 200+ yards with 207, a long of 61, and two touchdowns. Hoying passed for 272 and four touchdowns. The two teams combined for 980 yards, and it was the most points scored on a Lou Holtz Notre Dame team.

- The Buckeyes played a near-perfect first half, leading 56-0 just before halftime only to see Iowa score on the last play to make it 56-7, and the offense took the second half off in the 56-35 win. In the first half, George scored four times and Glenn twice, and Shawn Springs had a 60-yard interception return for a score. George finished with 110 yards, Glenn with 149, and Hoying with 273, with all of those in the first half. Greg Bellisari had two interceptions. Iowa had six more yards, 16 more plays, two more first downs, and 5:40 more possession time.

1996

- The offense had 317 yards on the ground and 315 passing in the 70-7 opening win over Rice. Freshman Michael Wiley had three touches for three touchdowns--a 49-yard run, a 60-yard catch, and a 51-yard catch. Pepe Pearson ran for 119 yards, and both Joe Germaine and Stanley Jackson passed for over 150.

- The offense had over 600 yards again in the 72-0 win over

Pitt, making it 126 points against the Panthers in the last two years. Joe Montgomery ran for 109 yards and Pearson for 103, and 11 Buckeyes caught a pass. Freshman David Boston had a 66-yard punt return for a touchdown--with only seven other teammates on the field.

- The Buckeyes outgained Penn State 565-211 in the 38-7 win. Pearson ran for 141 yards, both Jackson and Germaine passed for two scores, and Dimitrious Stanley had 105 yards receiving and two touchdowns.

- The Buckeyes dominated Minnesota both on the scoreboard, 45-0, and in yards, 452-104. Pearson ran for 123 yards, and four passers, including Pearson with a 21-yard completion, combined for 222 yards, to eleven receivers. Freshman linebacker Andy Katzenmoyer returned an interception 42 yards for a score.

- Joe Germaine had his only start of the year in the 13-9 loss to Michigan in Columbus. The Buckeyes dominated the first half, 220-62 in total yards, but they managed only three field goals. Pearson ran for 107 of his 117 yards in the first half. Like the Buckeyes' win in 1987, Michigan scored on a 70-yard drive on their first possession of the second half, scoring on the infamous slip by Shawn Springs that allowed Tai Streets to complete a 69-yard pass play from Brian Griese.

1997

- The Buckeyes had not played Northwestern the last two years, the Wildcats having gone to the Rose Bowl in the 1995 season, so they took out their frustration in a 49-6 win, trailing 3-0 after the first quarter. Three quarterbacks combined for five touchdown passes--three by Germaine and one each by Jackson and Mark Garcia. Tom Hoying's only catch of the year was for 29 yards and a score, and Pearson ran for two scores. Total offense was 563-164 in favor of the Buckeyes, and first downs were 32-9.

1998
- The defense held Penn State to 181 yards, Jerry Rudzinski scored on a fumble recovery, and Joe Cooper scored on a blocked punt in the 28-9 win over the Nittany Lions. Dee Miller had over 100 yards receiving against the Nittany Lions for the second straight year.
- The Buckeyes had a 9-0 record and were ahead of Michigan State, which would finish 6-6 on the year under Nick Saban, 24-9 with under 10 minutes left in the third quarter after a 73-yard interception return for a touchdown by Damon Moore. Moore's interception was so quick that, watching from the press box, I thought that the Spartans had completed the pass and the receiver was heading for the end zone, finally seeing that Moore was streaking the other way. The Spartans rallied for a 28-24 win, though the Buckeyes had a first-and-ten on the Spartan 15 with under two minutes left. There was no doubt in my mind that the Buckeyes would score, but Germaine misfired on all four passes, ending with an interception. The defense gave up only 22 points in the fourth quarter all year, but 10 in this game.
- It seemed as if Michael Wiley and David Boston were running at twice their usual speed in the 31-16 win over Michigan. Wiley had a 53-yard scoring run in the first three minutes, and Boston had 217 yards and two touchdowns, giving him three against Michigan

in the last two years. Germaine passed for 330 yards and three touchdowns. Michigan had 24 more plays, and Tom Brady passed for 375 yards. The defense held the Wolverines to four (no typo) yards on the ground, sacking Brady seven times. This made Michigan's rushing total 46 yards in the last two matchups. Counting this game, the Buckeye defense had given up only two touchdowns in the last 13 quarters at home against Michigan, both by Tai Streets.

1999

- Steve Bellisari passed for two touchdowns in the 42-20 win over UCLA in a night game. Wiley ran for 119 yards, and Reggie Germany had 115 yards in receptions, as the offense rolled up 507 yards. Wiley and Ken-Yon Rambo, both from California, each had two touchdowns in the game against a team from California.

2000

- The opening 43-10 win over Fresno State was in the renovated stadium, and it looked odd to see the field sunken and no track. The Buckeyes had four defensive touchdowns--two on fumbles and two on interceptions--with the first two scores of the game coming that way. David Mitchell had two of the scores on a fumble return and an interception, and the defense had a total of four interceptions. The game saw each team throw a touchdown pass in the last five seconds. After the Bulldogs scored, Coach Cooper had freshman Scott McMullen launch a 44-yard bomb to Ricky Bryant. All six Buckeye touchdowns were scored by players who had never scored before.

- Six different Buckeyes scored a touchdown in the 45-6 win over Penn State. The defense held the Nittany Lions to 213 yards.
- In the Michigan game, the Buckeyes led 9-0, fell behind 31-12, rallied to 31-26, but fell 38-26. It was the fifth straight game in the rivalry where the Buckeyes had more total yards, with a record of 1-4.

2001

- Jonathan Wells ran for 179 yards and three touchdowns--one of them 71 yards, the team's longest of the year--as the Buckeyes jumped out 38-7 and beat Northwestern 38-20 in a night game. Mike Doss had a 30-yard fumble return for a score.
- Chris Vance had a circus catch, a one-handed snag in the back of the end zone in the 35-9 win over Purdue. Vance finished with 138 yards, Bellisari passed for 263, and Wells had his third straight game of 100+ with 101 yards. Total offense was 429-211 in favor of the Buckeyes. Four different Buckeyes scored a touchdown, and the defense recorded two safeties.

2002

- The opening 45-21 win over Texas Tech was Maurice Clarett's debut, and he ran for 175 yards and three touchdowns, two of them 59 and 45 yards, adding four receptions to lead the team. The defense held the Red Raiders to 31 yards on the ground.
- The Buckeyes trailed Washington State 7-6 at halftime before winning, 25-7. Clarett ran for two touchdowns and 230 yards, with 194 in the second half.

- Chris Gamble intercepted Zack Mills and zig-zagged 40 yards for a touchdown in the 13-7 win over Penn State. Of his seven career interceptions, this was the only one with return yards.
- In the 14-9 win over Michigan, Clarett had the first touchdown of two yards, and Maurice Hall had the winning one of three yards--he also had the winning score in overtime the previous week at Illinois. For the seventh straight year in the rivalry, the losing team had more total yards. The Buckeyes had only 17 plays in the first half, with nine of them on the touchdown drive. Will Allen's interception on the last play was the only one for either team in a combined 62 passes. His two interceptions on the year that sealed the wins over Cincinnati and Michigan netted no return yards.

2003
- In the opening 28-9 win over Washington in a night game, Maurice Hall had the first touchdown of the game, meaning that the last three games of the previous season had a player named Maurice scoring the Buckeyes' winning touchdown, and now this Maurice score to kick off the season. The defense held the Huskies to seven yards on the ground, with a long of nine.
- Against North Carolina State, a 44-38 win in three overtimes, the Buckeyes led 24-7 in the fourth quarter, only to see Philip Rivers lead the Wolfpack rally to a tie with 21 seconds left in regulation. The two teams combined for 65 rushing yards and a one-yard per rush average. Rivers passed for 315 yards, with 217 after halftime. Craig Krenzel ran or passed for five of the six touchdowns. He

had three overtime touchdown passes, to three different receivers.

2004

- The game against Marshall appeared to be headed to overtime tied at 21, but Mike Nugent kicked a 55-yard field goal on the last play of the game for a 24-21 win. Justin Zwick passed for 324 yards and three touchdowns, with all three scores and 255 yards in the first half, two to Santonio Holmes for 80 and 47 yards. Holmes finished with ten catches for 224 yards, with 199 in the first half.
- The 37-21 win over Michigan seemed to come out of nowhere, the Buckeyes coming off a loss to Purdue and the 37 points being five more than any other output that year. The Buckeyes exploded on their first possession, with Anthony Gonzalez catching a 68-yard pass from Troy Smith, raising his arms in celebration as he scored. Ted Ginn's 82-yard punt return--touchdown #7 on the year for #7--where he started on the right sideline and flew to the left before sprinting down the left sideline for the score, was another highlight play. Santonio Holmes caught a 12-yard touchdown pass from Smith, which meant that the four players who scored touchdowns were freshmen or sophomores. Smith ran for 145 yards and passed for 241, accounting for all but 60 of the team's 446 yards.

2005

- Against Texas, a 25-22 Longhorn win in Columbus, Troy Smith saw his first action after a two-game suspension and threw a 36-yard touchdown pass to Santonio

Holmes in the second quarter. The defense had Vince Young bottled up in the first half, but he threw the winning touchdown, confirmed after video review, with 2:37 remaining.

- Halftime of the Michigan State game, a 35-24 win, was also the halfway point of the regular season, and that is when the Buckeyes turned the game and their season around. With the Spartans leading 17-7 and lining up for a 35-yard field goal, Nate Salley blocked the kick and Ashton Youboty returned it 72 yards as time expired. The Buckeyes had three other huge scoring plays, with passes of 46 and 51 yards to Holmes and a 57-yard pass to Ginn. The defense set an OSU record with 12 sacks.

2006

- Malcolm Jenkins and Antonio Smith returned interceptions--61 and 55 yards--1:24 apart in the fourth quarter of the 28-6 win over Penn State, although Jenkins may have deposited the ball short of the goal line. These were the two longest interception returns of the year.
- In the 42-39 win over #2 Michigan, six different Buckeyes--Roy Hall, Antonio Pittman, Ginn, Chris Wells, Anthony Gonzalez, and Brian Robiskie--scored a touchdown each as the teams combined for exactly 900 yards. Wells did a 360-degree turn in the backfield on the way to his 52-yard touchdown, his longest run of the year. Pittman also had his longest run of the year, a 56-yard run for his score, and finished with 139. Smith passed for 316 yards, giving him 857 total passing yards in three contests against the Wolverines.

2007

- The bid for an undefeated season ended with the 28-21 home loss to Illinois. Chris Wells and Maurice Wells scored the three Buckeyes touchdowns, but the Illini's Juice Williams passed for touchdowns to four different receivers, one of them to Jacob Willis, son of former OSU receiver Lenny Willis. Illinois may have caught a huge break when an apparent fumble at the OSU three-yard line was not detected. The Buckeyes had the ball for only three plays and 1:14 of the fourth quarter as the Illini held the ball for the last 8:09, covering only 48 yards.

2008

- In Terrelle Pryor's first start, four of his ten completions were for touchdowns, two to Brian Hartline, in the 28-10 win over Troy. Kurt Coleman had two interceptions.
- The score was only 14-7 at halftime, but the Buckeyes scored 28 unanswered to beat Michigan 42-7, outgaining the Wolverines 416-198. Chris Wells ran for 134 yards and a touchdown, making it into the end zone all three years against Michigan. In his last game at Ohio Stadium, Todd Boeckman threw an 18-yard scoring pass to Hartline. Between Pryor and Boeckman, three of the eight completions went for scores, two to Hartline and one to Brian Robiskie.

2009

- The Buckeyes led Navy 20-7 at halftime in the opener, but they were facing a possible tie as Navy lined up for a two-point conversion with 2:23 remaining. Brian Rolle intercepted the pass and returned it for two points in the

31-27 win, almost the identical score as the 1981 Liberty Bowl win (31-28) over the Midshipmen. The 27 points would be the most scored by any opponent this year.

- In front of a new stadium attendance record at night, the Buckeyes lost to USC, 18-15. The Buckeyes led 15-10, but the Trojans scored with 1:05 remaining. The two teams combined for only 206 rushing yards, 88 by the Buckeyes. Going back to the Fiesta Bowl of last year, those last two losses were by three points each in the closing moments. This was the third straight loss in a night game in Ohio Stadium.

- The Buckeyes had a 24-10 lead on Iowa in the fourth quarter, but they needed overtime to win 27-24 and clinch a trip to the Rose Bowl. Devin Barclay, who had switched jersey numbers from 12 to 23 during the year, kicked a 39-yard field goal after the defense had forced the Hawkeyes out of field goal range on their overtime possession. Anderson Russell had two of the Buckeyes' three interceptions.

2010

- The Miami Hurricanes scored 24 points, the same as in the championship game of the 2002 season, as the Buckeyes won in Columbus, 36-24. Pryor ran for 113 yards and passed for 233. The defense had four interceptions for 124 yards, with Cameron Heyward returning one for 80 without scoring. Devin Barclay made five of his six field goal attempts, the five tying the OSU record.

- The Buckeyes trailed Penn State 14-3 at halftime, but five different players scored in the second half to win 38-14. Dan Herron ran for 190 yards, as the Buckeyes had 306 of their 453 yards in the second half. As in the 2006 Penn State game, the defense returned two interceptions for touchdowns, by Devon Torrence and Travis Howard.

- After a scoreless first period, the Buckeyes scored 24 in the second and beat Michigan 37-7. Four different Buckeyes scored a touchdown, with Jordan Hall answering the Wolverines' only score with an 85-yard kickoff return. Dan Herron had 175 yards and the team's longest run of the year, an 89-yard carry from the OSU two-yard line to the Michigan nine. Pryor passed for 220 yards. It would be the last regular season game for Jim Tressel and for coach Rich Rodriguez at Michigan.

2011

- The Buckeyes beat Wisconsin 33-29 in an Instant Classic, with each team scoring a touchdown within a minute in the last 1:18. The Buckeyes had a 26-14 lead with 3:48 left before the Badgers scored twice to take a 29-26 lead with 1:18 remaining. Braxton Miller had only 89 yards passing, but he threw the winning pass of 40 yards to Devin Smith, Smith's only catch of the game, with 20 seconds remaining. Miller came dangerously close to the line of scrimmage on his heave to Smith, but video review confirmed that it was a proper pass. Herron ran for 160 yards. The Buckeyes had 104 yards and three points in the first half, and 253 yards and 30 points in the second. The teams scored 52 of the 62 points in the second half.

2012

- Bradley Roby had two of the team's three interceptions, including one of 41 yards for the first touchdown, in the 63-38 win over Nebraska in a night game. The Cornhuskers would have leads of 14-7 and 24-21. Miller ran for 186 yards, and Carlos Hyde for 140 and four touchdowns, as the Buckeyes rolled up 371 yards on the ground and the two teams combined for 935 total yards.

- For the second straight year, the Purdue game went into overtime, with the Buckeyes winning 29-22. The Boilers' first two touchdowns came on an 83-yard pass play on the first play of the game and a 100-yard kickoff return. With Miller injured late in the third quarter, Kenny Guiton led the last drive of the game, seven plays for 61 yards. With the Buckeyes down 22-14, Devin Smith had the longest Buckeye catch of the game, 39 yards, and Chris Fields had the shortest catch of the day for either team, two yards with three seconds remaining for the touchdown. Jeff Heuerman caught the conversion pass to tie it at 22, and Carlos Hyde had the winning touchdown in overtime.

- Drew Basil had half of his field goal total of the year by kicking four in the 26-21 win over Michigan, including a 52-yarder on the last play of the first half, his longest of the year, and two more in the second half, the only scoring in the second half for either team. Hyde ran for 146 yards, and Miller passed for 189. Michigan's 279 yards of total offense, including two scoring plays of 67 and 75 yards and with only 60 yards in the second half, represented the Buckeyes defense's second best performance of the year.

2013

- Five different Buckeyes scored in the first quarter as the Buckeyes scored 34 and cruised to a 76-0 win over Florida

A&M. In all, eight Buckeyes had a touchdown, and ten caught a pass. Jordan Hall carried four times and scored twice. Total offense was 603-80 in favor of the Buckeyes, and Florida A&M's longest play was ten yards.

- Nineteen years after losing at Penn State, 63-14, the Buckeyes beat the Nittany Lions by the same score in Columbus. Hyde, Miller, and Guiton each ran for two touchdowns. Hyde ran for 147 yards, and Miller passed for 252 and three touchdowns to three different receivers, as the Buckeyes rolled up 686 yards on offense.

2014

- In the 35-21 loss to Virginia Tech, the Buckeyes trailed 21-7 at halftime, but had tied it at 21 in the fourth quarter. It was the Buckeyes' first home-opening loss since losing in 1978 to Penn State.

- The Buckeyes trailed Michigan 14-7 before J.T. Barrett scored on an improvised 25-yard run that capped an 83-yard drive with seven seconds remaining before halftime in the 42-28 win. The Buckeyes were up 28-21, when on the first play of the fourth quarter, Barrett suffered a fractured ankle. Ezekiel Elliott ran 44 yards for a score on fourth and one, and Darron Lee had a 33-yard fumble return to extend it to 42-21, giving him the first and last touchdowns of the regular season games.

2015

- Penn State led 3-0 at the end of the first quarter before the Buckeyes scored three times in the second and cruised to a 38-10 win. Elliott ran for 153 yards, and

Barrett ran for 102 and was involved in 15 plays, producing four touchdowns, two on the ground and two in the air. Saquon Barkley had 194 of the Nittany Lions' 195 rushing yards. Of the Lions' 315 total yards, 112 came on two plays.

- In front of a new Ohio Stadium record crowd, Michigan State's Michael Geiger kicked a 41-yard field goal on the last play to pull the upset, 17-14. The Spartans had 22 more plays and more than 16 more minutes of possession, and the Buckeyes had only 132 total yards--86 yards rushing and 46 yards passing.

2016

- In the 62-3 win over Nebraska, Damon Webb gave the Buckeyes the only touchdown that they would need with a 36-yard interception return on the first possession of the game, and Malik Hooker added a 48-yard interception return in the third quarter. Barrett passed for 290 yards with four touchdowns, and total offense was 590-204 in favor of the Buckeyes.

- In the 30-27 double overtime win over Michigan, Malik Hooker's 16-yard interception return tied the game at seven in the second quarter, and Tyler Durbin, who had missed two earlier field goal attempts, nailed one from 23 yards with one second left in regulation to force the overtime. In both overtime games this year, Durbin kicked a field goal for the last points in regulation. In the second overtime, Barrett had the controversial run on fourth down to the 15-yard line, and Curtis Samuel leaped into the end zone on the next play for the win.

2017

- The Buckeyes lost to Oklahoma in Columbus, 31-16, in a game that was tied at three at halftime and had only a 17-13 Sooner lead after three quarters. The Buckeyes had only one touchdown, while Baker Mayfield passed for 386 yards and three scores.
- The 39-38 comeback win over Penn State was an Instant Classic, as Barrett hit Marcus Baugh with a 16-yard pass with 1:48 remaining. The Buckeyes had trailed 38-27 with 5:42 to go. With Penn State up 21-3, the scoring run for Penn State was 38-3 going back to last year. Penn State was allowing only 9.6 points on defense coming into the game.

2018

- In the opening 77-31 win over Oregon State, despite the weather delay for 80 minutes during halftime--at which point the Buckeyes led 42-14--this would be the shortest game of the year, in three hours and six minutes. Mike Weber ran for 186 yards and three touchdowns, and Dwayne Haskins passed for 313 and five scores. Ten Buckeyes had a reception, and eight Buckeyes scored, including Nick Bosa recovering a fumble. The teams combined for over 1,100 yards, 721 by the Buckeyes.
- The halftime score of the Michigan game was only 24-19, thanks to a Blake Haubeil field goal on the final play, but the Buckeyes erupted for 38 points in the second half for the 62-39 win. This was Chris Olave's coming out party, with two touchdown catches and an assist, blocking a punt that Sevyn Banks returned for a score. Mike Weber

ended his three-year career with a touchdown in all three years against Michigan State and the Wolverines, the two teams from his home state. The offense rolled up 567 yards, with Haskins passing for 396 and Parris Campbell with six catches for 192 and two scores.

2019

- The Wisconsin game had only a 10-7 lead in the third quarter, but the Buckeyes scored four more times to win 38-7. J.K. Dobbins ran for 163 yards and two touchdowns, and Olave had two touchdown receptions, as the total offense advantage was 431-191. The defense held the Badgers to 83 yards on the ground.
- The Buckeyes appeared to be cruising when the lead was 21-0 over Penn State in the third quarter, but two fumbles--they lost three in the game--got the Nittany Lions to within 21-17. Justin Fields' 28-yard pass to Olave in the right corner of the south end zone in the fourth quarter secured the 28-17 win. Dobbins ran for 157 yards and two touchdowns.

2021

- In the 35-28 loss to Oregon, C.J. Stroud passed for 484 yards, the offense racked up 612 yards, and Jaxson Smith-Njigba, Chris Olave, and Garrett Wilson each had over 100 yards receiving. After the game, OSU fans were hoping for a repeat of what happened in 2014 that led to a national championship: give up 35 points in a loss at home in the second game of the year, which was the first home game and a non-conference game, with a quarterback in his first full year. It would not turn out that way, but the Buckeyes averaged 54 points per game in the remaining six home games.

- In the 41-20 win over Tulsa, Treveyon Henderson set the Ohio State freshman rushing record with a 270-yard performance, breaking the record held by Archie Griffin, who had 239 against North Carolina in 1972.
- In the 66-17 win over Maryland, Stroud passed for 406 yards, Henderson ran for 102, and Smith-Njigba and Olave each had over 100 yards receiving.
- In the 33-24 win over Penn State, Stroud passed for 305 yards, and Henderson ran for 152. Jerron Cage returned a fumble 57 yards for a touchdown; my Facebook post the next day had his photo, with the caption "Cage Free!"
- In the 59-31 win over Purdue, Stroud passed for 361 yards, Miyan Williams ran for 117, and Smith-Njigba and Olave each had over 100 yards receiving.
- In the 56-7 win over Michigan State, Stroud passed for 432 yards and six touchdowns, and Smith-Njigba, Olave, and Garrett Wilson each had over 100 yards receiving.

CHAPTER 4

HIGH SCHOOL BROADCASTING

FOOTBALL

MY FIRST HIGH SCHOOL football broadcast was in 1984 for WCVO-FM. When I eventually had the task of doing the engineering– Dan McLaughlin trained me at the WCVO studio–it would take five trips to transport the equipment from my car to the press box, before I bought a two-wheel cart and trimmed the number of trips down to three. I would pick up the equipment at the WCVO studio on Reynoldsburg-New Albany Road and return it after the game. The equipment included a heavy 3,000-watt Marti transmitter (valued at $2,500), a mixer, a receiver, a pager, two headphones, an antenna, a heavy tripod for the antenna, "20' and 8' RF cords" (according to the full-page of instructions detailing the steps to start the broadcast, which I still have), a box of tapes containing public service announcements, and a machine to play the tapes. Some of the instructions are:

- Set up the tripod and connect the antenna with the crescent wrench.

- At Gahanna, aim the antenna just off to the right of the light pole adjacent to the press box.
- If the press box is in a "valley", prop the front leg of the tripod so that the antenna is aimed up.

If I needed an inspiration for this heavy equipment scenario, I would conjure up the memory of the legendary sportscaster Howard Cosell, who was a pioneer in sports interviews in his early years and was quoted as saying "When I would appear carrying my forty-five pound tape recorder ..." in the book *Howard Cosell: The Man, the Myth, and the Transformation of American Sports* by Mark Ribowsky. I also had my own bag for my notes and binoculars. How all of this fit into my 1980 Chevrolet Monza, I'll never know. The antenna would stick out of the trunk; at best, I should have had a bungee cord to close the trunk better. On one occasion, I thought that I was going to be cited by a police officer as I crept through a business district with the antenna protruding from my open trunk. I watched in my rear view mirror as he walked behind me, but he was only stopping traffic to let cars out of an office parking lot. At Gahanna Lincoln High School, I would need to transport the equipment through the concession building before the gates opened.

According to the *Columbus Dispatch*, Gahanna Lincoln had the fourth best winning percentage among Central Ohio teams in the 1980s, at 77%, which meant that the odds were good that we would see a win when they played. The coaches during my years were Phil Koppel at first, then Colin Messaros, and they would give me their starters before the game, on the field. The only visiting coach whom I can recall talking to before a game was Reynoldsburg's Rob Sass, who was very gracious. Gahanna and New Albany were the main schools that we covered due to the proximity to the studio, but we would also call several games from Westerville South, Worthington, and Bishop Hartley High Schools. At one game between Bishop Ready and Bishop Hartley in 1989, we learned that a group of Bishop Ready teachers had jogged to the game from their high school to Hartley in the rain, a 10-mile effort.

In 1982, WCVO-FM hired Stu Mason as the sports director and high school broadcaster, a lucky event for me, as we would call football and basketball games for several years. I still have a WCVO name tag on which Stu wrote "Steve Basford Ast. Sports Dir". Stu would also have me give a weekly report on high school football in Ohio, and since the Internet was a few years away, I would go to the Ohio State campus on Saturday mornings, to get as many out of town newspapers–the *Cleveland Plain Dealer, Cincinnati Enquirer, Dayton Daily News, Toledo Blade, and Akron Beacon-Journal*–as I could out of coin-operated boxes along High Street so that I could read up on the teams from those areas. After a while, I learned that I was mispronouncing towns such as Versailles (I assumed that it was the French pronunciation "Ver-sigh", instead of "Ver-sales") and Cincinnati Mariemont (I assumed that it was pronounced "Marie" as in Marie Osmond, when it should be "Mary-mont").

In 1985, I called the Gahanna vs. Eastmoor game, won by Gahanna 3-0 in overtime on a 34-yard field goal by Brad Hammock, who had missed two previous field goal attempts. Of course, this was on Friday the 13th. The games the week before for the two teams were decided by kicks, too. I had called the Gahanna vs. Westerville North game, where Hammock kicked a 23-yard field goal with 6:05 remaining in the 10-7 win. Eastmoor had lost 16-14 when Upper Arlington's Eric Johnson kicked a school-record 50-yard field goal off a free kick with 10 seconds left. The morning after the Gahanna vs. Eastmoor game, I realized that I had left our WCVO banner hanging outside the Eastmoor press box. In a panic, I looked up the phone number of the Eastmoor athletics department in the phone book and called it, reaching Coach Brian Cross. I was expecting him to be in a foul mood after the close loss, but he could not have been nicer; he arranged a time for me to meet him at the stadium and pick up the banner. Later that day, I worked the stats at the first

Ohio State night game ever played in Ohio Stadium, a 10-7 win over the Pittsburgh Panthers, which meant that I had worked games in consecutive days that were decided by three points each.

For a few years, my broadcast partner and I would alternate quarters of doing the play-by-play, but Stu later had us switch to having one person doing the play-by-play, rightfully so.

When we carried the Reynoldsburg at Gahanna Lincoln game in 1987, the Reynoldsburg quarterback and punter was Mike Matheny, the future major league catcher for the Milwaukee Brewers, Toronto Blue Jays, St. Louis Cardinals, and San Francisco Giants and the future manager of the St. Louis Cardinals (losing in the 2013 World Series) and the Kansas City Royals.

In 1988, Bill Walters joined WCVO-FM, another big break for me in starting a broadcast relationship with him that would extend over 30 years. One of Bill's duties before the football games was to find a phone in the high school before kickoff and call the studio to see if our transmission was working. It was always a relief when he returned to say that we were coming through loud and clear. At halftime of games, I would report on upcoming running races, and Bill would report on a variety of sports.

One of the best high school games that I ever called--seriously!--was the New Albany 2-0 win over Berne Union in 1988. I learned the opponents and year of this only by finding a cassette tape in 2022 of a game that I called in 1990 where I talked about that 2-0 game–"The teams just marched up and down the field." So, in the span of three years, I had called a game that was scoreless in regulation–Gahanna Lincoln vs. Eastmoor in 1985–and another game that had a 2-0 score. The week before, Berne Union had beaten Miller, 3-0, and they would be shut out three straight times later in the season. After two games, the Berne Union defense had not given up any points; in their last eight games, they gave up an average of 31 points per game.

In another New Albany game–I don't recall the year or opponent–the Eagles had one last drive. On one play in the drive, a receiver making his first appearance caught a long pass to keep the drive alive. Later, a perfectly thrown pass hit a different receiver in the midsection and knocked the wind out of him. On their last fourth-down play, the pass was thrown perfectly to the same receiver who had made the first catch ... and he dropped it. In another New Albany game, the opponent converted on fourth-down-and-10 plays twice and on a fourth-down-and-20 play another time in their late drive to score the winning touchdown.

One year, the visiting team at Gahanna Lincoln was Cleveland James Rhodes High School, which I assumed was named for the former Ohio governor. Luckily, in those pre-Internet years, a co-worker offered to do some research and informed me that this school was named for James Ford Rhodes, a businessman and historian.

I still have a 1988 memo from WCVO-FM General Manager Pat Patterson in which he referred to Stu Mason and me with "I've got some of the best men in Steve Bashford ...", but I assume that he was referring to me, despite the typo. Pat would call us "volunteers", which is accurate in that we did not get paid. It was not an issue; after 10 years with WCVO-FM, I could list about 200 more games on my resume. It was irrelevant to prospective employers that I had not been paid for them.

In 1990, we carried the Bishop Watterson at Westerville South game. A player for Bishop Watterson was Brian Kennedy, who would become the Eagles' head coach in 2017. I would call two of the games that he coached, when Watterson played Dublin Jerome in 2017 and 2018. When calling Gahanna Lincoln games that season, we had another future coach; the Lions' quarterback Bubba Kidwell would become the coach at New Albany.

In that same year, we had the Westerville South at Worthington game, matching two of the top running backs in Ohio–Ki-Jana Carter of Westerville South and DeWight Pickens of Worthington. Pickens ran for

111, and Carter for 155 yards in Worthington's 21-12 win. Worthington's Dimitrious Stanley was a sophomore quarterback/running back who also caught a 19-yard pass for a touchdown. Stanley would go on to play at Ohio State, Carter at Penn State (becoming the runner-up for the Heisman Trophy and the first player selected in the 1995 NFL Draft), and Pickens at Ohio. Both Stanley and Carter would score a touchdown in a Rose Bowl, two years apart. On the air, I said that "Stanley has all the tools."

Also in 1990, we had the 54-6 blowout win for Amanda Clearcreek over New Albany, a game that had no scoring in the fourth quarter. It was a typical game for Amanda Clearcreek; they outscored their opponents 428-33 that year, setting or tying four records for a season on defense, and were in the middle of a 22-game regular season streak of giving up nine points or less.

Stu Mason arranged two gigs for me with Time Warner Cable in northwest Ohio. The first was in 2000, where I was the color announcer for a doubleheader of grade-school boys football games in Upper Sandusky, called the Pumpkin Bowl, featuring four teams in the Wyandot County Midget Football League. During the warmups, I asked each player for his favorite NFL team and player, and shared that information during the game.

In the 2010-2011 school year, I took over from Jason Whitt as the football and basketball play-by-play broadcaster for WINF-FM in Delaware County. Before the first football game, I met with Jason at the WRFD radio station on North High Street, north of Worthington, to get trained on the broadcast system. Ironically, to the best of my knowledge, my mother had worked at WRFD before she was married. She would refer to it as the "Farm Bureau", since it was operated by an affiliate of Farm Bureau Mutual Insurance Company. Based on comments that she had made long ago, I think that she also worked at the WCOL station; her obituary has "... worked for local radio stations". I must have inherited my love of radio from her. I needed a broadcast partner, so I reached out to Steve Geiger. I knew him as a talented basketball analyst, but had no idea of his comfort with football. I told him that I wanted someone who was "smooth" on the air, and I was incredibly fortunate when he agreed to join me. A math teacher, Steve was also able to keep some individual stats while performing his duty as the analyst on our games. Actually, before asking Steve, I asked a former Ohio State football player, whom I ran into at a Kroger grocery store; however, he declined.

Our first football game was Olentangy vs. Olentangy Orange, and it took me a while to get over the fact that the Orange players have jerseys similar to the Florida Gators, having been at the national championship game of the 2006 season where Florida trounced Ohio State, 41-14. Olentangy featured junior Joshua Perry, who had already committed to Ohio State. Joshua was a star linebacker and a solid running back. On the air, I said "Let's take a poll. Text A if you think that Joshua Perry should play defense at Ohio State, text B if you think that he should play offense, or text C if you think that he should pull a Chris Gamble and play both ways." Note: Gamble had played both ways on the 2002 and 2003 Ohio State teams.

Again, with WINF-FM, I was doing my own engineering, but compared to the equipment that I had used in 1981 through 1990 with WCVO-FM, this was a piece of cake, as all of the equipment fit into a briefcase, and the broadcast used Bluetooth technology with a cell phone. I would pick up the equipment from Fred Shaffer at a studio off of Powell Road in the Polaris area of northern Columbus and return it after the game. Among Fred's many talents is the fact that he was involved in the voice-overs for the documentary, "I'm a Buckeye! The Earle Bruce Story". What was great about calling the games for WINF-FM was that during breaks, I could relax, since the studio would run ads. The engineer in the studio would give me a countdown to when the ad would end.

On two occasions, we broadcast the football game from Delaware Hayes High School, whose mascot is the Pacers, as in horses. The Little

Brown Jug harness races take place at the Delaware County Fair each September. The team had a tradition for many years--a horse and driver in sulky led the team onto the field. Athletic Director Steve Glesenkamp describes the tradition this way: "With the nickname the PACERS and the Brown Jug races several blocks away, the tradition was natural. The fans and the student body looked forward to Friday nights when the horse and driver in sulky ran onto the field leading the team. It was an exhilarating feeling. As the sod was replaced with turf and the horse aged, the tradition was discontinued as turf warranty became an issue." A unique feature of their field is that it is laid out east-west instead of north-south, which means that we never had to look into the sun, and that we had to avoid the cliche "He's a north-south runner".

I was fortunate to have Rick Middleton as my broadcast partner for three games. Rick is a graduate of Delaware Hayes High School--where he was honored by the Columbus Touchdown Club with the James A. Rhodes Award as the Ohio High School Player of the Year--and a football captain at Ohio State, becoming the 13th player selected in the 1974 NFL draft, by the New Orleans Saints.

We were able to follow Big Walnut High School through its three games of the 2010 playoffs, which took us to Canal Winchester and Westerville Central High Schools (a combined 68-32 score in the wins in the first two weeks), and to Ashland University's Jack Miller Stadium, where Big Walnut's season ended with a 42-14 loss to Uniontown Lake High School in the third round. For Uniontown Lake, running back Jim Luther had been playing with a torn knee ligament since the fourth week of the season.

In 2013, Aaron Cassady reached out to me to be the play-by-play broadcaster for Columbus Academy High School football on his Gameday Broadcasting Sports Network Internet streaming company. I was incredibly fortunate that Steve Geiger agreed to join me for our three years calling the Columbus Academy games. I saw Eric Welch sitting in the stands before a Thursday night televised game and told him that I needed a broadcast partner to fill in for Steve for three games. It turned out to be another lucky break for me when he jumped on it.

The software that we use for the high school games broadcast always has a 10-second pause from when I click the button to start the broadcast to when the system confirms that we are on the air. Those 10 seconds are the most nerve-wracking of the event. One thing that I need to pay close attention to is that when I set up the advertisement recordings, I need to remember to click on the setting so that when the recording ends, the system will revert to our live broadcast; otherwise, the recording will repeat. Amazingly, in hundreds of games over nine years, I am batting 1.000 for that!

The Columbus Academy Vikings had a 6-4 record in 2013, scoring at least 30 points in each of their six wins. The 42-40 win over the Whitehall-Yearling Rams was a shoot-out, as each team scored in each quarter. It was always a treat to hear Whitehall-Yearling's band; as a take-off on the Ohio State marching band's nickname of The Best Damn Band in the Land, Whitehall-Yearling's is The Best Ram Band in the Land. When Academy played at London High School, I had a chat at halftime about Dick LeBeau--who was a member of Ohio State's 1957 national championship team, a long-time NFL star as a defensive back for the Detroit Lions, an NFL assistant coach and head coach of the Cincinnati Bengals--with a gentleman who had seen him play for the London Red Raiders in the 1950s.

At one game, I interviewed a sportswriter who was a native of Buffalo, New York, and was an "extra" actor in the movie The Natural, which was filmed in Buffalo's War Memorial Stadium. He said that the star "Bob" Redford was very gracious!

Columbus Academy had a 4-5 record in 2014, scoring at least 38 points in each of their four wins, which included a 38-35 upset at Harvest Prep in Week 9. The staff at Harvest Prep treated us royally; they gave us one of the coaches booths to call the game, and the public address announcer on two occasions mentioned our broadcast staff--myself, Steve Geiger, and even Steve's son Max, who was there to assist. The Vikings had a 4-6 record in 2015, in Robin Miller's first year as the head coach, averaging 37 points in their four wins. The last game was a 28-14 loss to London, in which Michael Johnson of London rushed for 361 yards and four touchdowns. Johnson finished the season as the area's leading rusher with more than 2,900 yards.

In 2016, I switched to being the play-by-play broadcaster for Gahanna Lincoln High School football on the Gameday Broadcasting Sports Network, pairing with Milan Jordan, who is as good as they come. We were grateful to have a private booth in which to call the home games. Gahanna Lincoln started the year 4-0--including a 62-0 win over St. John's College from Brantford, Ontario, Canada--but finished with a 5-5 record. Four of the five losses were by seven points or less, playing in a tough conference and against playoff teams Dublin Coffman, Lancaster, Pickerington Central, and Pickerington North. When we carried the game at Grove City, I was reunited with public address announcer Tom Rutan, who was a teacher at Upper Arlington when I was a student. On the air, I said that Tom and I were at Upper Arlington in "Nineteen hundred and many years ago." One of the highlights of the year was calling the game at Lancaster High School, which had the best food at halftime, practically a buffet.

In 2017, I switched to being the play-by-play broadcaster for Dublin Jerome High football (their mascot is the Celtics, pronounced *Keltics*) on the Gameday Broadcasting Sports Network. Bill Walters joined me for the first three years. One year, we had games in four different counties--Union, Franklin, Delaware, and Fairfield--so to kick off one of our games, I played the "Spanning the globe" sound bite from ABC's Wide World of Sports.

Our first year was exciting, starting with a bang in a 41-7 win over Logan. The highlight of that game was running back Robert Cope–who would be a walk-on player at Ohio State–starting a run to the right side-line, getting hemmed in, then reversing to the left and racing 58 yards to the end zone. Robert's dad, Jeff, would join me in the spring to broadcast a Jerome baseball game. The Logan team had twin linebackers with the appropriate last name of Ruff.

The broadcast location for one of our road games was the roof at Olentangy Orange High School. My halftime interview for that game was with my long-time Ohio Wesleyan and high school broadcast partner Steve Geiger, who is a math teacher at Orange and was also doing the play-by-play for the Orange Pioneers' broadcast.

Against Dublin Scioto, Jerome won 21-17, scoring the winning touchdown on a hook-and-lateral play with 2:44 remaining. The most famous combination in sports history may be Tinker to Evers to Chance, but this was Schell (Hayden) to Ballengee (Trey) to Cope (Robert). Quarterback Schell flared a pass to wide receiver Ballengee in the left flank, and Ballengee flipped the ball to Cope, who, despite playing at less than 100%, took it to the end zone, a play that covered 79 yards. Earlier during this game, I said that we saw a new high school record--three measurements for a first down in the same series. In the pre-game segment at the next game, I said "In case you missed it, here was my call for last week's hook-and-lateral play", and then played Jack Buck's famous call of Kirk Gibson's walk-off home run in the 1988 World Series: "I don't believe what I just saw!" But, how many people know what Jack's next sentence was? He said "Is this really happening, Bill?"--Bill White was his analyst--which was perfect, having Bill Walters as my analyst. Eli Neverov, a Jerome student, captured the play on video--the play went down the sideline in front of him--and posted it on Twitter, gaining national attention.

By the way, on a play like this, the way to score it in the stats is that the receiver gets credit for a reception and yards to the point of the lateral, and the player receiving the lateral gets credit for the remaining yards as receiving yards, but not for a reception, since there can be only one reception per play. So, at the end of the year, you may see a player with receiving yards but no receptions, which also causes chaos for his average gain per reception!

Two weeks later, we had the Jerome vs. Thomas Worthington game, where Jerome scored the winning touchdown on a five-yard pass from Hayden Schell to Andrew Brim with six seconds remaining to win 33-32, rallying from a 26-7 deficit. Jerome had also scored a touchdown on a four-yard pass from Schell to Brim with four seconds remaining in the first half. After these two Instant Classic wins, both on the road, I said that this Jerome team was the modern version of the Kardiac Kids, referring to the Cleveland Browns of the 1980s. Bill had a better term--*the Kardiac Celts*. The very next day, I called the Ohio Wesleyan vs. DePauw game, which DePauw won 31-30. So, in the span of about 18 hours, I had called two one-point games. The team had a 7-4 record, losing in the first round of the playoffs.

In 2018, our first game was against Bishop Watterson High School, played at Mike Hagley Field, about a mile from the house that I lived in until age eight. Hagley Field at night reminds me of Wrigley Field, with the lights and the neighborhood houses in the background. The press box was too small to accommodate us--the athletic director called it a "cracker box"--so we called the game from the stands, with fans so close that often their voices could be heard on the air. Bill had a folding table that was perfect to set our equipment, and I ran my extension cord from an outlet inside the press box. The Celtics lost their next four games--including a tough 35-28 loss at Pickerington North, where they led by a touchdown at the end of the third quarter, but won four of their last five to finish with a 5-5 record.

In that year, the brand-new Olentangy Berlin High School opened and joined Dublin Jerome's conference. Our trip to Berlin for the football game had high winds and, as Coach Bob Gecewich described it, "rain coming sideways." Whenever Dublin Jerome plays Olentangy Berlin, I call it the Mispronunciation Bowl and remind our listeners that it's the Jerome "Kell-tics" vs. the "BUR-lin Bears", not the Jerome "Sell-tics" vs. the "Ber-LIN Bears".

The 2019 team had a 9-3 record, which included a first-round play-off 38-31 win over Springboro in five overtimes. In one of the overtimes, each team missed a field goal that would have won the game. In Week 2 of the regular season, against traditional power Columbus St. Francis DeSales--a team that would lose only one other regular season game, to Bishop Hartley in Week 10--Jerome dominated the Stallions, 45-14. The game at Dublin Scioto had a 90-minute weather delay--each time that lightning was spotted, the earliest that play can resume is 30 minutes later. I was able to fill some of the time by interviewing Lori Cecil, a photographer for *ThisWeek Community News*, who fortunately took shelter in the press box. Some of the parents spent part of the delay by walking up Hard Road to a restaurant on Sawmill Road. The Celtics made up for a history of losing to Hilliard Bradley by securing seven turnovers in the 43-14 win. The season ended in the second round of the playoffs with a loss to Springfield at Marysville's spectacular Impact Stadium that had opened that school year. That year, I was one of several local play-by-play broadcasters who would record a preview and send it to Marty Bannister to play on 98.9 FM before the games started. Often, it would take me 10 tries before I was satisfied with my recording. After the game, we would call Marty to report, live on the air, on the game that we had called.

The 2020 team finished with a 2-5 record in the COVID-shortened season, with one of the wins a 27-16 upset at Olentangy, which had a 4-0 record at the time and finished with a 6-3 record. Olentangy and Marysville had joined Jerome in a re-aligned conference in 2020. After losing to Marysville a second time--in the first round of the playoffs--Jerome, like any team that had been eliminated, was allowed to schedule another regular season game, which they did against Olentangy Orange.

With both teams in the stadium and our equipment set up, the game had to be canceled due to a COVID issue.

For football in 2020, the halftimes were shortened by 10 minutes, and the teams did not go to the locker room, instead going to an empty space near the stands where folding chairs were set up. I revised my first-half ending spiel to "As the teams head to their folding chairs, the score is ..."

The 2021 team had a 7-5 record, with the team setting a school record by scoring at least 24 points in each of its first six games. Three of the Celtics' five losses were by seven points or fewer. Chris Intihar and I made the trip to Perrysburg in the opener, which Jerome won 24-10. We were fortunate that our location was in the visitor's press box, because a Jerome quarterback entered the game late wearing a jersey number that we did not recognize. One of the Jerome dads seated below us informed us that it was the starting quarterback, who needed a jersey to replace his torn one. In Week 2, Jerome beat a Toledo Whitmer team that outscored the other 11 of its first 12 opponents that year by a margin of 441-161. In the battle for bragging rights in the city of Dublin, Jerome lost to Dublin Coffman, 49-42 in overtime and in front of a packed stadium at Coffman High School, a game in which Jerome may have set a record by returning three kickoffs for a touchdown--two by Luke McLoughlin and one by Preston Everhart.

For home games, we were able to patch our audio broadcast into the video feed that fans had subscribed to. The highlight of the season was on Senior Night in the home game against Olentangy High School, where Jerome won 27-24 on a 34-yard Hail Mary pass on the last play of the game from Zakk Tschirhart to David Adolph (a senior, appropriately), who got his feet down with inches to spare on the right edge of the end zone. In the pre-game segment of our next game, as I had done four years earlier after the hook-and-lateral game against Dublin Scioto, I said that if you missed it, here was my call of the play, and played Jack Buck's famous call of Kirk Gibson's walk-off home run in the 1988 World Series: "I don't believe what I just saw!", followed by the clip of University of California play-by-play announcer Joe Starkey's call of the 1982 California-Stanford game that ended on the multiple-lateral kickoff return for a touchdown: "Oh my God! The most amazing, sensational, dramatic, heart-rending, exciting, thrilling finish in the history of college football!"

How many sportscasters have called a season for a team that had a game with a Hail Mary win and a game that had three kickoff returns for a touchdown?

We closed out the season with a road trip for the second round of the playoffs to Springfield High School, which has an impressive press box and provided us with a private booth for our broadcast. Chris Intihar gave me a breather at halftime of three games during the season by interviewing former Major League Baseball catcher Mike Durant, Dublin Jerome Cheer Coach Carla Crawford, and Dublin Jerome Kick Off Club President Brian Izzo.

BASKETBALL

In 1976, I was the analyst for two games broadcast by WBBY-FM. Russ Merrin did the play-by-play; Russ is the brother of Keith Merrin, the successful coach at Mount Vernon High School, who had taken his team to the Class AAA state championship semifinal game in 1974. Keith would eventually become the coach at Gahanna Lincoln High School, where I would call some of his games when I broadcast for WCVO-FM from 1981 through 1990.

I was filling in for Bud Wilkinson--no, not the former football coach--who at the time was working for the *Delaware Gazette* and WDLR radio in Delaware, and would go on to be a state reporter and TV/Radio writer for the *Columbus Dispatch*. Bud writes that for him this was: "... one season of high school games. Wasn't planned. Knew nothing about basketball. I was horrible. I showed up at Delaware Hayes about a half-hour before tipoff to do color to find out I was calling the game. I'd never done play-by-play and had played prep school hockey in New England and knew nothing about basketball." *Hey Bud, we've all been there!* Bud would later be the TV/Radio columnist at The Arizona Republic in Phoenix, the entertainment editor/critic at Channel 10 in Phoenix, and a hockey reporter on Phoenix Roadrunners hockey telecasts on regional ASPN network, then launched a radio show that played Broadway music, which was an instant ratings success in Phoenix. He currently writes about classic cars and motorcycles for a newspaper in Connecticut and has a website on motorcycles.

The first game was on February 6–interestingly, Ohio State's Coach Fred Taylor, for whom I would work the stats on televised games a few years later, had announced his resignation the day before–with North Union playing Sunbury Big Walnut at the neutral site of Hayes High School in the city of Delaware. The *Columbus Dispatch* sports section that day showed North Union at Sunbury Big Walnut, without mentioning that the game was at Hayes High School, so perhaps someone wanting to attend the game may have shown up at an empty gym. North Union's Dave Cline had 15 points in the game; Dave was the son of Ollie Cline, who played football at Ohio State in the 1940s and held the OSU single game rushing record with 229 yards until Archie Griffin broke it in 1972 with 239 yards. The Big Walnut coach was Norm Nelson, whom I would see again at Grandview Heights for a game on WCVO-FM in 1983. The *Delaware Gazette* story the next day had the headline "In overtime thriller/ North Union 48-47 MOC victor over Big Walnut". MOC was the Mid-Ohio Conference, and the game the next week had two other teams from the same conference. The story had an extensive box score, including the OER (offensive efficiency rating) for each team. I can honestly say that this is the only time that I have seen the OER statistic referenced for a high school basketball game.

If that trip to the city of Delaware was a challenge–at least I knew where the city of Delaware was!--it was like being in my backyard compared to the trip a week later for my second game. On a Friday the 13th that turned out OK, Mount Gilead played at Sparta Highland in Morrow County, about a 70-mile round trip. That date was also the day after I started my career at The Ohio State University. Highland is the high school that produced Tim Belcher, the pitcher who won 146 games while playing for the Los Angeles Dodgers, Cincinnati Reds, Kansas City Royals, Chicago White Sox, Los Angeles Angels, Seattle Mariners, and Detroit Tigers. My brother Mark went with me and joined me in the press box. When the game ended, Russ asked me for my analysis. I gave a short, profound (at least, I tried to make it profound) answer, to which Mark pretended to wipe a tear from his eyes.

The "Radio Highlights" in the *Columbus Dispatch* did not list our two WBBY games on those dates, though it did list only one high school game being broadcast, on WWWJ-FM in Johnstown, which is farther from Columbus than was WBBY-FM in Westerville. The *Dispatch* sports section the next day in each case has hundreds of scores from around the state, but does not include my two games. The February 7 section shows that at least seven local games were postponed.

In hindsight, it's interesting to me that I have no recollection of what the engineering was for those broadcasts–Russ must have handled all of it–in order to compare to what I eventually had to do for three future outfits where I did the engineering. After a few months, a check for $20.00 for the two games arrived in the mail.

When doing some research for this book, I was amazed to find extensive information on www.crawfordcountybasketball.com related to those two games, such as:

- The Mount Gilead vs. Sparta Highland game was a 63-59 win for Sparta Highland.

119

- Jeff Jahn of Sparta Highland had 32 points, and Kent Baker of Mount Gilead had 34 points in that game.
- Kent Baker, Jeff Jahn, and Dave Cline were first, second, and fourth, respectively, in scoring in conference games.
- Baker (six), Jahn (three), and Cline (one) had the 10 highest scoring games in conference games that season. Baker had games of 46, 38, 34, 33, 32, and 29. Jahn had games of 39, 32, and 31, and Cline had a 29-point game.
- Kent Baker averaged 31 points per game, and Jeff Jahn averaged 25.8 points per game over all games of the season. Earlier in that 1975-1976 season, Jahn had a 52-point game, and Baker had a 48-point game.
- Kent Baker was still the all-time leading career scorer for players in Morrow County, according to a 2018-2019 entry.
- Sparta Highland had a 17-4 record that season in coach Jim Schoch's first season. Jeff Jahn and coach Schoch would be inducted into the Highland Local Schools Hall of Fame in 2012, along with MLB pitcher Tim Belcher.
- It was also the first season for Mount Gilead's coach Dale Creamer.

I also found that Jeff Jahn was a third team Class A All-Ohio in 1976, and that Kent Baker was a second team Class AA All-Ohio in 1977, as voted by the Associated Press.

In the 1977-1978 school year, I was the analyst for five high school basketball games televised on a pay-per-view basis on Warner QUBE. The first game of that season, which was the seventh game that I ever worked, had Euclid–coached by Doc Daugherty–at Upper Arlington. The very next game had Grove City–coached by Herb Russell–at Upper Arlington. So, in consecutive games, we had the visiting coaches who would be named the 1990 and the 1977 winners of the Paul Walker Award, presented by the Ohio High School Basketball Coaches Association. The first three games were decided by one, two, and two points.

We would do a live preview several minutes before the game started. During the game, the play-by-play broadcaster would pose multiple-choice questions to the viewers, such as: *Do you think that it will be a close game?* Viewers would register their vote using their consoles. Late in the game, we would pick three players as the candidates for the Most Valuable Player for viewers to vote on--usually, two from one team and one from the other--which had the possibility of fans from one school splitting their vote and allowing the third-best player to get the award. During the Upper Arlington vs. Euclid game, won by Euclid, 58-57, the camera caught the legendary University of Dayton coach Don Donoher in the stands. In that game, one of the Upper Arlington players was Dr. Pete Edwards--obviously, not a doctor at the time--who would become an owner of the Columbus Crew soccer team. Euclid had Cliff Kirchner, who would play for Ohio State. For at least one game, I wore a red polyester sport coat with a pattern that would have made the 1970s version of Bob Knight envious.

I have a pair of cassette tapes that contain the entire contest between Columbus West and Whetstone, played on February 3, 1978, a game which West won 60-45. Bob Vincent was the play-by-play broadcaster for that game. Let the record show that I was ahead of my time; there was a play where an official called for a jump ball, though simultaneous possession had not taken place. On the air, I said that the rule was unfair--the official chose the two players closest to the ball to do the jump ball--and that I would like to see the rule changed. A few years later, the alternating possession rule was implemented.

Some of the questions that Red Jamison and Bob Vincent posed to the viewers to vote on were:

- Multiple times late in the game: Who do you think will win?

- Should the Braves stall?
- Was that a good call? Push button number 1 if you think it was a good call, press button number 2 if you think it was a bad call. (73% voted that it was a bad call.)
- Do you think that this team should stop shooting from the outside and take it inside more? (56% voted to stop the outside shooting.)
- Do you think that the coach should put Jackson back in the game? (67% said yes.)
- Have you been to a high school basketball game in person? (86% said yes.)
- Do you want to see more televised high school basketball games? (88% said yes.)
- With Upper Arlington down to Euclid by four points with 10 seconds remaining: Can Upper Arlington win the game? (30% said yes.)

The first Upper Arlington vs. Grove City game that we broadcast had a 50-48 win for Upper Arlington. The *Columbus Dispatch* the next day had "The Greyhounds missed their final field goal." I have a DVD that includes our pre-game segment with Red and myself, and it shows my pocket calculator on the table, ready to calculate shooting percentages. The game and the *Dispatch* from the day of the game intersected the first three broadcast outfits for which I called games–Warner QUBE, WCVO-FM, and WBBY-FM. The *Dispatch* radio listings show that the game was also carried by WCVO-FM, the station that I would join three years later. The *Dispatch* TV/Radio column by Bud Wilkinson--whom I filled in for on WBBY-FM in 1976--mentioned that WBBY's stockholder William "Wild Bill" Bates had a restraining order issued by the Delaware County Common Pleas Court Judge, and that QUBE's December 1, 1977 start-up "generated a whale of national media coverage", and that

WBBY was one of four radio stations to have won the rights to carry Ohio State basketball. I don't know if someone with the power considered me for one of the Ohio State broadcast positions for WBBY, ha!

The next game, a week later, was another two-point game. I have a cassette tape that contains only the last quarter of the Independence 76ers at the Whetstone Braves game played on January 13, 1978, a game which Whetstone won, 59-57. That meant that our first three games were decided by a total of five points. The *Columbus Dispatch* the next day had "Whetstone lost ... in the final period when 14 trips down the floor failed to put a point on the board". I am guessing that the game was re-broadcast and that I positioned a tape recorder next to the TV speaker. The recording demonstrates that I kept player scoring and team turnover stats; I had the two teams combine for an incredibly high 66 turnovers, which computes to one every 29 seconds! Red Jamison said that the high number of turnovers may have been due to the fact that it was Friday the 13th.

After one game, my brother Mark pointed out that I had mistakenly said that the tournament games would start at the Franklin County Fairgrounds, instead of the Ohio State Fairgrounds. We're all allowed one mistake, right?

The year 1981 was the year that I showed up at a WCVO-FM game at Grandview Heights and asked if the broadcasters wanted someone to do the stats, which evolved into me becoming a WCVO-FM broadcaster within a few weeks and lasted for 10 years. The engineering for basketball was a breeze compared to the football operation; at Gahanna Lincoln, Paul Gierman ran a cable from our apparatus out of the gym, under some carpeting in the hallway, and to a telephone in an office behind the gym. We broadcast from a corner of the court at floor level, where the Gahana players entered from the locker room, which provided the shortest distance to the telephone. My instructions for the process, which I still have, include "Tape down the cable at doorways so that people do not trip over it". On some occasions, we would use the Marti-transmitter-and-antenna equipment. In my 10 years at WCVO-FM, we would also carry games from New Albany, Bexley, Mifflin, and Bishop Hartley.

Paul would often give us broadcasters a break at halftime by interviewing a school representative, including his son Morgan—also listed as an Engineer for WCVO Basketball broadcasting in a memorandum—talking about Grandview Heights' wrestling team, and Gahanna's football coach Phil Koppel, who talked about recruiting. Paul also called games with me in the 1981-1982 season.

The first game that I called was Groveport Madison beating Gahanna Lincoln, 72-66. Henry Grace of Groveport—who would play for Ohio State—had 22 points and 10 rebounds, and Mark Hensley of Gahanna had 22 points and 19 rebounds. Spoiler Alert: Mark would have a memorable game 14 days later.

The second game that I called was at Bexley between Dublin—there was only one Dublin high school at the time, as opposed to three now—and Bexley in 1981, two years before the Bexley Lions won the Class AA state championship, though their 1983 star Steve Willard was a sophomore starter on that 1981 team. I have a cassette tape of that game, in which I called Willard "the little guy"; I have a program from a 1983 All-Star game that listed him as 5'9" and 140 pounds as a senior. The tape demonstrates that I was keeping individual scoring stats while doing the play-by-play and that I had access to season field goal percentages for some of the players; the local newspapers would publish those every week. Dublin won, 59-55, taking a 57-55 lead on a shot with two seconds remaining. While listening to the tape, I had forgotten that games played at that time had a center tipoff to start each quarter!

We would often get the winning coach to join us for a post-game interview. Paul Gierman said that if Groveport Madison won, Bob Miller--the legendary coach who would move on to Thomas Worthington High School, record 573 career wins, and be inducted into the District 10 Basketball Coaches Association Hall of Fame in 2022--would gladly talk to us for as long as we would like. Gahanna player Mark Hensley told me that Coach Miller was always one of his favorite coaches, and that Coach Miller once found him after a game to congratulate him and talk about his future. Coaches Terry Reed and Andy Clark of Gahanna Lincoln, Larry Larson of Grandview Heights (known as "Mr. High School Sports" in Central Ohio for his coverage in print and on 610 WTVN radio for 19 years, and who was presented with the Ohio High School Athletic Association Media Service Award for the 1997-1998 school year for the Central District, and for whom Larry Larson Middle School in Grandview is named), Jim Duffy of Grandview Heights, Jon Daup of Worthington, Norm Roll of Dublin, Jeff Brenning of New Albany, Jim Hamilton of Upper Arlington, and Norm Nelson of Big Walnut also joined us after games.

The only time that I can recall that we had a player to chat with after a game was with Richie Hunt of New Albany. It may not have been after the 63-57 New Albany win in the 1987-1988 season over Lucas, when he scored 38 of New Albany's 63 points, one of two games that season where he scored 38. He also had 11 rebounds. The *Columbus Dispatch* headline was "NEW ALBANY"S HUNT BAGS 38".

My third game broadcasting for WCVO-FM--on February 13, 1981--was an Instant Classic, when Worthington (which was renamed to Thomas Worthington once Worthington Kilbourne opened) played at Gahanna Lincoln, a game that Gahanna won 67-66 in the last game of the season carried by WCVO. Coincidentally, that 1978 game on Warner QUBE that had a combined 66 turnovers was also played on a Friday the 13th, and for the Worthington Cardinals, this Friday the 13th also turned out to be bad luck. They had an 11-point lead during the game and a one-point lead with five seconds remaining, with one of their play-ers at the free throw line to try to seal the win. The player missed the free throw, Gahanna's Doug Patch launched a half-court shot that missed, but Mark Hensley put back the miss for the winning score ... all this in the span of five seconds, somehow. My analysis of the final play (I still have the cassette tape) was "Among our 10 starters, we had one freshman, one sophomore, seven juniors. How fitting it was that the one senior out there got the winning basket."

Thirty nine years later, I would rehash this game with Mark at Ohio Wesleyan, at a game when his daughter Madison played for Mount Union. In 2022, I sent Mark an audio clip containing those last five seconds, of which he said "It was a crazy ending". This game was so significant that a story about it appeared on the front page of the *Columbus Dispatch* sports section the next day, with the headline "Lions Nip Worthington". Steve Biffle was my broadcast partner, the first of several occasions that I would be part of a Steve and Steve broadcast pairing.

Matt Sobolewski, a freshman for Worthington who would play for the Air Force Academy and play against future NBA players David Robinson, Tim Hardaway, and Luc Longley, had 26 points, which I reported as "a career … you call that a career? … a career high?" During the game, I said that "His potential seems unlimited", and Gahanna Coach Terry Reed in our post-game interview called him "an exceptional freshman basketball player". I had a chat with Matt in April of 2022, and he mentioned that he had to contend with the Air Force Academy's height restriction. Matt was selected as the Player of the Week during the season by Warner QUBE Cable TV; my brother Mark, who worked for Warner, pointed out that Matt at age 14 needed a parent to drive him to the Warner studio.

Also on the Worthington team was Casey Close; I noted that he was averaging 8.5 assists per game, and that, at one point, Casey was close to getting a technical foul after two calls went against him in 10 seconds. He would play baseball for the University of Michigan–he is in the University of Michigan Hall of Honor for his accomplishments as the 1986 Baseball America National Player of the Year and U-M's career leader in home runs and runs scored–and the Columbus Clippers in the minor leagues, and would eventually become the agent for baseball stars Derek Jeter, Freddie

Freeman, Paul Goldschmidt, Zack Greinke, Clayton Kershaw, and Ryan Howard. I kept the final edition of the *Columbus Citizen-Journal* from December 31, 1985, and the Sports section has an article on Casey as one of "A few who stood out from the crowd", saluting local athletes from the *Citizen-Journal*'s history. It mentions that he was the *Citizen-Journal* baseball Player of the Year in 1981, when Worthington won the Class AAA state championship. In that tournament, he was the winning pitcher in the semifinal game, striking out 15 in eight innings. He gave up a run on a sacrifice fly by Youngstown Boardman's Bernie Kosar, future quarterback of the Cleveland Browns.

When I called the game between these two teams the following season, it was almost an instant replay, with Gahanna missing a shot with two seconds remaining and down by one point.

One of our games at Gahanna Lincoln was also televised by Warner QUBE, with Pat Hughes doing the play-by-play. Pat's broadcast position and mine were set up close enough that I learned later that my voice was heard on the Warner telecast, when I excitedly called an alley-oop play.

For a while, Gahanna's conference had three coaches named Miller–Bob at Worthington, Ray at Grove City, and Dave at Reynoldsburg–and Ohio State coach Eldon Miller was spotted in attendance at one of our games.

I have a cassette tape of a game where we had about ten minutes to fill in the pre-game because the junior varsity game ran long. I did my best, talking about the teams' previous games (twice), but I heard myself getting a bit antsy: "We're about seven minutes away from the start of the game" ... "We're about a minute away from the start of tonight's game" ... "We're about 24 seconds away from the start of the game" ... "We're about five seconds away from tipoff."

On February 3, 1984, I called the Gahanna Lincoln vs. Groveport Madison game, which Groveport won in two overtimes, 69-65. That game featured John Feasel scoring 11 points for Groveport, playing for his father, John W. Feasel. John the player says that the 11 points may have been his career high. John would go on to coach the Olentangy girls and boys teams, and has called Ohio Wesleyan games with me.

In 1986, Stu Mason and I had the best Central Ohio regular-season game of the year--Wehrle, ranked #1 in Ohio in Class A, at Bishop Hartley. Hartley had a 17-point lead in the first half but needed three overtimes to win, 80-79, snapping Wehrle's 34-game regular-season winning streak. I have a cassette tape of the game, and in our pre-game, I said that "this game has the potential to be the best game that you and I have ever seen on the WCVO High School Game of the Week", and "I guarantee you that we will not be disappointed." Interestingly, Stu said that this was not the game that he originally planned for us to broadcast. Hartley's Tony Lucas, a 6-5 sophomore, scored 39 points. Tony was later a McDonald's High School All-American, played at Youngstown State, and was inducted into the Greater Columbus Basketball Legend Association in 2019. Wehrle had won the first meeting 71-59, as Eli Brewster, who would play for Ohio State, scored 41 points. Wehrle would win the Class A state championship in 1986, one of several that they won in the 1980s, and this would be the only game that they would lose that season. They would have another three-overtime game that season, in the state semifinal game to beat Van Buren, 83-79. During the third overtime, Stu was getting anxious; he said that if the game went another overtime, he would have to leave in order to do his radio job in Springfield. I still have a letter addressed to the WCVO Sports Department from Bishop Hartley coach and athletic director Tom King, expressing his gratitude "... for your excellent coverage of our recent DeSales game."

The varsity game started so late that I talked eight minutes non-stop setting the stage for the game, and another six minutes non-stop with my "This Week in High School Basketball" report, covering local games and statistics, and some statewide news. One of the topics was the possibility of implementing a three-point shot. Stu and I surmised that it would not catch on with most coaches in Ohio! At halftime of that game, I interviewed sportswriter Bob Whitman and legendary coach Jack Ryan.

At some time in the 1980s, while setting up for a basketball game at Bishop Hartley, a broadcaster for another outfit dropped by and introduced himself. At first, I thought that it was Chuck Underwood, assuming that he had grown a mustache, but it was Randy Rhinehart. I would cross paths with Randy a few more times--such as at Ohio State women's basketball games, when I would get player interviews for WCVO-FM--before starting a steady position of working stats for him in 1990.

In the 1990-1991 school year, Stu arranged for me to be his analyst for six Lancaster High School boys basketball for WLOH-AM. What was unusual was that teams from as far as Findlay, Dayton, Toledo, and Fremont came to Lancaster for regular season games. Coach Jack Greathouse of Lancaster--the school's all-time winningest basketball coach and now a member of the Ohio Capital Conference's Hall of Fame, the Ohio High School Basketball Coaches Association Hall of Fame, and the Ohio High School Basketball Hall of Fame--was always a pleasure to chat with on the post-game interview. After the season, I received a letter from Stu and Scott Haskins, the Program Director, thanking me " ... for the fine effort and representation you displayed during this basketball season. You represented us well. We heard a lot of good comments from the staff, fans, school officials and towns people about how professional the broadcasts went."

Stu also asked me if I wanted to be a WLOH-AM disc jockey for four hours on Saturday nights. I turned it down, but that would have been fun, especially if I could have majored in my specialty of 1960s oldies.

In December of 2001, Stu arranged for me to do the play-by-play for Time Warner Cable in northwest Ohio for the Oregon Clay at Findlay boys basketball game, which is the last time that I have appeared on camera (no wisecracks, please), both pre-game and post-game. I was able to contact Dave Hanneman, sportswriter for the *Findlay Courier* newspaper to get some background information on the two teams, and he gave me a page of notes, which I still have. In writing this book more than 20 years later, I didn't have the name of the contact, but I found Dave's email address–being fortunate that he was still at the *Courier*–and he confirmed that he was the one. *Note: Dave was presented with the Ohio High School Athletic Association Media Service Award for the Northwest District for the 2000-2001 school year.* In preparing for that game, I wanted to demonstrate whatever knowledge I had of former Findlay High School athletes, so I mentioned basketball star Dave Sorenson (an Ohio State 1970 graduate who also played for the Cleveland Cavaliers and the Philadelphia 76ers in the NBA) and Indiana University's Harry Gonso (quarterback of their Rose Bowl team in the 1967 season) on the air. I was told that there was a Findlay graduate on the Miami University football roster by the name of Ben Roethlisberger. I was given a list of several ads to read during the game, and I had to ask how to pronounce "Granary", for The Granary Gifts & Furniture store, and "plyometrics" for a fitness gym.

Findlay's Jim Rucki was in his third season as their coach and would eventually record his 500th career coaching victory. A story on WFIN.com has "One of his best players was in his first year as coach when Ben Roethlisberger was a senior." I reached out to him on Facebook to ask if he had any details on this game, and he sent me images of the scorebook. I remembered that the game was a blowout, and the score shows Findlay winning 69-34. The *Toledo Blade* story the next day had the headline, "CLAY TURNS ICE COLD AT FINDLAY". Clay actually led 6-0 and 10-9, but Findlay had a 23-0 blitz in the third quarter as part of a 50-7 run. I recall saying during the third quarter, "Fans, if you're just now tuning in, that score is not a misprint." Coach Rucki–who complied 100 years of Findlay basketball into the book, "Findlay Trojan Basketball"-- pointed out that Justin Thomas of Clay, who led his team with 12 points and four rebounds in the game, would go on to pitch in the major leagues for the Seattle Mariners, Pittsburgh Pirates, Boston Red Sox, and the New York Yankees.

I was the play-by-play broadcaster–with Steve Geiger as my broadcast partner–for basketball games on WINF-FM in Delaware County for the 2010-2011 school year, with three of our 10 games being girls' games; the station let me pick the games. This included my first connection with John Feasel, who was coaching the Olentangy girls team at the time and would later become the Olentangy boys coach and a broadcast partner for Ohio Wesleyan games. Our last game was an Instant Classic boys game, with Olentangy Liberty beating undefeated Westerville South, 66-64. South's Trey Jackson–Jim Jackson's son who would play at Wisconsin–had 18 points. By a coincidence, Westerville South was one of only two Division I Central Ohio teams with a 19-0 record heading into that last regular season game, and Randy Rhinehart called the other game for Upper Arlington Radio, with previously undefeated Upper Arlington also losing to Dublin Coffman in overtime. By another coincidence, this was 30 years after the Instant Classic game that I called in 1981, also the last broadcast of the year, with the home team Gahanna Lincoln upsetting Worthington by one point in that game.

For the 2011-2012 school year, Aaron Cassady arranged for me to call New Albany High School boys games for the Gameday Broadcasting Sports Network. In the 22 years that had passed since I last called a few New Albany games for WCVO-FM, their new high school buildings, gym, and football stadium were sights to behold.

In April of 2013, Stu Mason arranged for me to do the play-by-play for the Jump25.com 5th Annual Ohio College All-Star Classic, four basketball games in one day--men's and women's teams composed of college seniors, and boys' and girls' teams composed of high school seniors--at Ohio Dominican University. Unprepared without food, my nourishment was limited to two cans of Hawaiian Punch over the eight hours, but it was a great time. To get the starting lineup for one of the women's college teams, I spoke to their coach Pete Gaudet, who had been the head coach at Army, an assistant coach and the interim coach at Duke when Coach Mike Krzyzewski had a health issue, an assistant men's and women's coach at Vanderbilt, and an assistant coach for the Ohio State women's team. Former Ohio State player and long-time Buckeyes radio analyst Ron Stokes had his daughter and Ohio State graduate Amber playing in the college women's game, and his son Ronnie playing in the high school boys' game. I still have the rosters, and my notes for Jett Speelman of Newark Catholic show that he would play at Ashland University. Ohio Wesleyan and other teams in its conference probably wish that he would have stayed there, instead of playing his last two seasons at Denison, where he was a dominant player. In attendance, watching her daughter play, was Georgeann Wells, who was the first woman to dunk a basketball during a collegiate game, which was in 1984 while playing for West Virginia University. After the college men's game, my broadcast partner Cody Inverso interviewed former Ohio State player Evan Ravenel, who was one of the stars in the game. The souvenir program shows the Jump 25 Hall of Fame inductees, which includes Coach Dave Feyh of Columbus Independence High School, 35 years after I called one of his games for Warner QUBE.

Starting with the 2017-2018 school year, I have called Dublin Jerome High School boys games on the Gameday Broadcasting Sports Network Internet stream. Before each game, Jerome coach Richie Beard graciously records an interview with me. I play it at halftime, because we can't count on the varsity game starting at a standard time, given that the freshman and junior varsity teams play beforehand.

In the first year, the Jerome Celtics had a 13-10 record, with five of the ten losses by four points or less. The 2018-2019 team had a 14-9 record, ending their season with a 60-59 tournament loss at Canal Winchester, a game extended into overtime when Jerome's Dan Lee hit a deep three-point shot.

The 2019-2020 team won its first three games by a total of four points, but finished with a record of 11-13. Again, the Celtics were tough in the tournament, winning 45-44 against a higher-seeded Olentangy Orange team on Orange's court before losing at traditional power Dublin Coffman 50-45.

During the pandemic that encompassed the 2020-2021 school year, basketball was pretty much business-as-usual for our broadcasts, though Dublin Jerome, like many schools, scrambled to schedule games late into the season. The athletic directors of the schools that we visited went out of their way to accommodate us. Ellie Geiger at Licking Heights even supplied us with a 100-foot extension cord that ran from an outlet in the hall outside the balcony to our broadcast location. Halftimes were usually shortened from ten to eight minutes, with the teams staying at their benches. It was also impressive to see the freshman and junior varsity players for Dublin Jerome sanitize both their own chairs and the visitors' chairs after their game was over.

In December of 2020, Dave Purpura of *This Week Community News* ran a story–also available on the dispatch.com website of the *Columbus Dispatch*–about the Internet broadcasts such as ours during the pandemic, emphasizing our value, given that the number of in-person fans was severely limited. The headline was "Online broadcasts keep fans connected to teams", and the story quoted my cohorts Eric Welch and Aaron Cassady, who said that listenership increased by a factor of five or six for his New Albany football broadcasts. The story included a photo of Chris Intihar and me calling a game, courtesy of photographer Shane Flanigan. For the calendar year 2020, Shane earned first place in portrait and third in game action in Division 4 by the Ohio Prep Sportswriters Association.

The 2020-2021 team had a 9-14 record and pulled another first-round upset in the tournament, 52-41 at Watkins Memorial, before ending the season with a loss at Reynoldsburg. One highlight of the year was the 42-40 win over Worthington Christian, the only regular season loss for the Worthington Christian team that made it all the way to the state championship game in Division III.

When a Jerome player–usually CC Ezirim–threw down a dunk, I would play an audio clip of Bill Raftery's iconic call of "Send it in, Jerome!", from the 1988 game where Pittsburgh's Jerome Lane shattered a backboard with a dunk. Chris Intihar, a broadcast partner, later bought a T-Shirt online with the wording "Send it in, Jerome!" on a shattered backboard background.

The 2021-2022 team had a 21-5 record–the third most wins in its short history–including a 10-0 record in the Cardinal Division of the Ohio Capital Conference, which was its first conference title since 2008. The team set a school record on defense by giving up 46.1 points per game and had a 3-1 record in overtime games. The last regular season game of the season was an overtime win at home over Hilliard Darby on February 18, exactly 11 years after I called the Olentangy Liberty home win over Westerville South in the last regular season game of 2011.

Unfortunately, the one overtime loss came in double overtime to undefeated Westerville South in the fourth round of the state tournament. That ruined my opportunity to say that I had called two games where the team that we followed gave Westerville South its only loss late in the season, referring to that loss to Olentangy Liberty in 2011, when Westerville South had a 19-0 record coming into the game. Jerome had also lost to Westerville South in the regular season by a score of 54-49, so this was my second chance of the season to call South's first loss. Two of the three overtime wins were in the first and last games in conference play. In four of the five losses, the Jerome deficit at the end of regulation was 0, 3, 5, and 5 points. This was the second time in four years that Jerome's season ended with a loss in overtime in the tournament. This also meant that two of the three basketball teams that I covered that season, including the Ohio Wesleyan women's team, had its season end with an overtime loss in a tournament game. Both Jerome and the Ohio Wesleyan women's team finished with 21 wins.

For the 2021-2022 season, I was able to record a pre-game interview with a few opposing coaches—Sean Luzader of Thomas Worthington, Mark Tinklenberg of Marysville, Henry Stolly of Bellefontaine, Ed Calo of Westerville South, Anthony Calo of Olentangy Orange, Greg Nossaman of Olentangy Liberty (the 2022 winner of the Paul Walker Award, presented by the Ohio High School Basketball Coaches Association), Pat Murphy of Columbus St. Francis DeSales, Vince Lombardo of Bishop Watterson, Chris Maul of Hilliard Darby, and Shaun Fountain of Licking Heights.

Again, the athletic directors at the schools when Jerome played on the road were incredibly accommodating. In some cases, we set up in the balcony, provided with a table and chairs; at other places—Westerville North High School (twice), Jonathan Alder High School, and Ohio Dominican University—we were at courtside. At St. Francis DeSales High School, we were on the stage at one end of the court, close enough to the baseline that we could have reached out and exchanged high-fives with the players if we wanted to. The gym at DeSales has windows high along one side, letting in daylight and giving a Hinkle Fieldhouse—at Butler University in Indianapolis—effect during the afternoon games.

Many times, when I arrive at a school other than Dublin Jerome, toting my broadcast equipment in a two wheel luggage, the staff member admitting people into the venue will ask me "Do you know where you are going?", thinking that I am an official! The officials often have luggage like mine.

When I would go to a game to check out an upcoming opponent, I would take notes and chart the shots on a page that looked like a basketball court. It would not take long before a fan in the stands would see what I was doing and ask if I was a coach who was scouting one of the teams. I guess that my clipboard was a clue for that.

Note to rookie broadcasters: when calling a high school game, it's imperative to check the scorebook that each coach brings to the scorer's table during the warmup, since coaches often add players from the junior varsity team at the last minute.

BASEBALL

In 2012, Aaron Cassady asked me to call four New Albany High School baseball games for the Gameday Broadcasting Sports Network, which was both exciting and scary, since it was my first ever baseball experience, and I was afraid that I would have nothing to say to fill in the gaps. All turned out well, thankfully; the pace was fast and I relied on my years of listening to baseball broadcasters.

Both the first and last games that I called in that season had a 1-0 score, with the lone run scoring in an inning where the ball never left the infield. The first game had New Albany beating Delaware Hayes, a team that featured at shortstop and pitcher 6'5" Jacob Bosiokovic, who would play first base for Ohio State and be drafted by the Colorado Rockies. I had called some of his high school basketball games, too. In the last game, a tournament game that ended the season for New Albany, Nick Jensen-Clagg of Pickerington Central, who would play at Kent State, struck out 16 New Albany batters in seven innings--eight swinging and eight looking. The September before, Jensen-Clagg had thrown a 43-yard touchdown pass in the Kirk Herbstreit National Kickoff Classic football game when I worked the stats.

In that first game, I hadn't thought beforehand what to say if the game had a dramatic conclusion, so the only thing that popped into my head was "And this one belongs to the Eagles!" ... plagiarizing Marty Brennaman, the Cincinnati Reds' radio broadcaster.

In 2014 and 2015, the Gameday Broadcasting Sports Network switched to broadcasting Gahanna Lincoln baseball games. The 2014 team included Evan White, Brad Hull, and Cael Baker, all of whom would play college baseball at the Division I level. Evan White would go on to play at the University of Kentucky–where he was an All-America honoree, two-time Rawlings Gold Glove award winner, and ranked among UK's all-time batting leaders–and was the 17th overall pick in the 2017 Amateur Draft by the Seattle Mariners, reaching the big leagues in 2020. The 2014 team finished with a 17-14 record and had lost eight of their last ten regular season games heading into the tournament, but made it all the way to the Division I State Championship Semifinal at Huntington Park--a game that Eric Welch and I called--where they lost to North Royalton, 3-0. I was able to record a pre-game interview with Gahanna's coach Mike Shade a few times. Coach Shade won his 500th game in 2022, and is a member of the Central District Baseball Coaches Association Hall of Fame.

The 2015 team saw Gahanna's season end with a 3-0 loss to Pickerington North at Ohio Dominican University in the tournament. Like their football stadium, Ohio Dominican's ballpark, Panther Valley, is in a scenic setting. The team had pitcher Jackson Wolf, who would play for West Virginia University and was selected 129th overall by the San Diego Padres in the 2021 draft.

In 2018, I called a few Dublin Jerome games. Jeff Cope, the father of Robert–who played baseball and football for Jerome and was a football walk-on at Ohio State–called a game with me, pressed into duty on short notice. We carried a road game at Bishop Watterson High School, and Ohio State football coach Urban Meyer was in attendance to watch his son Nate play for the Watterson Eagles. Nate would play both football and baseball at the University of Cincinnati.

CHAPTER 5

NCAA DIVISION III BROADCASTING

IN THE SUMMER OF 2013, Steve Geiger informed me that Ohio Wesleyan University, where he played basketball and was on their 1988 Division III National Championship team, needed new broadcasters for their Internet stream, and was I interested in applying with him? *Yes, Captain Obvious.* We decided to update our resumes and dress up for the interview (one of the last times that I have worn a tie?) with Sports Information Director Mark Beckenbach, and we were hired on the spot. That led Steve and me to also call Ohio Wesleyan football games starting in 2013, and me to calling Ohio Wesleyan baseball and softball games starting in 2017. Ohio Wesleyan is a member of the North Coast Athletic Conference (NCAC).

I don't do the engineering for Ohio Wesleyan's broadcasts, but it is very similar to what I do for my high school games on the Gameday Broadcasting Sports Network, which has been very helpful the few times that we had a minor glitch.

In 2017, Ohio Wesleyan student-athlete Megan Parker–she was on the Track and Field and Cross Country teams–interviewed me to talk about my broadcasting experience, which she published in an online story titled "Meet Steve Basford of StreamOWU".

BASKETBALL

I filled in for Randy Rhinehart, the regular play-by-play broadcaster, on two occasions to do the play-by-play for a Capital University game--a men's game against Mount Union in 2012 and a women's game against Wilmington in 2013–with Jim Hamilton as the analyst. The men's game included a post-game interview with Capital's coach Damon Goodwin, whom I had seen play for the Dayton Flyers against Ohio State in St. John Arena in 1986. To get familiar with the Mount Union team, I made the 190 mile trip to New Wilmington, Pennsylvania the week before, to see them play at Westminster College. In hindsight, I did not check if that game was being streamed online–most small colleges do that–to save me a trip.

Fans who are accustomed to watching major college games on TV or in person, and broadcasters such as myself, will find a different experience at a Division III game. With fewer media timeouts–which started only in the 2021-2022 season–and shorter timeouts, basketball games run approximately 90 minutes. On more than one occasion, I saw a coach holding his infant child an hour before the game started; would you expect to see Division I coaches doing that?

I started as the play-by-by-play broadcaster for the Ohio Wesleyan Battling Bishops on their Internet stream in the 2013-2014 season–for both men's and women's games–with Steve Geiger as the analyst. OWU plays in the Branch Rickey Arena, named for the noted baseball executive who had played baseball and football at Ohio Wesleyan; when he became OWU's athletic director, he also coached football, basketball, and baseball. One good omen was the fact that I once had a date with Branch Rickey's granddaughter; we went to a basketball game, of course.

When I obtain a first-time color analyst to fill in for Steve Geiger on the few occasions when he has a conflict, I have to smile at some of their questions:

- "Where is the media entrance?" *Umm, there is only one entrance.*
- "How do I get my press pass?" *I'll give your name to the admission representative, but If I forget, just say that you are the color analyst.*
- "How should I dress?" I inform them that we do not get on camera (no wisecracks, please), but, by the way, it would be in bad taste to wear an Ohio State shirt.

Division III basketball coaches--Ohio Wesleyan's Mike DeWitt and Stacey Ungashick Lobdell, and the visiting coaches--are incredibly accommodating to work with when I ask if I can record an interview of about three minutes. In the beginning, I assumed that I would need to get permission from the visiting team's athletic director to interview the coach. After a while, I learned that an email to the coach was good enough. And, after a few years, I learned which coaches give long answers and which coaches give short answers, so that I can calculate how many questions to compose.

It's interesting that coaches refer to opposing players not by their name, but by their jersey number, such as "I'm really impressed by #5." I imagine that this is normal, that players when assigned an opposing player would identify that player and their tendencies based on the jersey number and not the name. This also happens when I ask a fan if they have a player on the team; the response is "Yes, #5".

I have to give a special shout-out to Sean Strickland, the former University of Pittsburgh at Greensburg coach. His team was to play in the second game of a NCAA Division III tournament session at Ohio Wesleyan in 2016, and I had arranged for him to chat live at halftime of the first game, instead of recording an interview, as I usually do. During the first game, I received a text from Coach Strickland, whom I had never met: "Hey Steve, this is Sean. We should arrive around 4:00." It was so informal, as if we had been buddies for years!

While they are all a pleasure to work with, below are the NCAC coaches with whom I have had the most experience.

On the men's side:

- Dan Priest of Kenyon was my very first visiting coach to interview, in 2013. Along with Bill Fenlon of DePauw, Coach Priest is the only coach whom I interviewed in each of my first nine years calling Ohio Wesleyan games. That took some doing, as his Kenyon team canceled all of their games for the 2020-2021 season; however, he showed up at an Ohio Wesleyan game during the season, and we were able to chat live at halftime. I also ran into Coach Priest in Fort Wayne one year at the Division III national championship game.
- Steve Moore of Wooster (a member of the Ohio Basketball Hall of Fame with 846 career victories) and Bob Ghiloni of Denison (190 career victories), both of whom retired after the 2019-2020 season.
- Bill Fenlon, who was the DePauw coach since 1992-1993 before retiring at the end of the 2021-2022 season with nearly 600 career wins coaching in Division III, was always laid-back and good for a quote, as in the time that he told me that "shooting is ethereal"; I had to look up what *ethereal* meant. Coach Fenlon had a minor in English from Northwestern, where he played for the Wildcats and played in the game when they beat Magic Johnson's Michigan State team in 1979. Northwestern had an 0-7 record in Big Ten play before that game, and the Spartans would win 15 of their next 16 games, winning the national championship. I have a program from when

he played against Ohio State in 1978; it has his photo, accenting his long hair (at the time). He had all nine of points (and all four of his fouls) in the second half of that game, an Ohio State 103-76 win. One of the players whom he coached was Brad Stevens, who went on to coach the Butler Bulldogs to play in the NCAA championship game in 2010 and 2011, and would hold the positions of coach and head of basketball operations for the Boston Celtics. In 2022, DePauw played at Ohio Wesleyan twice, and, at the second game, Coach Fenlon informed me that his mother had watched our first broadcast from Dallas, Texas and mentioned to him that our broadcast team had been very nice when talking about him. He asked me to give her a Hello on the air, which I did.

- Isaiah Covaco of Oberlin is a native of Hawaii and attended high school in southern California, before playing at Yale and coaching at Oberlin in the snow belt near Cleveland. In my first year's interview with him, I asked how that climate change worked out for him, and he said "I like snow, I guess."
- Bob Simmons of Allegheny; with Allegheny leaving the NCAC after the 2021-2022 season, I will miss my chats with him.
- Matt Croci of Wittenberg
- Kyle Brumett of Wabash

On the women's side:

- Kris Huffman of DePauw, who has two NCAA Division III national championships and over 600 career victories. Coach Huffman played for the University of Northern

Iowa, in Cedar Falls, Iowa, the city adjacent to my dad's home town of Waterloo.

- Sara Lee of Denison, who had 503 wins in 33 years as their head coach. At the end of the 2021-2022 season, she was promoted to the roles of Senior Associate Director of Athletics, Deputy Title IX Coordinator for Athletics, and Senior Woman Administrator for the Big Red athletics department.
- Kate Costanzo of Allegheny, whose last season was 2020-2021.
- Alex Dellas of Hiram
- Suzanne Helfant of Kenyon
- Sarah Jurewicz and Kelly Mahlum of Wittenberg
- Kerry Jenkins of Oberlin

I arrive 90 minutes before tipoff, which is around the time that the visiting team arrives, in order to interview the coaches and to get the players' pronunciations. The Denison University's website saves me the effort of getting their pronunciations, since each player profile has an audio clip of the players pronouncing their name. Whenever Wabash College visits, I can always count on Brent Harris, their Athletics and Campus Wellness Communications Director, to supply an impressive document of their stats and game notes.

Many times, we have a doubleheader with the women's game first, followed by the men's game. Typically, the visiting women's and men's teams are from the same college, but, on rare occasions, the visiting teams are from different colleges. On a weekday, the women's game starts at 6:00 and the men's at approximately 8:00. On Saturdays, the games start at 1:00 and approximately 3:00.

In the last week of each year in December, the women's team hosts the Bishop Classic Hoops for Hope, with three visiting teams and two games in each of two consecutive days; the donations are used to raise money for breast cancer awareness, education, and research. On the first day, the games are at 6:00 and 8:00, and the next day, the championship game is at 3:00, with the game for third place at 1:00--which means that one of the teams is playing 15 hours after ending the night before.

The structure of the NCAC tournament after the regular season is that the highest seeded team of the four winners of the first round hosts the two semifinal games and the championship game, so Steve Geiger and I called the men's games when Ohio Wesleyan was the host in 2015, 2016, and 2017. In 2015 and 2016, the fourth-seeded team--DePauw and Denison, led by veteran coaches Bill Fenlon and Bob Ghiloni, respectively--won the tournament and received the automatic bid to the NCAA Division III tournament. In the tournament one year, before the renovation of the Branch Rickey Arena, the arena was so hot that the doors to the outside had to be opened ... and this was in February!

In the first year that Steve Geiger and I called the games, 2013-2014, the men's team had a player doing double-duty--Taylor Rieger was on the basketball and soccer teams at the same time. The team had a record of 20-8 and earned an invitation to the NCAA Division III tournament. Reuel Rogers set a team record for blocked shots in a home game, season, and a career, leading the NCAC in blocks three years in a row.

The women's team in 2013-2014 had their best season in four years, with an 18-9 record, and won their last seven regular season games. Julia Grimsley, a defensive specialist, and Tamra Londot were the only two seniors, and Londot finished among the career leaders in rebounds and played in three sports during her OWU career--also in volleyball and softball. On February 22, 2014, we had an Instant Classic for the women's game against traditional power DePauw, which was on winning streaks of 77 games in the regular season and 55 games in conference play, and ranked first in the nation. In the pre-game, I said that there were a couple of omens: DePauw's regular season win streak was 77, and the UCLA men had an 88-game streak snapped 40 years ago at Notre Dame, with a team from Indiana involved in each case. The other omen was that Steve Geiger and I had called a boys' high school game three years previously--also in Delaware County, where Ohio Wesleyan is located, and also in February, and also the last game of the regular season--where Olentangy Liberty gave Westerville South, 19-0 at the time, its only loss of the regular season. OWU freshman Taylor Dickson scored with 17 seconds remaining to cap a 6-0 run in the span of 1:05 in this 65-64 win over DePauw.

The men's game that followed in the doubleheader was just as suspenseful, as DePauw's Adam Botts hit a three-pointer with one second remaining to give his team a 64-63 win.

The men's team had a 22-6 record in 2014-2015, earning another invitation to the NCAA Division III tournament. The women's team had their second straight winning record at 15-13, winning six of their last eight games, and beat DePauw for the second straight year, on DePauw's court in the NCAC tournament. LaNiece McRae finished her OWU career with the team record for blocked shots in a game, season, and career, and Sarah McQuade, who would become an assistant coach for the Bishops, finished second in Bishop history in career assists.

The men's team had a 25-5 record in 2015-2016 and hosted the first two rounds of the NCAA Division III tournament--which Steve Geiger and I called--winning the two games against Pittsburgh Greensburg and the University of Lynchburg by scoring a combined 211 points. The 25 wins were the second most in team history, behind only the 27 of the 1987-1988 team that won the NCAA Division III national championship. The team averaged 88 points per game, and had four players--Claude Gray, Ben Simpson, Seth Clark, and Nate Axelrod--each score at least 20 points in the win over Lynchburg. Each of those four players would finish his OWU career with more than 1,300 points.

The 2015-2016 women's team had to cope with a squad of only nine players and finished with a 6-20 record, but when the calendar flipped to

January, they played much better, with a two-game win streak--including a 101-94 win over Wooster in double overtime--and a streak of three wins in the span of four games. Five of the six wins were in conference play. Like Tamra Londot two years previously, Mercedez Wood was not only a player on the hardwood; she also played on the softball and volleyball teams. The team was first among all NCAA Division III teams in 3-point percentage--38.3%--with Taylor Dickson fifth among individual players at 46%.

The 2016-2017 men's team had a 7-6 record after 13 games but won their next 14 straight and finished with a 21-7 record, hosting the NCAC tournament for the third straight year. During that 7-6 start, John Feasel, who was calling a game with me, predicted that the Bishops would finish strong. I have learned not to doubt him!

The 2016-2017 women's team had a 12-14 record, winning six of their last seven regular season games. Both Megan Kuether and Taylor Dickson finished her OWU career with over 1,100 points.

The 2017-2018 men's team had a 19-9 record, winning both of the first two games of the NCAC tournament in overtime--Seth Clark had 44 points, tied for the fourth-most in OWU history, in the semifinal win over Wooster--before losing in the championship game. Nate Axelrod finished his OWU career with the second-most points in OWU history--2001, a number that is appropriate for this book! He led the NCAC in assists all four for his years--breaking the OWU record for career assists--and was a three-time NCAC Player of the Year.

The 2017-2018 women's team won only one of their 25 games, but the team improved to 11-16 in 2018-2019, winning at Kenyon in the first round of the NCAC tournament.

The 2018-2019 and 2019-2020 men's teams had a 12-14 record in each season. The 2018-2019 team had a tough loss at home to Wittenberg in overtime. The Bishops had a two-point lead with one second remaining. Whereas Duke had 2.1 seconds to throw a similar pass from Grant Hill to Christian Laettner to beat Kentucky in the 1992 NCAA East Regional Final, Wittenberg had only one second to throw the inbounds pass from the Bishops' baseline to the Wittenberg foul line, drawing a foul and converting both free throws to send it into overtime.

Before the 2019-2020 home game against rival Wooster, Ohio Wesleyan had a ceremony to honor Wooster's legendary Coach Steve Moore, who was retiring at the end of the season. In November of 2019, the men's game against Adrian College--located in Adrian, Michigan--coincided with the Ohio State-Michigan football game, played in Ann Arbor. I always promote our basketball broadcasts on Twitter and Facebook, and knowing that most sports fans would be watching the Buckeyes-Wolverines game, I included in my posts that our game was the "other Ohio vs. Michigan matchup" that day.

The women's team in 2019-2020 had an Instant Classic 75-73 overtime win over Wittenberg. Down by five points with seven seconds remaining in regulation, the Bishops hit a three-pointer to draw within two points. Wittenberg inbounded at center court, but Cierra Joiner stole the pass and converted a layup with three seconds remaining to force the overtime. To conjure up memories of a similar play in basketball history, in the pre-game segment of the next home game, I played an audio clip of the Boston Celtics' broadcaster Johnny Most's famous call in 1965 of "Havlicek steals it! Havlicek stole the ball", when John Havlicek of the Celtics stole the inbounds pass in the closing seconds to preserve the win over Philadelphia in the NBA East Division playoff series. The team had a 14-13 record, and Claire Sterling finished her OWU career as one of only eight players at the time with at least 1,000 points and 600 rebounds.

In addition to the men's and women's teams having a unique, abbreviated 2020-2021 schedule--as in: all games were in February or March, the only games were conference games, the conference did not have a postseason tournament, and season series were on a back-to-back, home-and-home basis--the other noteworthy story of the season was playing in the renovated Branch Rickey Arena, improving the 44-year-old arena with new flooring, bleachers, scoreboards with statistics panels, lights, sound system, and air conditioning. Steve Geiger and I had a different point of view for the games, as we were relocated to the side of the court facing the benches, as opposed to our previous location behind the benches. For the first few games, no spectators were allowed, with limited spectators allowed after that.

The men's team had a 6-6 record in 2020-2021, achieving the .500 record in the final game by winning 84-82 in overtime at Hiram as sophomore guard Jack Clement hit a jumper at the buzzer.

The women's team in the 2020-2021 season featured several talented freshmen and finished 8-2, with both losses to traditional power DePauw. They won their first four games for the first time since the 1999-2000 season, and won their last four games by an average of 35 points.

The men's team had a 15-11 record in the 2021-2022 season, with the highlight being a rally from 10 points down with 4:50 remaining to beat the rival Wooster team in a home game. Henry Hinkle, a freshman playing with four fouls, scored the last nine points in that rally, including two free throws with four seconds left for the winning points.

The women's team had a 21-7 record in the 2021-2022 season, missing a chance to play in the NCAA Division III tournament by losing in overtime in the championship game of the NCAC tournament. The last time that the team had at least 21 wins was in the 2001-2002 season (21-8), and the last time that the team had a better winning percentage was in the 2000-2001 season (26-7). Cierra Joiner finished her career as only the ninth player in OWU history with at least 1,000 points and 600 rebounds.

FOOTBALL

The first year that Steve Geiger and I started calling Ohio Wesleyan games on their Internet stream was 2013. With no media timeouts, Division III football games run about two and a half hours, often shorter than high school games, which have a 23 minute halftime. We have a 10-minute pre-game segment, and Coach Tom Watts graciously allows me to record an interview beforehand, which I play during the pre-game. Coach Watts is a fourth-generation football coach, and his grandfather was the coach at East Liverpool High School in Ohio, which led me to stump Steve Geiger with a trivia question: "Who was Coach Watts's grandfather's most famous player at East Liverpool?" See the end of this section for the answer.

Something that I have observed at OWU football games that you would never see in Division I football was the men's basketball coach setting up the end zone pylons before the game and being stationed on the sidelines during the game to fetch footballs that leave the field of play.

Ohio Wesleyan often has an Honorary Captains game, where former captains take part in team activities, including having two of them chat with me during a game. It seems as if during each chat, the Bishops would score a touchdown.

In 2014, Steve Geiger and I were sidelined for one game when the Buckeye Cable Sports Network, which carries games for teams in northwest Ohio and southeast Michigan, carried an Ohio Wesleyan home game and used their own broadcasters. At halftime, the broadcasters interviewed Steve and me to talk about our experience calling Ohio Wesleyan games. I wrapped by saying that for our broadcasts, "They couldn't get Mike and Mike, so they had to settle for Steve and Steve."

The 2013 team had a 5-5 record, with Mason Espinosa setting team records for passing attempts, completions, touchdowns, and yards in a career, and for passing attempts, completions, and yards in a season. The 2014 team improved to a 6-4 record.

The 2015 team had a 5-5 record, with a non-conference 42-3 loss to traditional power Mary Hardin-Baylor in a night game at home in Selby Stadium. Ohio Wesleyan would play at Mary Hardin-Baylor in 2016. In one of my pre-game interviews with Coach Tom Watts, he agreed with my assessment of Ohio Wesleyan's Tim Shadoan as a Swiss Army Knife; Tim was fifth on the team in rushing, fourth in receiving, first in punt returns, first in kickoff returns, second in scoring, successful on six of eight on field goal attempts, and successful on 16 of 17 on extra point kicks.

The 2016 team had a 6-4 record. Tim Shadoan was third on the team in receiving, first in punt returns, first in kickoff returns, and first in scoring, successful on all 25 of his extra point kicks.

The 2017 team had a 5-5 record, as Brian Berry passed for 2,436 yards and 22 touchdowns. The 2018 team had a 4-6 record, with the defense returning three interceptions for touchdowns.

The 2019 team started 4-0 and finished with a 7-3 record, with the defense holding the opponents to 14.9 points per game, the program's best effort since the 1999 season. Zane Ries, who passed for 1,768 yards and 11 touchdowns, would go on to shine on the basketball court for the Bishops once the football season was over. Defensive end Kyle Hogan finished his Bishop career with a typical Kyle Hogan season; he blocked multiple kicks in 2017, 2018, and 2019.

The 2020 season was canceled due to the pandemic, but in the spring of 2021, they played two official football games, plus a third designated as an exhibition, with a fourth having to be canceled. Steve Geiger and I called the Denison game, a tough 38-37 loss in a 43 degree night game on March 19 where Denison kicked a field goal with 23 seconds remaining. Zane Ries played both in a basketball game and a football game in the span of 13 days.

In November of 2020, Mark Beckenbach arranged for me to record a voiceover of the classic 51-47 Ohio Wesleyan football win over Allegheny on November 10, 2001. In that game, the two teams combined for 1,094 yards of total offense, with Ohio Wesleyan's Joe Clinton accounting for 248 receiving yards, two touchdown catches, and a 61-yard punt return for another score. I added the play-by-play commentary to the existing 30-minute condensed video as if I were calling it live, referring to the printed listing of every play. Though the video was 30 minutes long, it took about 90 minutes to complete my recording, needing to stop and re-record at times when the action went by too fast. Mark said that this would not quite be like Lindsey Nelson's Notre Dame highlights productions in the 1960s and 1970s, where he would edit in "As we pick up the action later in the quarter...".

The 2021 team had an 8-2 record, recording their most wins since the nine in 2012 and outscoring the opponents by an average of 33.9 to 19.5. The first two games that I called were a 24-23 loss to Wittenberg and a 35-28 overtime win over Wabash, which meant that including the 38-37 loss to Denison in March, I had called three straight OWU games in calendar year 2021 where the difference in the score at the end of regulation was 1, 1, and 0 points. On the flip side, I called the game against Kenyon, where they scored 52 points.

The answer to "Who was Coach Watts's grandfather's most famous player at East Liverpool?" is Lou Holtz.

BASEBALL

In 2017, I asked Mark Beckenbach if I could call the Ohio Wesleyan baseball games, and he said *Yes, and how about softball, too?* If you are following along, the dominos fell like this: In 1991, I gave up broadcasting high school games to do stats for Randy Rhinehart ... and continued with Randy in 2007 with Columbus Sports Network ... which went out of business in 2008 ... which led me to reach out to WINF-FM to work stats for high school games ... which led me to meet Steve Geiger ... which led me to ask Steve to join me in calling high school football and basketball for WINF-FM in 2010 and for the Gameday Broadcasting Sports Network in 2013 ... which led Steve to ask me if we should pursue the Ohio Wesleyan basketball broadcasting job in 2013 ... which led us to ask if we could call Ohio Wesleyan football games, too ... which led me to calling Ohio Wesleyan baseball and softball games starting in 2017.

The 2017 team of Coach Tyler Mott had a 14-26 record, and the 2018 team improved to 19-20. On April 8, 2018, Ohio Wesleyan lost to Wooster 34-1, then three days later beat Defiance 20-0. Eleven days later, it was a doubleheader split with Heidelberg University that saw a combined 29 runs in each game. Ten days after that, the Bishops scored 20 runs in each game of a doubleheader sweep of Hiram College.

The 2019 team had a 15-22-1 record. Canyon McWilliams as a position player led the team in at bats, hits, runs, doubles, home runs (tied), total bases, batting average, slugging percentage, and stolen bases. As a pitcher, he led the team in wins (tied, with a 3-0 record), saves, and lowest opponent batting average, and had 35 strikeouts in 18 ⅔ innings.

In 2020, due to multiple rainouts and the NCAC canceling the entire conference schedule due to the pandemic, Ohio Wesleyan managed only one home date and six games in Florida, finishing with a 4-4 record.

The 2021 season was more back-to-normal, with 33 games played, the Bishops winning eight. The last home game of 2021 saw Ohio Wesleyan give up four runs in the top of the first inning against DePauw but pour it on for a 27-12 win. The Bishops were to have had one more home game, but it was canceled due to weather, spoiling the story that I had prepared: "The 39 runs in the DePauw game is not the most that Bishops' pitching coach Dave Koblentz has seen. He was the coach at Columbus West High School in 1975 when they won the Class AAA state championship game by a score of 28-20, a game where they led 25-4 in the middle of the fifth inning."

The 2022 team had a 10-28 record, which included a 5-3 win over rival Wooster. Amazingly, we had good weather, sunny and temperatures around 50 degrees, for the March 2 single game and the March 4 doubleheader, though the second game on March 4 was terminated in the ninth inning due to darkness. Five weeks later, Central Ohio would have light snow. Major League Baseball was in the middle of a 99-day work stoppage when I kicked off the March 2 broadcast with "Stoppage? What stoppage? We have baseball for you!" Naturally, almost two months later, our softball doubleheader was canceled, with temperatures in the low 30s, a wind chill in the low 20s at game time, and snow on the ground in the morning. Freshman Sammy Stoner, whom I had covered when he played football for Dublin Jerome, may have set a record by hitting in all 10 games that he started and as a pitcher recorded the win in the first game of the year and a save in another game. He had also played as a strong safety on the 2021 OWU football team.

When I visited the Ohio Northern dugout in 2022 to get their player pronunciations, the person who supplied them was their coach Gene Stechschulte, who was a relief pitcher for the St. Louis Cardinals between 2000 and 2002, had a total of five official at bats as a hitter, but is one of an elite group of players to have hit a home run on the first pitch that he saw in the majors, which he did as a pinch hitter.

In 2019, I had my first-ever experience calling a game in another state, when Aaron Cassady, who calls Marietta College baseball games for WMOA radio in Marietta, asked me to be his analyst for a doubleheader at La Roche University in Pittsburgh. As I got closer to Pittsburgh, I saw that Aaron had texted me that the games would be delayed due to the recent heavy rain, which was not a big deal, but when I got home, I bought a smart watch that syncs with my phone, so that I am more likely to see notifications on a more timely basis. Since the games were on radio, and I was accustomed to broadcasting on an Internet stream, it was the first time since I called Delaware County high school football and basketball games for WINF-FM in the 2010-2011 school year that I heard a studio engineer in my headset. The Marietta Pioneers split the doubleheader, losing the first game 12-0 and winning the second 5-4, scoring three in the top of the ninth inning.

SOFTBALL

I also started calling Ohio Wesleyan softball in 2017. Whenever Coach Cassie Cunningham joined me for a pre-game interview, she would always end her talk about what she wanted the team to do with "and have fun."

The 2017 team had a record of 17-18-1. The 2018 team improved to 16-14, including a doubleheader sweep against Hiram by the scores of 2-0 and 1-0. The 2019 team had a 11-27 record, and the 2020 team had a 5-5 record, managing to play only 10 games, all in Florida, before the remainder of the season was canceled due to the pandemic.

The 2021 team got off to a great start; in the first date of the season, the Bishops won the first game of the doubleheader 3-2 in 10 innings, a game that was scoreless in the regulation seven innings, with the Bishops answering with a run in the bottom of the eighth and ninth. With no lights at Margaret Sagan Field, the second game of the doubleheader was called due to darkness with Ohio Wesleyan holding a 7-1 lead after three innings. The team finished with a 6-12 record after a 6-4 start.

The 2022 team, composed of all freshmen and sophomores, had an 11-21 record.

CHAPTER 6

OTHER DUTIES AS ASSIGNED

IN 1975, MY ROLE for the Ohio State-Penn State football game televised by Time Warner Cable was to wind and rewind the broadcast tapes in the production truck outside the stadium. Before sunrise, our crew met up at an office in Worthington to get on the truck. I had a part-time job for Time Warner; one of my tasks was to go to a transmitter building on Morse Road in the middle of nowhere, now across the street from the Easton Town Center, and press two switches to bring the Pittsburgh Pirates broadcast to our subscribers. I quickly became a fan of Bob Prince, their play-by-play announcer.

In 1981, Ohio State soccer coach Al Bianco had me chart the plays that the team was running in one of their practices. What do I know about soccer, besides the fact that the team with the most goals wins? *Next question, please.* Al did give me credit for my effort in his PhD dissertation, "The modification of general practice and soccer specific behaviors on an intercollegiate soccer team" with "To ... Steven Basford and the rest of the students who so enthusiastically assisted in the collection of data, I am most grateful."

In 1985, Stu Mason allowed me to do a weekly report for WCVO-FM on any topic of my choosing, for his Sports Showcase program. One of them was on the Ohio State football spring game, in which I said that the theme was whether Jim Karsatos or Tom Tupa would be the front-runner as the starting quarterback in the fall, taking over for three-year starter Mike Tomczak. Another was my opinion on why the four Ohio State basketball seniors--Troy Taylor, Ron Stokes, Joe Concheck, and Dave Jones--deserved consideration for the NBA draft. Taylor and Stokes were tough guards who could score, Concheck was a tall forward who could shoot from the outside, and Jones was known for his defense, having played well against Indiana's Steve Alford. Another was a report on a high school baseball playoff game. I still have the *Columbus Dispatch* article from its TV/Radio section on February 13, 1986 that describes the Sports Showcase program in general terms. The TV listings in that section show a total of two college basketball games televised that Saturday and two more that Sunday, with none on networks such as ESPN!

In 1986, Stu worked for WUCO-AM in Marysville, and I would call in a report on high school football every week during the season, to be included as part of his show. I logged the game score for every team in Central Ohio into a text file on my NEC PC-8201A laptop–which was similar to the Radio Shack TRS-80 Model 100, and still works!–and wrote a program using the BASIC language to sort the games so that every team's games were together. I would print each team's results in order using my Hewlett Packard ThinkJet printer.

I have a cassette tape of his show that contains one of my reports–Stu referred to me as his "Information Coordinator"--which was more than 19 minutes long. My report included information on future University of Minnesota quarterback Scott Schaffner of Cincinnati Moeller as an all-Ohio prospect, Scott's twin brother Todd at center, future Ohio State players Carlos Snow of Cincinnati Academy of Physical Education and Patrick Rogan of Urbana, and future Penn State player O.J. McDuffie of Gates Mills Hawken (who would play for the Miami Dolphins). In a few years, I would work the stats for Ohio State games that had Scott

Schaffner, Snow, and Rogan. I also mentioned Columbus Academy's all-Ohio prospect Aaron Clark as a running back; he had a "60-yard touchdown romp". In another report, Stu Mason interviewed Academy's coach Paul Bernstorf, who said that Clark had led the team in rushing, receiving, punt returns, kick returns, and interceptions in 1985. Aaron would play basketball for Wittenberg, and I would call Ohio Wesleyan basketball games in the 2010s, where Aaron's son Seth would star for four years. In his OWU career, Seth had the fourth highest scoring game, with 44, and ranked seventh in career points.

The show included Stu interviewing Eastmoor High School's football coach Brian Cross (I had met up with him the year before and would interview him 24 years later), who described his quarterback, Scott Reeves: "He's the best quarterback that I've ever coached, he throws the ball well, he runs the ball, he's an intelligent young man." Scott would play basketball for Ohio State and would join me to call an Ohio Wesleyan basketball doubleheader. This taped show is from September 5, 1986, and here is proof that fact is stranger than fiction: Stu reported that Cal Ripken's streak of playing in consecutive games had reached 736 that week; Ripken would tie Lou Gehrig's record of 2,130 exactly nine years later, on September 5, 1995.

For one game in the girls high school basketball state tournament championship semifinals, my duty as the spotter was to identify every play--the player who shot, fouled, rebounded, stole the ball, committed a turnover, assisted--to the staff member who keyed these into the software for the official stats. For that game, the poor soul was Tim Stried of the Ohio State Athletics staff, who would become the Director of Media Relations for the Ohio High School Athletic Association. I give myself credit for asking Tim at halftime what I needed to do better. He said to make sure that I was calling out the plays in the terms that he needed, not as a play-by-play broadcaster. For example, I was saying "put-back by #5" instead of "offensive rebound by #5, shot good by #5." That's a good lesson for anyone starting out in sports work--always ask the more seasoned person for feedback.

In 1993, Randy Rhinehart arranged for me to attend a tennis exhibition at the Greater Columbus Convention Center--Billie Jean King vs. Margaret Court and Monica Seles vs. Arantxa Sánchez-Vicario--with the hope of interviewing Billie Jean King after the match. It turned out that I had no chance at an interview, as her entourage surrounded her as she left the court. This was shortly before Monica Seles was stabbed in the back at a match in Hamburg, Germany.

I worked several boxing matches one day, held in a ring in the parking lot of the Veterans Memorial building, relaying Mark Bishop's scoring for each round to the TV graphics staff. It was a hot afternoon in July of 1995, and the boxers' sweat poured off their trunks as if it were raining. Mark and Randy probably sweltered in their tuxedos, too.

Stan Anderson, who input the stats into the software for Ohio State games and coordinated the official stats for the high school football state championships in Canton and Massillon for a few years, arranged for me to work at the 2005 Sugar Bowl in New Orleans. The job was to set up the stat monitors for the game between undefeated Auburn and Virginia Tech. After attending the 2004 Alamo Bowl and returning to Columbus and spending one night at home, I was back on a plane to New Orleans. I took the bus on a foggy New Year's Eve from the New Orleans airport to downtown, where the bus dropped me off a few blocks from the hotel connected to the Superdome. This was eight months before Hurricane Katrina.

My pass allowed me into all the media events. While waiting for a press conference in a lobby, Virginia Tech coach Frank Beamer came in and sat caddy-corner from me on a couch. I was able to eavesdrop on his laid-back chat with his Sports Information staff. I went to a media event where players were available for one-on-one interviews and asked Virginia Tech kicker Brandon Pace if he was looking forward to kicking in a dome and if he had watched Ohio State's Mike Nugent kicking in a dome a few days ago. If he noticed that I was not taking notes or recording his comments, he was very gracious.

At the Sugar Bowl game, I was watching the local news on TV in the press box dining area when the sports anchor whom I had just seen on the air came in and sat down. I did not have an assigned seat in the press box, but I found one and jotted down the plays as if I were a media person, never getting busted. After the game—which Auburn won, 16-13—we collected the monitors, and Stan wrapped them in a gigantic shrink-wrap and placed them on a skid to be transported back to their home. On the day after the game, I went to a press conference where Archie Manning spoke, and another where Auburn's coach Tommy Tuberville and quarterback Jason Campbell talked about the disappointment of being the odd-team out; they were one of the three undefeated teams at the end of the regular season, but Oklahoma and Southern California qualified for the BCS championship game.

In 2009, I was the timeout coordinator for the ESPN-televised boys' high school basketball game between Columbus Northland and Findlay Prep--a team based in Henderson, Nevada, and ranked #1 in the nation. Jared Sullinger--who would go on to star at Ohio State and play for the Boston Celtics and Toronto Raptors--scored 32 points, had 21 rebounds, and made a pair of free throws in the final seconds to lead Northland to a 53-52 win in the contest at Otterbein University. It snapped a 45-game win streak for Findlay Prep, which entered the game averaging over 100 points per game.

In the 2010s, Stu Mason allowed me to submit reports for his Mega Sports News website; I was able to sit in the press box and submit game reports at Miami University, when the RedHawks played Army in football; the University of Toledo, when the Rockets played Boise State, with quarterback Kellen Moore, in football; Bowling Green State University, when the Falcons played Idaho in football; the University of Dayton, when the Flyers played Duquesne in basketball; Wright State University, when the Raiders knocked off a powerful Butler University basketball team; Middle Tennessee State University, when the Blue Raiders played Memphis in football; Huntington Park for Columbus Clippers baseball; and Bill Davis Stadium for Ohio State baseball. On another occasion, I submitted a report on a Cincinnati Reds vs. Pittsburgh Pirates game.

At some places, when I picked up my credential, I would get the question "Where is Mega Sports News?", and I would get a funny look when I said Columbus, Ohio. Part of my motivation for doing a report at remote college football games was to pursue my goal of seeing each of the 130 Football Bowl Subdivision teams—I am up to 125 as of this writing—in person. This allowed me to add Boise State, Middle Tennessee State, and Memphis to my list. When the Clippers played Akron in an exhibition game in 2011, my story included the fact that Jason Kipnis—future member of the Cleveland Indians—was making the switch from an outfielder to a second baseman while in the minor leagues. On the road, I would upload my report using the computer at my hotel, and Stu would add photos of the players mentioned in my report.

My experience as a public address announcer was for two high school basketball all-star games at Olentangy High School in 2016, at the request of Olentangy Coach John Feasel. It turned out that two of the girls and three of the boys would play for Ohio Wesleyan or other teams in OWU's conference, and I would eventually call their games. Late in the girls game, a coach yelled out to his team that one of the players had not scored, and to set up a play for her. One glitch in the girls game was that two players on the same team in the game at the same time had the same jersey number, and I announced the wrong player. A coach yelled over to me to fix the mistake. I could make the excuse that this would never happen in a normal game, but lesson learned!

In 2017, I was the parabolic microphone operator for the high school football playoff game between Cincinnati Winton Woods and Cincinnati

Anderson, played in West Chester, Ohio. I received on-the-job training for that job, and had the parabolic microphone dangling from a strap around my neck during the game.

I was the timeout coordinator for two televised Ohio State lacrosse games played in Ohio Stadium in 2018, one for ESPN and one for the Big Ten Network. This duty is known as the "red hat", due to wearing a red hat (go figure) so that the official can find you easily. I learned two things. First, be on your toes, because you are on the sideline and players come running off the field to their bench, near your position (Yes, getting run over will get you on ESPN's SportsCenter, but not worth it.) Second, when the TV staff member tells you in your headset to relay to the head official that we are 20 seconds away from resuming play, add a few more seconds, since the official is anxious to resume and will count down on his own. Better to under-promise and over-deliver, right?

To illustrate my versatility: a WCVO-FM staff member had me go to the Ohio Democratic Party headquarters at a hotel in downtown Columbus on Election Day of November of 1986 to get some interviews and phone in a report. I was given a tape recorder and equipment to hold up to a pay phone to transmit the recordings to the radio station. I interviewed Thomas Ferguson, who was elected the Auditor of State. I called in a report about John Glenn's re-election as a United States senator, and I noted that his wardrobe included scarlet and gray. For this, I was paid $10.00, which was the only pay that I received in my ten years with WCVO-FM, while broadcasting basketball and football at that volunteer radio station.

CHAPTER 7

INTERVIEWS

SINCE HIGH SCHOOL FOOTBALL games have a 23-minute half-time, I need ways of filling the time. There is also the risk of a weather delay, which means that I have begged someone in the press box to join me for a chat to fill the time. Live and pre-recorded interviews have been my salvation.

SOME LESSONS LEARNED ...

- RULE #1: instead of concentrating on your next question, listen to the interviewee! The response may lead to a better next question. Don't be That Guy like Handsome Dan in the movie *Wayne's World 2*--played by Harry Shearer--who interviewed Wayne and Garth but wasn't paying attention, to the point that Wayne says "You're not really listening to me, are you?"

  Me: "Did you play baseball in high school?"
  Interviewee: "Yes, I was a pitcher"
  Me: "Based on your size, I am guessing that you were a catcher?"

- RULE #2: Get your facts right!

Me: "Talk about the play of your freshmen, Seth Clark and Matt Jeske?"
Ohio Wesleyan men's basketball coach Mike DeWitt: "Well, Matt's a sophomore ..." *Note: Coach DeWitt bailed out this sports-caster who was in his first year of calling OWU games by adding that Jeske had been limited to nine games as a freshman.*

- RULE #3: Try for provocative questions.

Me (first question):"Definitely a very physical game out there tonight."
Basketball player: "Umm, yeah."

In one interview for a basketball game, I wrapped up by asking the coach "What do you need to do to win today?", and she replied with a smile, "Score more points." I have learned since then to phrase it as "What do you need to do well today for a win?"

In 1988, I would get Ohio State football player interviews after the games for WCVO-FM and take the cassette tapes to the studio on Reynoldsburg-New Albany Road. Luckily for me, this was before the common practice of having some televised games that would end near midnight. I did not keep a log of who I interviewed, but I know that the list included Jeff Graham, Judah Herman, David Brown, and Pat O'Morrow. After the game against Syracuse, John Cooper's first game as the Ohio State coach, I asked Pat if he was aware that he had tied the Ohio State record of kicking five field goals, which Bob Atha had done in 1981 against Indiana.

From 1988 through 1992, I had a media pass to Ohio State wom-en's basketball games and would interview players after each game for

166

WCVO-FM. It took some adjusting at first, having followed OSU men's basketball for years--*Wait, Northwestern's women's team is near the top of the Big Ten, and Michigan's is near the bottom?* Since I wanted to interview every player by the time that the season was over, occasionally, a player who had played minimally in the game wondered why someone would want to interview her. I did not keep track of everyone whom I interviewed, but I know that the list included Stacie Bruce, Vicki Pullie, Cheryl Perozek, Jai Jones--I still have a cassette tape with interviews of those four--Sharon Geary, Gennifer Johnson, Nikita Lowry, Averrill Roberts, Nicole Sanchez, Mindy Smith, and Jill Snavely. In those five seasons, the Buckeyes had a combined record of 93-53 under coach Nancy Darsch. As (bad) luck would have it, I would stop doing this the year before Katie Smith joined the team and helped lead them to the 1993 national championship game, where they lost to Texas Tech, 84-82, the game where Sheryl Swoopes of Texas Tech scored 47 points.

I had taken up running in 1979 and competed in several races over the next several decades, including the 1981 Columbus Marathon and the 1993 Athens (Ohio) Half Marathon. In the 1993 Columbus Marathon, I finished among the leaders! The asterisk for that comment is that Randy Rhinehart had arranged for me to ride in the media van for the entire race. This was on a chilly day, with a low of 35 degrees at 8:00 that morning--it was so cold that it was hard to bend my fingers to write my notes--the day after the Toronto Blue Jays won the World Series on Joe Carter's walk-off home run. Afterwards, I was able to pose a few questions, while other members of the media were interviewing him, to Brad Hudson--the men's winner--and I had a one-on-one interview with Jennifer Martin, the women's winner. I still have the cassette tape of those interviews. On many other occasions, I would interview the winners of a 5k, 5-mile, or 10k race after running it myself. I have the cassette tapes of interviews with Brock Merriam, Marie Burelson, Andrew Herr, Dave Rubadue, Donna Eramo, Alan Choma, Christine

Tinsley, Paula Ehrle, Kris Detwiler, Curtis Holbrook, Phil Howard, and Dawn Wallace.

On New Year's Eve of 2003, Stu Mason arranged for me to be in the press box at the Columbus Blue Jackets vs. San Jose Sharks game at Nationwide Arena–won by the Sharks, 1-0–and get player interviews. I know that one of them was with Geoff Sanderson. Stu's equipment filled a large piece of luggage, whereas these days, I could use my digital recorder that is the size of a candy bar and send audio files as an attachment. I transmitted my interviews to a company in Phoenix, which was ironic in that the next day, I took off for Phoenix for the Ohio State Fiesta Bowl game against Kansas State, flying into Las Vegas.

My technology has evolved from a cassette tape recorder, to a digital recorder that I can either plug into the mixer for my broadcasts or transmit to my computer using the Windows Sound Recorder, to a digital recorder that has a built-in USB connection, to using the Google Voice app that allows me to record phone calls.

Some of my interview subjects follow. This is a case of name-dropping, since the list includes a few Olympians, NFL players, and NBA players.

Brian Agler, former General Manager and Head Coach of multiple championships in the Women's National Basketball Association, and the eventual Vice President and Director of Athletics and Recreation at Wittenberg University, joined me at halftime of a high school basketball game in 2011 where his daughter was playing. He was a 2014 inductee into the Ohio Basketball Hall of Fame.

Bob Atha, Ohio State quarterback and kicker from 1978 through 1981. I tracked him down in 1990 by looking for his phone number in the White Pages--which I realize that younger generations have no idea what that is. I used the interview meeting to ask him if he had any advice for my running injury. I did not tell him that he was the subject of the trivia question that I devised for WOSU-TV in the 1980s. To prepare for the interview, I had researched my 1979 Ohio State Football Official Press Guide and found that he "… was a conventional straight-on place kicker in high school but now has adopted a soccer-style kick." When I asked him about making the transition to a soccer-style kicker, he said, "I don't know where you got your information …".

Nate Axelrod, Ohio Wesleyan basketball star who is the second-highest career scorer in OWU history with 2,001 points and the record holder in assists, was an assistant coach at Oberlin College the year after he graduated from OWU, and allowed me to interview him when Oberlin played at OWU. When Oberlin won that game, it meant that Nate had a perfect winning career record at Ohio Wesleyan's Branch Rickey Arena when OWU played Oberlin, since as a player, OWU never lost to Oberlin.

Greg Beatty, a receiver on the Ohio State football team, joined me after the Buckeyes' 1989 spring game, and I was able to ask him about his touchdown catch, which Tim May of the *Columbus Dispatch* described as "a 28-yarder from Cochran to Greg Beatty, who bobbled it but still was awarded the score." He said that Kirk Herbstreit would become a great quarterback; ironically, three years later, the two of them would hook up on Kirk's last touchdown pass as a Buckeye, in the 13-13 tie against Michigan.

George Bell, the long-time public address announcer for Dublin Coffman High School, joined me at a Dublin Coffman vs. Dublin Jerome basketball game. George is a community volunteer and former president of the Dublin Citizens Police Academy, and he led "Dublin's Greenest, Grandest St. Patrick's Day Parade" as the 2018 Grand Leprechaun.

Mike Bellisari chatted at halftime of a Columbus Academy High School football game, where his sons played, and shared his experience of playing football at the University of Cincinnati, including a trip to Florida State University.

John Betz, currently the athletic director at Olentangy Berlin High School. He was on the 1983 Bexley High School basketball team that won the Class AA state championship (I worked the stats for that game for television), and recounted the last two games, played in St. John Arena, including the semifinal win over Akron St. Vincent-St. Mary, which had Jerome Lane, who played for Pittsburgh in college and for the Denver Nuggets, Cleveland Cavaliers, Milwaukee Bucks, and Indiana Pacers in the NBA; Curtis Wilson, who played for Ohio State; Frank Stams, who played football at Notre Dame and in the NFL; and future Ohio State football player Ed Taggart. I still have my program for those games, and, looking at the team photo, he has changed a bit. John is modest; in my chat, he did not mention that he was an Associated Press third-team all-Ohio honoree in 1985. His teammate Rich Gatterdam informed me of that. I called two of his games in 1985 for WCVO-FM, and he scored 13 points in a win over Grandview Heights to help the Lions clinch the league championship, earning a quote in the Columbus Dispatch: "Sharing it is no fun."

Neal Billman, former Upper Arlington High School assistant and Gahanna Lincoln High School football head coach. Coach Billman was named the *Columbus Citizen-Journal* Coach of the Year in 1973 and was honored as the Central Ohio District Coach of the Year in 1972, 1973, and 1977. He was the *Columbus Dispatch* Coach of the Decade for the 1970s and was inducted into the Ohio High School Football Coaches Association Hall of Fame in 1992. He led Gahanna Lincoln to the Class AAA state championship game in 1976, losing to

Cincinnati Moeller, which was coached by Gerry Faust. I found his phone number in the telephone book and made arrangements for the interview. He was the perfect person to describe the rivalry between Upper Arlington and Gahanna Lincoln when he was my halftime guest during the matchup in 1990. One question that I had for him was: "Something that has been bothering me for the last 25 years is: How did you get the nickname of Cazzie Billman?" This was a reference to the time that he was a coach at my Jones Junior High School and had his photo in the school newspaper playing basketball, with the caption of "Cazzie Billman", a nod to the Michigan Wolverines star Cazzie Russell. He replied "Cazzie? You must have gone back a long way to drag that one out. How did you know that? You were there ... I'm quite impressed that you remember that."

Joe Bline, Dublin Jerome High School athletic director and former Jerome boys basketball coach, set the stage for me in an interview in 2017, my first year of calling Jerome games.

Liz Bulman, a triathlete and Ironman competitor. To do my research for interviews at a triathlon in 1988, I had bought the current issue of *Triathlete* magazine. This helped for one of my questions--"With so many triathlons in the country this weekend, why did you choose this one?"-- since the magazine included a schedule. When my recording had a technical difficulty, Liz was gracious to re-record it, with the benefit being that she knew what questions were coming.

Jay Burson, former Ohio State basketball star. I interviewed him when he was involved in organizing a 5k race that I ran in, which started and ended in Ohio Stadium on a Mother's Day weekend. Jay was the all-time scoring leader in Ohio high school basketball at the time, and was a 2006 Charter Class inductee into the Ohio Basketball Hall of Fame.

Dave Butcher, highly successful girls high school basketball coach in the Pickerington system, granted me an interview after one of his state championships. Coach Butcher is a member of the Ohio Basketball Hall of Fame, and was once named the National Coach of the Year by the *USA Today*.

Chris Carlisle, Dublin Jerome Assistant Athletic Director. He had been the Jerome boys basketball coach in 2009-2010, when I called one of his games as a fill-in for WINF-FM.

Lori Cecil, photographer for *ThisWeek Community News*, joined me during a lightning delay in 2019 at the Dublin Jerome vs. Dublin Scioto high school football game.

Sos Codispoti, community events organizer and public address announcer for Dublin Jerome High School football and basketball games, shared his vast experience in Dublin athletics and community events, which includes a Beat MIchigan dinner every year on the Monday before the game.

Robert Cope, former Dublin Jerome High School baseball and football player and football walk-on at Ohio State. Robert was the recipient of a hook-and-lateral play that went for the winning touchdown against Dublin Scioto in 2017. Robert has the distinction of being the ball carrier on the only two plays that quarterback Quinn Ewers participated in as a Buckeye in 2021.

Carla Crawford, Dublin Jerome High School Cheer coach, joined me at halftime of a Jerome basketball game. With no preparation, I ad-libbed all of my questions.

Brian Cross, former head football coach at multiple high schools in Ohio, joined me at halftime of a high school basketball game in 2011. Since he had previously coached at Grove City in its heyday--he was the winningest coach in Grove City High School history and was selected as the State Coach of the Year twice during his tenure--one of my questions was if he could have ever imagined that Grove City would have had to suspend its football program in 2009. In that year, the school board canceled all extra-curricular activities after voters failed to pass an operating levy. My first encounter with Coach Cross was in 1985 when he was the coach of Eastmoor High School; I had to call him on a Saturday morning following my broadcast of the Gahanna Lincoln vs. Eastmoor game to retrieve our WCVO-FM banner. Coach Cross was noted for wearing shorts at football games, no matter what the weather was. During one high school basketball game where he was in attendance, I said on the air: "It's a cold night in Central Ohio. How cold is it? It's so cold that Brian Cross is wearing long pants." A few years ago, Coach Cross did wear long pants at a televised football game; I informed Jeff Logan about his penchant for wearing shorts, and Jeff asked him if he had softened up. He is a member of the Ohio High School Football Coaches Association Hall of Fame.

Jeff Dalpiaz, who has the dream sideline job of relaying stats to the television production staff for football and basketball games, usually in states adjacent to Ohio. Jeff once worked a Friday night college football game in Buffalo and decided to drive to Columbus overnight without sleeping to work at the Ohio State game the next day. He and I spend the hours leading up to an Ohio State football game by quizzing each other on Buckeye football and basketball trivia. When I was in the University of Toledo's Glass Bowl stadium press box to write a report on the Toledo vs. Boise State football game in 2011, there was Jeff, working the talent stats for the ESPN broadcast. Jeff and I often are side-by-side at Ohio State football home games, but we recorded the interview at the Allen County War Memorial Coliseum in Fort Wayne, Indiana, before the NCAA Division III men's basketball championship game in 2019. Jeff can often be spotted on Ohio State basketball telecasts when the camera trains on the scorer's table, communicating with the production staff.

Steve Devine was an assistant football coach under Earle Bruce at Ohio State and at Washington under Don James, and at Ohio University, Bowling Green, Toledo, and San Diego State, and was a scout for college talent for the New York Giants for 20 years, earning two Super Bowl rings. I came across him when I learned that he was currently a volunteer assistant coach at Marysville High School, his alma mater.

Trey Dixon, running back for Ohio Wesleyan's football team, joined me at halftime of an OWU basketball game.

Craig Dunn, sports editor of the *Logan-Hocking Times* in Logan, Ohio, filled me in on the Logan High School football and basketball teams when they played against Dublin Jerome. Craig was elected to the Ohio Prep Sportswriters Association Hall of Fame in 2019, and was presented with the Ohio High School Athletic Association Media Service Award for the 2007-2008 school year for the Southeast District.

Chip Engelland played for the Columbus Horizon of the Continental Basketball Association. He had served as a ball boy for John Wooden's 1975 NCAA Championship UCLA team, was a team captain for Mike Krzyzewski's 1982-1983 Duke team, and has had an extensive professional coaching career, most recently as a long-time San Antonio Spurs assistant coach. Chip was noted for wearing black gloves when he was on the bench while on the Horizon squad.

Brent Ford, who broadcasts Westerville Central High School sports on the Central Ohio Sports Network, has chatted to give me updates on the Warhawks football team.

Rich Frimel, Ohio State football defensive lineman, joined me after the Buckeyes' 1989 spring games.

Bob Gecewich, Dublin Jerome High School football coach from 2015 through 2020, joined me at halftime of a Dublin Jerome vs. Dublin Scioto basketball game to recap the football season. He and I would also record a five minute interview each week of the football season, to be played in our pre-game segment.

Steve Glesenkamp, Athletic Director at Delaware Hayes High School, joined me at halftime of a Pacers' boys basketball game.

Jeff Graham, Ohio State wide receiver. I interviewed him in the locker room after the 1988 Illinois game. One of my questions was if he might see action as a punt returner, given the team's injuries at that position. He said that he was a backup; ironically, he would return a punt 66 yards for a touchdown in 1989 against Illinois.

Archie Griffin--a man who needs no introduction, but if you must: he is the all-time leading ground gainer at Ohio State and the only two-time Heisman Trophy winner--came to the WCVO-FM studio in the 1980s to join me in a live interview. Archie graciously postponed a trip to Cincinnati to do the interview. I was filling in for Stu Mason on WCVO's Sports Showcase program. One of my hard-hitting questions for Archie was "Would you say that the NFL is more of a business than a sport?" We discussed a linebacker playing at Massillon Washington High School by the name of Chris Spielman. At some point in the 1980s during my career in the Office of Human Resources at OSU, a Channel 4 news team came to my office to film a feature ... not on me, but on Archie Griffin. He and I shared an office in his short time in the HR department.

Taylor Harle, Dublin Jerome golf coach and assistant basketball coach, joined me at halftime of basketball games a few times. The first time was on-the-fly without any preparation, so I asked some general questions about the golf season. He had led Jerome to the Ohio Division I state championship each of his three seasons as their coach. What do I know about golf, other than the purpose is to put the ball in the hole and the fact that the player/team with the fewest strokes wins? *Next question, please.* I do know a lot about movies, so I asked him for his favorite golf movie. When he said Tin Cup, I had to agree.

Mike Heller: about 35 years after I called games for WCVO-FM when Mike played basketball for Gahanna Lincoln High School (I have a cassette tape of a game in which I described him as "a very stockily built young man"), Mike was the public address announcer at his alma mater for a football game, and granted me an interview. When Mike was a student at Gahanna Lincoln, he also was a color analyst for his high school's football games on WCVO-FM.

Clint Hikes, Whitehall-Yearling High School broadcaster, joined me at a Dublin Jerome vs. Whitehall-Yearling basketball game to talk about Whitehall-Yearling sports.

Brad Hudson, who ran his first marathon at age 12 and went on to coach Olympians, won the Columbus Marathon for the second straight year in 1993, and I was able to pose a few questions along with the other media.

Rick Huhn, who has written baseball books on Eddie Collins, George Sisler ("The Sizzler"), and "The Chalmers Race", which is about the 1910 American League batting title race between Ty Cobb and Napoleon Lajoie. Rick gave me so much time in the interview that I was able to break it into two parts, which gave me two games worth of down time at halftime of football games.

Bob Hunter, former *Columbus Dispatch* sports reporter. Bob has authored several books on Ohio State football, in addition to *Thurberville*, a book about the humorist and author James Thurber, a Columbus native. We recorded the first of two interviews outside the Book Loft bookstore in the German Village section of Columbus after he gave a talk, and during the recording, it started to rain. We ducked under an awning, which you would never know from the interview, since Bob, the true professional, never broke stride in his conversation. I first saw Bob when I worked the stats for TV at the Liberty Bowl in 1981, enjoying his pre-game meal in the press box.

Julie Isphording, a member of the first-ever Women's Marathon Team in the 1984 Olympics and the winner of the Los Angeles Marathon in 1990, joined me at the 1990 Archie Griffin Run. I still have the cassette tape of that interview.

Vlade Janakievski, a kicker on the Ohio State football team from 1977 through 1980, who holds a share of the record for the most field goals in a Rose Bowl, with three in the 1980 game. He said that he was hoping for one more chance in the 17-16 loss to USC. I recorded an interview with him in 1990 at the Easy Living delicatessen that he owned and which drew national attention from Brent Musburger on televised Ohio State games. He had also been a car salesman, and I had bought a car from him, not recognizing him until he gave me his business card that had his initials VJ in bold type.

Cade Kacherski, former Dublin Jerome High School football player and Ohio State walk-on, who his coach Bob Gecewich told me had blocked around 10 kicks during his Jerome career.

Bob Kennedy, two-time Olympic distance runner. I interviewed him when he was a senior at Westerville North High School, after he won a 5k race in Newark. Bob would go on to star in Track and Field and Cross Country at Indiana University, and when I attended an Ohio State basketball game there in 2011, I saw his IU Athletics Hall of Fame photo on the wall in Assembly Hall.

Wynn Kerins, distance runner, gave me an interview after winning a 5k race in Waldo, Ohio in 1988. (If you are tempted to ask *Where's Waldo?*, it's in southern Marion County.) Wynn would later appear in a *Sports Illustrated* story that highlighted his speed for someone of his weight, which was around 200 pounds.

Craig Krenzel, quarterback for the 2002 Ohio State National Championship team and the Chicago Bears. I had two strokes of luck in interviewing Craig. First, the interview took place on November 24, 2021, which was exactly 20 years after the historic 2001 OSU upset of Michigan in Ann Arbor, in Jim Tressel's first year. The *Columbus Dispatch* ran a story on the 20-year anniversary that morning; otherwise, I would not have known about that coincidence. Second, the interview took place only because it so happened that I was broadcasting a Dublin Jerome basketball game that night, and Craig was in attendance, watching his son play for the junior varsity team.

Joe Lang, who had a 534-366 record while coaching the Bishop Ready girls basketball team for 40 years and had served as the school's director of admissions, joined me at halftime of a football game that I called for WCVO-FM.

Ron Lewis, the Assistant Director of Bands for Dublin Jerome High School, joined me for an impromptu interview at halftime of a Jerome football game,

Wade Lucas, Olentangy Local Schools Superintendent, was presented to me on the spur of the moment. Thankfully, he shared that he had been the Superintendent in the Coshocton school district, and I was able to fill part of the interview by discussing Roscoe Village, the historic site in Coshocton.

Ron Maciejowski, Ohio State quarterback from 1968 through 1970, chatted with me at halftime of the 1990 Bishop Watterson vs. Westerville South high school game, a game in which his son Matt played at tailback. In the first half, I posed a trivia question to our listeners: "In the last 25 years, can you name an Ohio State quarterback who had a perfect record as a starter? The answer is our halftime guest." I asked Ron for his favorite Woody Hayes story, and he talked about Woody's fits during practices.

Ed Marion, an NFL official for 28 years who worked playoff games in 20 consecutive seasons and officiated in the Super Bowls in 1971, 1975, and 1977, joined me in 1985 after he was the guest speaker at the 62nd Rules Interpretation Committee of the Ohio Association of Football Officials at the Park Hotel north of the OSU campus, a hotel that no longer exists. I still have the cassette tape of that interview. One thing that I asked him about was the fact that at the time in college football, a defensive player could not advance a fumble, but in high school and the NFL, he could, and what was his opinion of that? I asked him about the NFL using instant replay in pre-season games, and he was against it, saying that would take an awful lot of time. I also asked him if he agreed with the implementation of overtime to occur in high school football that year, and he said that he was against it. Coincidentally, I would call a game that went into overtime that season.

Brian Martin played for the Columbus Horizon of the Continental Basketball Association and had played for the University of Kansas.

Jennifer Martin gave me a one-on-one interview after winning the Columbus Marathon in 1993, the same year that she was inducted into the Allegheny College Sports Hall of Fame.

Matt McGowan, Bishop Watterson High School cross country coach and track coach for both the boys and girls team, recorded an interview with me after a 5k race. Matt started the RUNOHIO publication in 1988 and the www.runohio.com website, which covers Ohio and national running. To introduce the interview at a high school football game, I said that it sounded like the interview would be with six different people, given all of his roles

Dirk Miller, one of the career leaders in scoring, assists, and free throw percentage in Ohio Wesleyan basketball history, joined me at halftime of an OWU game.

Dustin Miller, Dublin Jerome High School principal, helped set the stage for my first year of calling Jerome games in 2017. This particular visit with a principal turned out well.

Andrew Moore, Reynoldsburg High School basketball coach. I rarely have time to interview the opposing coach when I call Dublin Jerome games, since in regular season games, coaches are engaged in the freshmen and junior varsity games, but Coach Moore was available before a tournament game in 2021, which made him the only opposing coach whom I interviewed that season.

Leo Panetta, who operates the baseball almanac website www.nationalpastime.com. I first connected with Leo in 2011, when I was looking for such websites. He and I had a routine of meeting up in a different major league ballpark every year between 2012 and 2019--stopped by the 2020

pandemic--and I recorded interviews with him at Pittsburgh's PNC Park and Minnesota's Target Field.

Paul Pennell, former baseball head coach and assistant basketball coach at Columbus East High School. He also coached his Columbus Briggs High School basketball team to the Final Four in 1991. I interviewed Coach Pennell after a presentation by author Wil Haygood on his book *Tigerland: 1968-1969: A City Divided, a Nation Torn Apart, and a Magical Season of Healing*, about the Columbus East High School squads that won the 1969 Ohio basketball and baseball state championships when he coached.

Larry Phillips, author of the books on Ohio football history *Ohio's Autumn Legends: Vol. 1* and *Ohio's Autumn Legends: Vol. 2*.

Tim Raab, author of the book *Powerhouses of Ohio High School Football*, chatted with me after an event to promote his book at the Book Loft bookstore in the German Village section of Columbus.

Reggie Rankin had played basketball at Linden McKinley High School in Columbus, and I interviewed him after his Ohio University team beat Ball State, 83-63, in Athens in 1988. *Note: I attended the post-game press conference of Ball State's coach Rick Majerus, who was in his first year and fourth overall as a head coach, and who would win 517 games and lead Utah to the 1998 NCAA final game against Kentucky.* Reggie had 14 years as an assistant coach at the Division I level with stints at Bowling Green, Nebraska, Wyoming, Ohio, and Georgia before becoming an ESPN high school basketball recruiting analyst and a college scout with the Golden State Warriors.

Aaron Rhinehart, a television sports production video wiz who manages the replays and highlights and has worked at events at the Tokyo

Olympics in 2021, in Germany, in Saudi Arabia, in a Connecticut studio for the 2022 Beijing Olympic Winter Games, and on Stanley Cup Playoff games, among others. He has worked for Fox Sports, ESPN, NBC, and Program Productions, the Columbus Blue Jackets and Columbus Crew on Bally Sports Ohio, CBS Sports Network, Spectrum News 1, and Time Warner Cable SportsChannel.

C. Trent Rosecrans, who has covered the Cincinnati Reds for *The Athletic*, the *Cincinnati Enquirer*, and the *Cincinnati Post*, and has also covered Major League Baseball for CBSSports.com. I asked Trent on the spot if he had time for an interview at a book event in Cincinnati, and he graciously obliged.

Kevin Rouch, Grandview Heights High School sportscaster, joined me when I called a Columbus Academy game at Grandview. Kevin is a high-energy guy. At the conclusion of the interview, I said "I apologize to our audience. I had hoped to have someone with a lot of enthusiasm, but I had to settle for Kevin."

Jack Ryan, the legendary football, basketball, baseball, and golf coach for 45 years at St. Charles and Bishop Hartley High Schools, joined me at half-time of the classic 1986 three-overtime basketball game between Hartley and Wehrle. The Ohio High School Basketball Coaches Association website points out that "Jack has the unique honor of being the only Ohio high school coach to be inducted into the Hall of Fame for football, basketball and baseball."

Tom Skladany, former kicker for Ohio State–he was a three-time all-American as a punter–the Detroit Lions, and the Philadelphia Eagles. My buddy Bill Walters had given me a tip to ask Tom about the fact that he had beaten Butch Reynolds in a race once--the catch being that it was for charity. In the interview, he described that the outcome of his injury against Michigan in 1973 was that it actually built up his kicking leg.

Caleb Spinner, an Ohio State University student and sports broadcaster, writer, and podcaster at Ohio State University who broadcasts seven Buckeye varsity sports, including men's basketball and hockey on Scarlet and Gray Sports Radio and the Big Ten Network, joined me at halftime of an Ohio Wesleyan basketball game.

Kerry Stringer joined me at halftime of a Columbus Academy football game, when his son Nick was the quarterback.

J.J. Sullinger, former Ohio State basketball star, chatted with me at a high school game where his son Jalen was playing for Thomas Worthington. J.J. was the Ohio High School Basketball Coaches Association's Division I Player of the Year in 2001.

Satch Sullinger, former Northland High School basketball coach who won the Division I state championship in 2009 and coached stars such as his sons—Jared and Julian—and Trey Burke. Coach Sullinger chatted with me at Dublin Jerome high school games when his grandson Jalen was playing for Thomas Worthington.

Gary Trent, former basketball player at Ohio University, the Portland Trail Blazers, the Toronto Raptors, the Dallas Mavericks, and the Minnesota Timberwolves, chatted with me after a 1993 Mid-American Conference tournament game at the Greater Columbus Convention Center. His Ohio Bobcats team lost to Toledo, 85-84 on a Rockets bucket with one second remaining in overtime; he scored 34 points and had given the Bobcats the lead with two free throws shortly before. Before my interview,

I eavesdropped on the late Dick Fenlon of the *Columbus Dispatch* asking Gary his questions, which were much more incisive than mine, needless to say. Gary was a 2018 inductee into the Ohio Basketball Hall of Fame, and was the Ohio High School Basketball Coaches Association's Division II Player of the Year in 1992.

Vince Trombetti, long-time football head coach at Columbus Beechcroft and Worthington Kilbourne High School, joined me at halftime of a Worthington Kilbourne vs. Dublin Jerome game.

Jeff Warstler, boys basketball coach at Columbus Academy High School, who was our host at the football games from 2013 through 2015 for the Gameday Broadcasting Sports Network, joined me to talk about his basketball team.

Spencer Waugh–The *Logan Daily News* described him as "The foremost authority on Logan High School's sports history", who "... compiled a complete statistical history of LHS football that is unmatched statewide". His website is www.loganfootball.com, and he sends a detailed Game Notes document previewing each game. He has joined me when Logan plays Dublin Jerome.

Scott Weakley, Worthington Christian High School boys' basketball coach, joined me after one of his games that I scouted in the 1980s. A few years later, he would become the Capital University men's basketball coach.

Bob Whitman, former high school sports reporter for the *Columbus Citizen-Journal,* joined me at halftime of the classic 1986 three-overtime high school basketball game between Hartley and Wehrle. This was 17 days after the *Citizen-Journal* ceased publication on December 31, 1985, and we talked about its final days. Bob was presented with the Ohio High School Athletic Association Media Service Award for the 2009-2010 school year for the Central District.

Tom Wilson, sportswriter for the *Lancaster Eagle-Gazette*, joined me at halftime of the Gahanna Lincoln vs. Lancaster high school football game in 2016. Tom was presented with the Ohio High School Athletic Association Media Service Award for the 2015-2016 school year for the Central District.

Trevor Zahara, author of the book *Confessions of an OSU Usher.* Trevor also gave me advice on how to go about publishing a book.

Local sports media who graciously took time to chat with me:
- Steve Blackledge of the *Columbus Dispatch*, who is a member of several Halls of Fame, including the Ohio Prep Sportswriters Association (OPSWA) Hall of Fame, Ohio High School Athletic Association Media Service Hall of Fame, District 10 and District 11 Basketball Coaches Association Hall of Fame, and the Ohio Track and Cross Country Coaches Media Hall of Fame. Whenever I see Steve, I ask him if he is still using his Radio Shack TRS-80 Model 100 laptop computer from the 1980s; he assures me that it is securely housed at a Smithsonian Institution Museum.
- Zach Fleer, who runs the www.270hoops.com website and was presented with the Ohio High School Athletic Association Media Service Award for the 2019-2020 school year for the Central District.
- Mark Znidar of the *Columbus Dispatch,* who was presented with the Ohio High School Athletic Association

Media Service Award for the 2008-2009 school year for the Central District.

- Brad Emerine of *This Week Community News*
- Scott Hennen of *This Week Community News*. For the calendar year 2020, Scott was runner-up for the Sportswriter of the Year in Division 4 by the OPSWA.
- Dave Purpura of *This Week Community News*. For the calendar year 2020, Dave earned first place in feature stories and columns in Division 4 by the OPSWA. He was presented with the Ohio High School Athletic Association Media Service Award for the 2013-2014 school year for the Central District. Dave also has been a host of a weekly high school football preview show on Facebook.
- Mike Rich of *This Week Community News*, and formerly with the *Delaware Gazette* and the *Mount Vernon News*
- Jarrod Ulrey of *This Week Community News*. I once saw Jarrod composing his post-game report for a Gahanna Lincoln High School football game in his "office" (his car). For the calendar year 2020, Jarrod was named the Sportswriter of the Year in Division 4 for the second consecutive year and third overall by the OPSWA. Jarrod also has been a host of a weekly high school football preview show on Facebook.

Former Ohio Wesleyan women's basketball players who chatted with me during halftime of a game: Pam Quigney, Megan Kuether (who had also played on the softball team), Taylor Dickson (another who had also played on the softball team), Erin Delaney, Claire Sterling, and Meg Dunning. Except for Pam, I had called games when they had played, but for Pam, I had to do some crash-course research on her shortly before the interview took place.

CHAPTER 8

SPORTSCASTERS FOR WHOM
I WORKED THE STATS

NOT TO NAME-DROP (the list include several Hall of Famers), but
here are some of the sportscasters for whom I worked the stats.

Debbie Antonelli, who has over 30 years in sports broadcasting, covering college basketball for ESPN, CBS, Raycom, and Westwood One--
including the Women's National Basketball Association--was the analyst
for two Ohio State women's games that I worked in 1993 for the Coaxial
Communications Cable TV company.

Amy Backus was the color commentator for the McDonald's All-Ohio
Classic high school girls basketball game televised on Warner QUBE in
1984. She was the head coach at Otterbein University at the time and
went on to similar positions at Middlebury College and Northwestern
University and was the head coach at Yale University. She would become
the senior associate athletic director at Yale University, and is currently the
James C. Wyant Director of Athletics and Chair of Physical Education at
Case Western Reserve University. She is a member of the New England
Basketball Hall of Fame.

Dave Bacon, sportscaster in the Cleveland area, called some televised college basketball games for Spectrum Sports in 2017. He was presented with the Ohio High School Athletic Association Media Service Award for the 2013-2014 school year for the Northeast District.

Marty Bannister, who has broadcast every sport in the book. According to my log, I first did stats for Marty for the Sports Medicine high school football all-star game on August 2, 1991 for Coaxial Communications. Obviously, Marty was a teenager at the time!

Todd Bell, who has called Columbus Clippers baseball, Ohio Dominican University basketball and football, you name it, called high school baseball state championship games from Huntington Park, home of the Columbus Clippers.

Mark "Munch" Bishop, currently a Cleveland radio sports talk radio host. I worked the stats for Mark for a Columbus Clippers game on low-power TV station Channel 8 (W08BV) in 1987, and for boxing matches in 1995, I relayed his scoring decisions to the TV production staff.

Tim Bray did the play-by-play for some high school football and basketball and Columbus Clippers games that I worked in the 1980s. Tim spent twenty years as the Director of Communications at Kentucky Speedway, a race track which featured NASCAR racing, and has called games for Bowling Green State University, Ohio State, University of Cincinnati, Xavier University, and numerous high schools. For the past two decades, Tim has been associated with Miami University in Ohio.

Dwight Burgess—I worked the stats for Dwight at some televised Dayton Flyers basketball games for Spectrum Sports in the 2015-2016, 2016-2017, and 2017-2018 seasons. Dwight has been the men's soccer coach at Wittenberg University and at Capital University--both men's and women's. He has been the long-time TV play-by-play broadcaster for the Columbus Crew and has called the action for a variety of national and international soccer events, including XM Satellite Radio's 2006 FIFA World Cup coverage.

Mike Cairns, former sportscaster in Washington, D.C. and Cleveland, called the televised Akron-Kent State football game in Akron in 2013. He was presented with the Ohio High School Athletic Association Media Service Award for the 2008-2009 school year for the Northeast District.

Dave Cecutti, who has been a Capital University basketball head coach, an Ohio State assistant coach, and Commissioner of the Ohio Capital Conference, a central Ohio high school conference. Dave also was my color announcer for a Dublin Jerome High School basketball game, a great pleasure for me in working with someone who had such vast experience.

Vince Chickerella, who won high school basketball state championships as the head coach at two Columbus high schools--Linden-McKinley and St. Francis DeSales--and was the coach at Capital University. He was a 2014 inductee into the Ohio Basketball Hall of Fame, and was inducted into the Ohio High School Basketball Coaches Association Hall of Fame and the Ohio High School Baseball Coaches Hall of Fame. Coach Chickerella was the color analyst for the Ohio State vs. Maryland basketball game at the Brendan Byrne Arena in the New Jersey Meadowlands for WTVN-AM in 1983.

Jonathan Coachman was the play-by-play announcer for the Big Ten softball tournament championship televised from Ohio State on ESPN in 2007. His voice was so strong that I could hear him doing the pre-game segment on the field while I was in the press box.

John Cooper, former Ohio State football head coach, who has the second most wins at OSU and is the only coach to win the Rose Bowl for a Big Ten team and for a Pac-12 team. Coach Cooper was the analyst for some televised high school football games. I still have my index card from one of his games--Pickerington Central vs. Dublin Coffman in 2003--showing the halftime stats, which I accumulate after each quarter and share with the graphics staff and the broadcasters. Coach Cooper wrote some notes across the card, including the 196 passing yards by Coffman's quarterback Jack Rafferty. This meant that I needed to compose a new card for the remainder of the game, but it also meant that I had a souvenir from a hall of fame coach, as he is a member of the National Football Foundation & College Hall Of Fame.

Mark Cooper did the play-by-play for a televised Ohio State women's volleyball match. As a member of the Ohio State marching band, he "dotted the I" in *Script Ohio* in the 1979 homecoming game against Michigan State. He went on to get sports jobs at WKBN in Youngstown, WNYT in Albany, New York, WTVH in Syracuse (where Mike Tirico was his student intern!), and WKBW in Buffalo, where he anchored and hosted the Jim Kelly Show. Mark came on board as the weekend sports anchor and reporter in May of 1992 for Channel 6 in Columbus. The next year, he became the 6:00 and 11:00 sports anchor and sports director through December of 1993.

Bob Costas, world-famous sportscaster. I worked the stats for him and Fred Taylor for two Ohio State men's basketball games at St. John Arena televised on NBC, in 1982 and 1983. Bob was named the winner of the Baseball Hall of Fame's 2018 Ford C. Frick Award for broadcasters. He started broadcasting for the Spirits of St. Louis in the American Basketball Association in the 1974-1975 season, and I called my first game in the 1974-1975 season, That's where the similarity ends.

Paul Cox was the play-by-play broadcaster for a Columbus Clippers baseball game on low-power TV station Channel 8 (W08BV) in 1987.

Ray Crawford, an Emmy and Associated Press Award Winning Anchor/ Reporter, Host and Play-by-Play broadcaster who has called a multitude of sports, filled in to complete the play-by-play of an Upper Arlington High School baseball game that was interrupted one day and completed another.

Jimmy Crum, WCMH-TV sports anchor, who was inducted into the Ohio Associated Press Broadcasters Hall of Fame in 2002. I grew up listening to Jimmy's voice when he called Ohio State basketball games on television, and some 20 years after first hearing him call the games, I worked the stats for high school basketball tournament games at St. John Arena that he called in the 1980s. He was presented with the Ohio High School Athletic Association Media Service Award for the 1998-1999 school year for the Central District.

Matt D'Orazio, star quarterback at Columbus St. Francis DeSales High School, Otterbein University, and in the Arena Football League, where he was a league Most Valuable Player and a two-time ArenaBowl Most Valuable Player. I also worked the stats when he threw a touchdown pass in the Sports Medicine Grant Central Ohio All-Star Game in 1995. Matt was the analyst for some of the high school football games that I worked.

Audrey Flaugh, who had been an Ohio State volleyball player and American Volleyball Coaches Association All-America honoree, was the color announcer for televised OSU women's volleyball matches.

Greg Frey, the only Ohio State quarterback to date to pass for at least 2,000 yards in three straight seasons and who was also a member of the Buckeyes baseball team, was the analyst for some high school football games. I also recorded an interview with Greg in 1992 after one of his games as the quarterback of the Ohio Glory--a team in the World League of American Football--where he tried to lead a late comeback. One of my questions was if he was flashing back to his three memorable comeback wins at Ohio State against Louisiana State in 1988, Minnesota in 1989, and Iowa in 1990.

John Gordon, who has broadcast for the Baltimore Orioles, New York Yankees, and Minnesota Twins, was the play-by-play broadcaster for Ohio State football and Columbus Clippers baseball games on Warner QUBE cable TV from 1979 through 1981. He has been the sports director for WBNS-TV and WTVN-TV; and the football and basketball voice of Ohio State on WBNS radio, for the University of Virginia, and for the Naval Academy. As an actor, John portrayed broadcaster Wally Holland in the movie *Little Big League*. One of the stats that he cited in the movie was "Last year, though, he was sixth in the American League in hitting right handers he was facing for the first time after the seventh inning at home", of which I was envious.

Cornelius Greene (he later changed his spelling to "Green"), who had been an Ohio State quarterback, was the analyst during the 1981 season for WOSU-TV. I saw him outside the stadium before the National Championship game in Glendale, Arizona in 2007, the 41-14 loss to Florida, and had a chat about the WOSU-TV days. Cornelius was inducted into the Rose Bowl Hall of Fame in 2019, most notably for quarterbacking the Buckeyes to a 42-21 win over Southern California in the 1974 game, which I attended.

Dave Grube, who had been a Capital University men's basketball head coach, was the analyst for two high school basketball games in 1980 televised by Warner QUBE.

Jim Hamilton, who served 25 years as a coach and athletic director at Upper Arlington High School. He coached basketball and golf from 1968 to 1986 and went on to serve as athletic director until 1993. The basketball court at Upper Arlington was named "Jim Hamilton Court" in his honor, and he was a 2021 inductee into the Ohio Basketball Hall of Fame. Coach Hamilton was the color announcer for Capital University games for many years, and I also was the play-by-play announcer for two Capital games--one men's and one women's--being fortunate to have Coach Hamilton as my broadcast partner. I tell Coach Hamilton that I gave him the biggest break of his coaching career--I tried out for the ninth game team in the Upper Arlington school system, did not make the team, and never tried out in future years, thereby sparing him the experience of seeing me on the court. I once brought a high school yearbook to a televised game so that the production staff could show his photo--featuring a flat-top haircut--on the air. I didn't get off scot-free; they also showed my yearbook photo on the air.

Pete Hanson, former Ohio State volleyball coach--who won NCAA national titles in 2011, 2016, and 2017; is a member of the USA Volleyball Hall of Fame and the American Volleyball Coaches Association Hall of Fame; and the National Coach of the Year four times--was the color analyst for some televised Ohio State women's volleyball games.

Wayne Harer, who accumulated 999 hits while playing in the New York Yankees and Boston Red Sox minor league organizations. Wayne was the color announcer for Columbus Clippers games for many years, and he bailed me out once. I was on a headset talking to a production staff member, who asked me who the Clippers manager was. Having a brain freeze, I said "Stump Mitchell", who was an NFL football player at the time. Luckily, Wayne overheard and corrected me to "Stump Merrill". Wayne also does a perfect impersonation of the late Harry Carey, who is most famous for calling Chicago Cubs games.

Jeff Hogan, former WBNS-TV sports anchor before moving on to be the news anchor for WRAL in Raleigh, North Carolina. I worked with him on some Ohio State baseball broadcasts, and he demonstrated his diplomacy in one game. The camera caught Ohio State fans posting the "K's" for strikeouts on a fence. I handed Jeff a note with "The fans can't count, it should be eight strikeouts, not seven". On the air, Jeff modified it to "The fans shorted him, it should be eight strikeouts, not seven."

Herb Howenstine, who has called Ohio State hockey, baseball, and women's basketball games, was the analyst for the second half of the Ohio State at Iowa football game for WOSU-TV in 1983, when I took my first-ever flight with the WOSU-TV crew. In the pre-game segment, Herb mentioned Iowa Coach Hayden Fry's saying, "We'll take what the other teams give us. We'll scratch where it itches."

Chris Huesman, Dublin Jerome High School baseball coach, was the analyst for some high school games.

Pat Hughes. The current radio voice of the Chicago Cubs, Pat called games for several sports for Warner QUBE Cable TV in Columbus. Pat was inducted into the Chicagoland Sports Hall of Fame in 2021. The https://www.mlb.com/cubs/team/broadcasters#hughes website has "He joined Cubs radio broadcasts in 1996 after spending the previous 12 years teaming with Bob Uecker on the Milwaukee Brewers Radio Network. Hughes began his baseball play-by-play career in the minor leagues, calling action for the San Jose Missions (1978-1981) and the Columbus Clippers (1982). He worked as a play-by-play voice for Marquette University's basketball team from 1988-2004, including working with Al McGuire during the 1996-2000 seasons. Hughes' collegiate play-by-play career also includes stints with Northwestern University, San Jose State University, the University of Wisconsin and ESPN. He worked in Minnesota in

1983 as the TV voice of the Twins and as the hockey host/interviewer on North Stars telecasts. Hughes was named the Illinois Sportscaster of the Year in 1996, 1999, 2006, 2007, 2009, 2014, 2015 and 2017. He earned Wisconsin Sportscaster of the Year Award honors three times (1990-1992)."

Red Jamison called several high school games for Warner QUBE Cable TV in Columbus in the 1977-1978 season. He also hosted the Talent Search show on Warner QUBE, featuring local amateur acts, where viewers would vote on the performers by using their consoles.

Harry Kalas, play-by-play broadcaster for the Houston Astros and the Philadelphia Phillies, called the 1981 Liberty Bowl game between Ohio State and Navy for television. Harry was a recipient of the Baseball Hall of Fame's Ford C. Frick Award.

Jim Karsatos, an Ohio State quarterback from 1983 through 1986. I did the stats for Jim and Randy Rhinehart for the Columbus Thunderbolts arena football games—played at the Coliseum in the Ohio Expo Center—and for high school football and college Division III football, in 1991. These games were broadcast on WMNI radio and Coaxial Communications Cable TV.

Kaye Kessler, who had been a sports writer for the *Columbus Citizen* and the *Columbus Citizen-Journal* since 1941, was the analyst along with Tim Bray for some Columbus Clippers games on Warner QUBE Cable TV in 1983. Kaye is in the Colorado and Ohio golf halls of fame.

Jack Kramer--For 36 years, his primary occupation was the director of marketing and public relations at two community colleges. On the side as avocations for 50 years, he has officiated soccer, baseball, and softball, and has also performed high school sports play-by-play online, on television, and on several different radio stations in western Ohio. The *Sidney Daily News* published a story when Jack called his 3,000th game on February 9, 2018. In 2012, Jack asked me to start managing his website–www. scoresbroadcast.com–that allows fans to listen to his broadcasts of games played in western Ohio. I already had some experience in HTML, but I quickly learned the basics of PHP, creating graphics, and creating an animated GIF. He was the play-by-play voice of the Ohio State football games shown on a delayed basis on WOSU-TV when I was his statistician from 1981 through 1990. Jack writes: "While viewing the game replays, we had the chance to evaluate our own performances, from the producer and director to those of us in the broadcast booth. Steve's stats were always spot on!" In 2021, I recorded an interview with Jack that was long enough to be split into segments for two high school football halftime breaks. He was presented with the Ohio High School Athletic Association Media Service Award for the 2011-2012 school year for the Southwest District.

Mike Lanza, long-time high school basketball and football coach in the Columbus area, was the analyst for high school football games on 820 AM when I did the stats in 2011 and 2012. He would bring cookies that his wife had made, and they were the best!

Scott Leo is one of those broadcasters who has called all kinds of sports, including Columbus Clippers baseball and Wittenberg University games. I did the stats for Scott at Wright State men's televised basketball games on Spectrum Sports in 2017.

Jeff Logan, former Ohio State running back and captain, and football analyst for over 40 years. I first worked with Jeff in 1979 on an Ohio State football game televised by Warner QUBE, and he calls me the "cornucopia of worthless information", based on my knowledge of trivia. I also recorded an interview with Jeff in 1990, in which we gave our thoughts for the upcoming Ohio State vs. Southern California game, the game that was terminated early due to lightning in the area. Jeff put me on his pre-game radio show in New Orleans the day that the Buckeyes played Louisiana State in 2008 in the National Championship game; one of his questions was: which Buckeye had the most rushing yards in a bowl game? Put on the spot, I incorrectly said, "Tim Spencer with about 160 yards in the 1982 Holiday Bowl." Once off the air, I realized that it was Raymont Harris in the 1993 Holiday Bowl, looked up the number using my T-Mobile Sidekick, jotted it down on a piece of paper and handed it to Jeff. At least I had the right bowl game and opponent (Brigham Young in each case)!

Andy MacWilliams has done it all--hockey, basketball, football (including the Cincinnati Bengals), baseball (including the Cincinnati Reds)-- and I worked the stats for him for the Division I high school football and the girls' and boys' high school state basketball championships in 1983 for WXIX-TV.

Paul Maguire, who had been a punter for the Los Angeles/San Diego Chargers and the Buffalo Bills, was the analyst on ESPN's production of the Ohio State vs. Syracuse football game in 1980.

Thom McDaniels, highly successful football coach at Canton McKinley, Warren Harding, and Jackson High Schools, and father of NFL assistant coaches Josh McDaniels and Ben McDaniels, was the analyst for some televised high school games in the Columbus area. Thom is a member of the Ohio High School Football Coaches Association Hall of Fame.

Tom McDonald, former Groveport Madison High School football coach, was the analyst for some televised high school games. Tom also joined me to call a Gahanna Lincoln High School football game in 2016, when the Gahanna quarterback was Mike Lowery, whose dad Tony had played for Tom at Groveport Madison. My favorite Tom McDonald story: we had a high school football game at the old Cooper Stadium, where the Columbus Clippers played baseball. A defender intercepted the ball on his own 10-yard line and ran laterally to avoid tackles. Describing the replay, Tom said "he's at the 10, the 10, the 10!" Tom is also on the Ohio State football official stats crew, with the task of tracking every player who makes an appearance in the game.

Ray Miller, former Grove City High School basketball coach who had over 400 career wins to go along with a great sense of humor, was the television analyst for an informal basketball game for charity. In the postgame wrap-up, Randy Rhinehart asked Ray "What can we learn from this game?", to which Ray said "Absolutely nothing."

Michelle Mimna, analyst for Time Warner Cable SportsChannel and Fox Sports Ohio, called girls high school volleyball state championship matches.

Keith Morehouse called the televised Ohio University vs. Central Michigan football game in Athens, Ohio in 2013.

Larry "Buck" Owen, who had been a catcher for the Atlanta Braves and the Kansas City Royals, was an analyst for some televised Columbus Clippers games.

Mike Pagel, who had been a quarterback for the Baltimore/Indianapolis Colts, the Cleveland Browns, and the Los Angeles Rams. Mike was the analyst for televised high school football playoff games in Cleveland in the 1990s, along with Randy Rhinehart doing the play-by-play. The three of us had lunch at a restaurant before one of the games, and the server asked for his autograph--not for herself, but for a customer who asked her to be the middle-person. I had worked the stats for Warner QUBE in 1980 when he quarterbacked his Arizona State team against the Buckeyes. When some staff at games mispronounced his name, he would point out that it rhymes with "bagel".

Dave Parr, who was a Columbus radio personality, was the analyst for the Upper Arlington vs. Westerville High School basketball game for Warner Cable in 1975, a game in which future Westerville South coach Ed Calo played.

Red Pitcher was the play-by-play broadcaster for the 1982 high school football Division I state championship game at Ohio Stadium between Massillon Washington and Cincinnati Moeller for WXIX-TV.

Marty Reid was a sports anchor for WCMH-TV in Columbus before moving on to ESPN, and I worked some high school basketball games for him.

Randy Rhinehart, who has called 16 different sports--at least, that is the count that he listed in a 2004 story in the *Columbus Dispatch*, so it may be higher now--gave me one of my biggest breaks when he asked me to be his statistician in 1990. The sports that I have worked on with Randy are: high school football, high school basketball, high school baseball, high school volleyball, high school ice hockey, high school lacrosse, high school field hockey, college football, college basketball, college baseball, college volleyball, college ice hockey, minor league baseball, Arena Football League football, and women's semi-pro football. He has been the voice for the state football, basketball, baseball, volleyball, and soccer championships, and for the Columbus Clippers, Columbus Destroyers, and

Capital University. He has called the action on TV for 10 different Ohio State sports–football, basketball, baseball, hockey, volleyball, softball, tennis, wrestling, gymnastics, and track and field. He has also done events that have aired on the YES Network, ESPN, Sport TV, CNNSI, Sports Channel, SportsTime Ohio, Columbus Sports Network, Prime Sports, the Big Ten Network, Fox Sports Ohio, and Ohio News Network. I found a YouTube video of the 1986 Gahanna Lincoln vs. Reynoldsburg high school football game that Randy and Jim Anderson, a former high school coach in Columbus, called for Coaxial Communications cable TV. Randy has quite a wit; my favorite quote from him was when he was kidding with a broadcast partner by saying "I've worked with a lot of analysts, and you are definitely one of them."

Toni Roesch, former Ohio State women's basketball player who is in the Ohio Basketball Hall of Fame, was the analyst for some high school games. She has been a color analyst for Big Ten, Metro Atlantic Athletic Conference, Ohio Valley Conference, and Mid-American Conference contests, as well as the Women's National Basketball Association as a broadcaster for ESPN, Comcast, and FOX.

John Sanders was the play-by-play broadcaster when I worked the stats for the Ohio State vs. Syracuse football game for ESPN in 1980.

Sandy Schwartz, former sports writer for the *Columbus Citizen-Journal*, was the analyst for Columbus Clippers games on Warner QUBE in 1983.

Gib Shanley, Cleveland Browns play-by-play broadcaster for 24 years and TV sports anchor at Channel 5 in Cleveland for 20 years, did the play-by-play for my very first Ohio State football game, at the University of Indiana in 1978, a game that turned out to be Woody Hayes's last true road game and last win as the Ohio State coach.

Allie Sherman, who had been a quarterback with the Philadelphia Eagles, but more noted for coaching the New York football Giants when they played in the NFL championship games of 1961, 1962, and 1963, was the analyst for that Ohio State vs. Indiana football game in 1978. My brother Mark and I had the task of returning his rental car to the Indianapolis airport.

Neil Sika was the play-by-play broadcaster for basketball games televised by Spectrum Sports at Northern Kentucky University in 2017. At one NKU game, I spotted Jim Kelch, the Cincinnati Reds broadcaster who also calls NKU games, and Neil graciously introduced me to Jim for a chat when I told him that I was a Reds fan.

Bob Spears, Ohio State pitcher who was the team captain, four-year baseball letterman, the team leader in wins in 1996 and earned run average in 1995, was the analyst for some televised Ohio State baseball games.

Frank Stams, former football player at Akron St. Vincent-St. Mary High School, Notre Dame University, and for the Los Angeles Rams and the Cleveland Browns, was the analyst for college football games on Spectrum Sports in 2013. I told him that I had seen him play high school basketball in the state championship semifinal game in St. John Arena in 1983, and I still have that program.

Bob Starr, former Groveport Madison High School football coach and principal of Berne Union High School, was the analyst for some televised high school games. Bob was also on the Ohio State football official stats crew with me, with the tasks of identifying the players who made the tackle or broke up a pass.

Matt Sylvester, former Ohio State basketball player, was the analyst for some high school state championship games in the Jerome Schottenstein

Center. I pointed out to him where I was sitting behind the Illinois bench when he hit the three-pointer to give the Illini–ranked #1 with a 29-0 record at the time–their only regular season loss in 2004-2005.

Craig Taylor, former Ohio State basketball player, was an analyst for high school basketball games on Warner QUBE. Craig and Pat Hughes also hosted a high school basketball show on QUBE. The Big Ten was loaded with centers when he played in the 1970s, and I felt that he more than held his own. I have an Ohio State program from 1975 with his auto-graph. Craig was a 2017 inductee into the Ohio Basketball Hall of Fame.

Fred Taylor, Ohio State basketball coach who won the 1960 National Championship. I worked the stats for two Ohio State basketball games on NBC for Coach Taylor and Bob Costas in 1982 and 1983, and for some Cleveland Cavaliers and Ohio Wesleyan games. Coach Taylor was the first coach in NCAA history to take his team to three straight Final Fours, and is a member of the Naismith Memorial Basketball Hall of Fame and a 2006 Charter Class inductee into the Ohio Basketball Hall of Fame. During a down time once, he described to me the defense that he drew up for a late inbounds play to force a turnover when the Buckeyes upset Marquette in the 1971 NCAA tournament. Coach Taylor sent me a letter of thanks after I worked a Cavaliers game for him in 1977.

Joe Theismann, a member of both the NFL Hall of Fame and College Football Hall of Fame as a quarterback, was the analyst for the 1981 Liberty Bowl between Ohio State and Navy, where I was the statistician for the Metrosports TV production.

Chuck Underwood, former Ohio State football and basketball play-by-play broadcaster, called the Sertoma All Stars high school basket-ball game, along with Fred Taylor for Warner QUBE in 1983. I also worked the stats for his broadcast of the Ohio State vs. Maryland game in the New Jersey Meadowlands for WTVN-AM that December. I still have a thank-you letter from Chuck following that 1983 all-star game, with "Thank you very much for the fine statistics work". Chuck moved on to become the founder and principal of the generational consulting firm The Generational Imperative, Inc., and has written books and produced videos on the various generations. He also granted me an interview in 2021, talking about his broadcasting and his venture into the field of generational studies. My favorite Chuck Underwood story is from an Ohio State basketball game when he described a player from another team who had a legal issue as being "in trouble with the local *gendarmes*."

Chris Vail, who has coached boys and girls basketball, football, soft-ball, baseball, and golf, has called high school football games that I have worked. On the drive back from Zanesville following a playoff game, the four of us quizzed each other on music trivia, and I stumped them with the Sir Douglas Quintet.

Tara VanDerveer, the all-time winningest coach in women's college bas-ketball, a three-time national championship winner, and a member of the Naismith Memorial Basketball Hall of Fame. During her time as the Ohio State coach, before she went on to Stanford–where she won her national championships–I worked the stats for her and Tim Bray at a girls' high school basketball all-star game at Otterbein University in 1983. I have a DVD with a brief clip that includes her commentary.

Jon Warden--while mainly known as a pitcher on the 1968 World Series champions Detroit Tigers, he was the color announcer for a high school basketball doubleheader televised by Warner QUBE at the Ohio State Fairgrounds in 1979. I have a program from the 1979-1980 Wehrle vs.

DeSales high school basketball game that shows Jon as the head coach and athletic director of Wehrle, with his wife, Karol, as the cheerleading advisor.

Paul Warfield, former Ohio State football player and NFL Hall of Fame receiver for the Cleveland Browns and the Miami Dolphins, was the analyst for WOSU-TV's delayed telecasts of Ohio State football games from 1983 through 1990. Paul was the No. 11 draft pick in the first round, by the Cleveland Browns in 1964, and led the NFL in receiving touchdowns twice.

Tony White, former Ohio State basketball player, was the analyst for televised Dayton Flyers games on Spectrum Sports in the 2015-2016, 2016-2017, and 2017-2018 seasons. I told him that during an Ohio State game that he played in, the play-by-play broadcaster mispronounced his hometown as "Pat-a-lask-a", instead of "Pataskala." I also told him that I was at the game when his Watkins Memorial High School team lost a heartbreaker in the tournament to Beechcroft, which featured future Ohio State player James Bradley.

Ed Whitson, a pitcher who won 126 games during his career with the Pittsburgh Pirates, San Francisco Giants, Cleveland Indians, San Diego Padres (pitching in the 1984 World Series), and New York Yankees, was an analyst for some televised Columbus Clippers games.

Jason Whitt was the play-by-play announcer for high school basketball and football on WINF-FM during my two years—the 2008-2009 and 2009-2010 school years—of keeping the stats, before turning the microphone over to me for the 2010-2011 school year. Jason also came out of retirement in 2011 to be my analyst on a high school basketball game. Jason is talented enough to keep player scoring stats during the game, of which I am envious. I owe a debt of gratitude to Jason for the fact that he employed Steve Geiger as an analyst for some basketball games in 2010, which led Steve and me to a long collaboration of broadcasting Ohio Wesleyan basketball and football games and high school basketball and football games.

Jacki Windon. In addition to working basketball stats for Jacki, I would be calling some Ohio Wesleyan games where she was officiating. Jacki is the former head women's basketball coach at Case Western Reserve University, and has broadcast games for the Mid-American Conference men's and women's college basketball, the Ohio High School Athletic Association, FOX, FOX SportsOhio, Spectrum Sports Channel, and ESPN3.

CHAPTER 9

BROADCAST PARTNERS

IN MY VIEW, a broadcaster is only as good as the broadcast partner. I have been fortunate to have been joined by several extremely valuable partners. One of the favors that I ask of them is "When (not if) I identify the wrong player, please point to the right name on the roster instead of correcting me on the air, and I will do the same for you."

MY BROADCAST PARTNERS INCLUDE:

Mary Armentrout was part of our three-person broadcast team for an Upper Arlington vs. Grove City High School basketball game on Warner QUBE in 1978. I have a photo of Mary, Bob Vincent, and myself at that game.

Blake Baker was a senior at Gahanna Lincoln High School when he joined me for Gahanna Lincoln baseball games for the Gameday Broadcasting Sports Network. A former player himself, he got a kick out of the fact that he was calling games where his younger brother Cael--who would go on to play in college at Cincinnati, Ole Miss, and Ohio University--was a four-year star catcher on the team, named the 2017 State Player of the Year, and set the all-time school record for home runs. Cael was also on the Gahanna football team, and Blake would call him "the big boy" on the air.

Ryan Baker has been a sportscaster and studio host, and he joined me for the Ohio Wesleyan vs. Oberlin men's and women's basketball games in 2016, producing a complimentary email from Mike Mancini of the Oberlin Athletics Communications staff.

Jacob Barker joined me for a Columbus Academy High School football game for the Gameday Broadcasting Sports Network. I see Jacob frequently at games, doing television production work.

Mike Basford of the Ohio State Athletics Sports Information staff has joined me for high school basketball games for WINF-FM and the Gameday Broadcasting Sports Network, and for Ohio Wesleyan basketball games.

Charlie Beaver, who played on the Ohio Wesleyan NCAA Division III national championship basketball team of 1988, joined me for an Ohio Wesleyan football game in 2021. Charlie appears in a huge framed photo of the 1988 team at the entrance of the Branch Rickey Arena, where the basketball team plays.

Mike Carsey smoothed things out for me with his experience when I filled in to call high school football and basketball games for WINF-FM in 2008 and 2009.

Aaron Cassady, who founded the Gameday Broadcasting Sports Network in 2009, gave me my big break when he reached out to me to start calling high school football, basketball, and baseball games in 2013. He and I also called high school basketball and baseball games together, and he arranged for my only broadcast outside of Ohio, joining him at a Marietta College vs. La Roche University baseball doubleheader in Pittsburgh for WMOA radio, based in Marietta. At one basketball game, the multi-tasking Aaron called the action with me while holding his two young, well-behaved daughters, who were busy coloring, on his lap.

Jeff Cope was pressed into duty at the last minute when I needed an analyst at a Dublin Jerome High School baseball game for the Gameday Broadcasting Sports Network. He passed his public address duty to someone else, allowing him to call the game that had his son Robert, who would be a walk-on football player at Ohio State, in action.

Charlie Danis, who calls Capital University games among his many talents, joined me for an Ohio Wesleyan basketball game.

Seth Duckworth, former Ohio Wesleyan catcher, joined me for Ohio Wesleyan softball, calling games when his daughter Aimee–who had four hits in a game as a freshman, to tie the school record–played. Seth would often utter "mmm!" when he disagreed with an umpire's call of a called strike with Aimee at bat. Seth also called Ohio Wesleyan baseball games with me when his son Ryan played for OWU. He is connected with the OWU baseball and softball communities and writes: "Parents, alumni, recruits, and extended families love watching the games and are very grateful for the quality of broadcasting Steve and crew have offered." Note that he is very modest, since he is a major part of the crew.

David Eastman, former faculty member at Ohio Wesleyan University, called Ohio Wesleyan baseball games with me. Dr. Eastman introduced me to the term "Johnny All-Staff" to describe the fact that the OWU pitching staff, having been overworked, would need multiple pitchers to see some action on the mound in a game that we were calling. He was also able to keep the official stats using an app on his phone while serving as analyst.

Martina Ellerbe, former Ohio State basketball player, joined me for an Ohio Wesleyan women's basketball game.

Doug Evans was a good luck charm in his only New Albany High School baseball game with me in 2012 for the Gameday Broadcasting Sports Network, as a New Albany player hit the only home run that I witnessed in the four games that I called that year.

John Feasel, Olentangy High School boys basketball coach. I first met Coach Feasel in 2011 when he was the Olentangy girls coach–he was named the Associated Press State Coach of the Year in 2016–and I told him that I thought that I had called some of his games as the opposing coach when I called games in the 1980s for WCVO-FM; he said no, that was his dad, who has the same name and was inducted into the District 11 Basketball Coaches Association Hall of Fame. He has joined me to call several Ohio Wesleyan games. I am fortunate that John is a Notre Dame fan instead of an Ohio State fan; he had no problem with not watching the Ohio State at Michigan football game on TV in 2017 in order to call an Ohio Wesleyan basketball game with me. Whenever I call a game that has his Olentangy team, John always sends me his team's stats without me even asking. John's sense of humor is legendary. He tells the story that as a player in high school, he held Scott Tedder, a Whitehall-Yearling opponent who would go on to be the all-time leading scorer in Ohio Wesleyan history, to 40 points in a game. For Halloween in 2021, he dressed as Dr. Evil from the Austin Powers movies, with a spot-on likeness. I could write a book on his wit, for example:

Me, chatting with him before one of his games that he was coaching: "Coach, can I get some pronunciations?"

John: "FEE-zel"

Me, referring to Jordan Holmes of the Denison University women's team, who is 6'1" and the only player in Division III history to have over 1,000 points, 1,500 rebounds and 500 blocked shots: "As Al McGuire would say, she's an aircraft carrier."

John: "Yeah, they have an aircraft carrier, and we have PT boats."

John, referring to Oberlin men's Coach Isaiah Cavaco: "I don't see how a graduate of Yale can run the Princeton offense."

John, referring to DePauw's Blair Carlin: "Her grandfather George would have been proud."

John, describing one of his boys' teams: "We're short, but we're slow, too."

Doug Flowers. About 30 years after I called some of his basketball games when he played for New Albany High School, Doug joined me to call New Albany games for the Gameday Broadcasting Sports Network.

Gordon Gaiten joined me for Dublin Jerome High School basketball, calling games for the Gameday Broadcasting Sports Network in 2018 when his son Joseph played.

Steve Geiger was a member of the 1988 Ohio Wesleyan Division III basketball national championship team and a second-team all-conference honoree in 1991, and I owe a huge debt of gratitude to him for getting started in Ohio Wesleyan broadcasts. Steve appears in a huge framed photo of the 1988 team at the entrance of the Branch Rickey Arena, where the basketball teams play. A former basketball coach at Danville High School in the 1990s–his OWU teammate Mick Shimp was an assistant–Steve has been my broadcast partner for Ohio Wesleyan men's and women's basketball, and Ohio Wesleyan football since 2013, high school football and basketball in Delaware County for WINF-FM in 2010-2011, and Columbus Academy high school football for the Gameday Broadcasting Sports Network from 2013 to 2015. Similar to Mike and Mike, we are Steve and Steve. He has also done the play-by-play for Ohio Wesleyan football and basketball on occasion. His son, Max, was a commentator for some basketball games for Olentangy Orange High School while a student there. Steve is a native of Delaware County, having attended Olentangy High School. In doing research for this book, I found a recap of one of his high school games against Dublin High School in the *Columbus Dispatch* archives: "Brad Baldridge added 15 points for Dublin. Steve Geiger's 18 points led Olentangy." Steve and Brad would continue their battle over the years when Brad's Wittenberg team played Ohio Wesleyan. Coincidentally, that same *Dispatch* high school basketball section has a report on the Columbus Academy game and shows Academy's Aaron Clark scoring 10 points. Steve and I would call the games for the four years of Aaron's son Seth's OWU career, and Steve would battle Aaron when OWU played Wittenberg.

Bruce Gerber started as a last-minute fill-in at an Ohio Wesleyan basketball game and has been a valuable asset ever since. Bruce played at Kenyon College, which is in Ohio Wesleyan's conference, and was able to call some games when his son Jaret and his daughter Lauren played for Ohio Wesleyan. Bruce was pressed into duty once to be the spotter for an OWU women's game, a task that I had once for a high school tournament game. I refer to Bruce as "the second most famous person from Orrville, Ohio", behind only Bob Knight.

Phil Golovin had been a basketball official, which came in handy when he joined me for a Delaware Hayes High School game for WINF-FM in 2011. Phil's photo appears in the "Columbus Radio" book, from when he was a disc jockey for WCOL.

David Hejmanowski, who had called baseball games for the Delaware Cows of the Great Lakes Summer Collegiate League, joined me for Ohio Wesleyan baseball games.

Bob Hull. We once had three generations of the Hull family in action for a Gahanna Lincoln High School baseball game on the Gameday Broadcasting Sports Network. Brad was the shortstop, his dad Brian was on the Gahanna staff, and I drafted grandfather Bob about 10 minutes before the first pitch to join me in calling the game, filling in for Brian. I asked him if he had any broadcasting experience, and he said that he had read the comics on radio for the benefit of the blind, which was more than good enough for me. As a bonus from the Hull family, Bob's wife Shirley provided us with delicious cookies.

Brian Hull, who was on the Gahanna Lincoln High School baseball coaching staff before becoming an Assistant Coach and Recruiting Coordinator at Ohio Dominican University, joined me to call Gahanna Lincoln games for the Gameday Broadcasting Sports Network when his son Brad was the shortstop.

Chris Intihar has called Dublin Jerome High School football and basketball games for the Gameday Broadcasting Sports Network, and Ohio Wesleyan basketball and baseball games with me. Chris joined me for an Ohio Wesleyan men's basketball game in 2022 and a women's basketball doubleheader at Ohio Wesleyan in 2018, after which we received a complimentary email from the Wisconsin-Oshkosh sports information director. At basketball games, Chris has the gift of being able to track a few team stats—turnovers, three-point field goals made, and free throws shot and made—which is very helpful. Chris is the only person whom I have trained to run a broadcast for a game on the Gameday Broadcasting Sports Network—he filled in for the play-by-play when I had to pass—and he pulled it off without a hitch. At one game, the halftime score was 52-25, which he described as "palindromic". His son Wil was on the Dublin Jerome baseball and football teams, and I once called a football game where he returned a fumble 92 yards for a touchdown. I was able to interview Wil for a short time at halftime at a Jerome basketball game, four years after he graduated.

Cody Inverso joined me to call four Jump25.com all-star basketball games in one day at Ohio Dominican University in 2013 for Mega Sports News.

Ben Jandrain was a good-luck charm; his only Ohio Wesleyan men's basketball game with me saw the Bishops score 123 points and have six players in double figures, against Hiram College in 2016.

Tim Jewell called Dublin Jerome High School basketball games with me for the Gameday Broadcasting Sports Network in 2020, while his son Jason was on the team.

Turner Johnson, former Ohio Wesleyan pitcher, joined me for a baseball doubleheader and was another good-luck charm in a rare Bishops' win over traditional power Wooster. Turner's career ERA of 0.00, in three innings, may stand as a record for some time.

Milan Jordan is one of those sportscasters who does it all, and I was fortunate to call Gahanna Lincoln High School football games with him in

2016 for the Gameday Broadcasting Sports Network. I also appreciate his gift of gab, allowing me to take a break at halftime.

Bob Kennedy is the original Mr. Microphone; you can hear his voice as the public address announcer in Ohio Stadium, the Jerome Schottenstein Center, and at just about any other major game in Central Ohio. Bob also broadcasts high school games on radio and joined me for a New Albany High School basketball game for the Gameday Broadcasting Sports Network.

David Kinder, before becoming the WHIZ-TV sports anchor in Zanesville, joined me for a Columbus Academy High School football game for the Gameday Broadcasting Sports Network.

Mike Klein, broadcaster of New Albany High School games for the Gameday Broadcasting Sports Network, and former two-term New Albany-Plain Local school board member, joined me for some Ohio Wesleyan basketball games.

Kyle Kuhlman was a good-luck charm in calling Dublin Jerome High School football games for the Gameday Broadcasting Sports Network, at least for a game and a half. His first game was an Instant Classic in 2017, where Jerome won on a pass with six seconds remaining, and his second game in 2018 saw Jerome take the lead over traditional power Dublin Coffman at halftime, before losing. Kyle can often be spotted on Ohio State basketball telecasts when the camera trains on the scorer's table, doing his stats work.

Cliff Lanthorn, former Ohio Wesleyan assistant women's basketball coach, joined me for some Ohio Wesleyan games.

Steve Leppert and I are members of the local Hank Gowdy chapter of the Society for American Baseball Research (SABR) organization, and he has joined me for Ohio Wesleyan baseball and softball games. Steve was jinxed in 2020, as every time that he was scheduled to call a baseball game, it was rained out, but we were able to call the 2021 season's games, and he joined me for some OWU softball games in 2022. Similar to Mike and Mike, we are Steve and Steve.

Stu Mason covers just about every sport imaginable for his Mega Sports News website, and I was fortunate to hook up with him in the 1980s at WCVO-FM for high school football and basketball and in the 1990-1991 school year for high school basketball on WLOH-AM in Lancaster.

Don Masters, former Van Buren High School football coach, joined me in 2001 on Time Warner Cable when I did the play-by-play for the Oregon Clay at Findlay High School boys basketball game. The football field at Van Buren is named in his honor.

Russ Merrin was the play-by-play broadcaster for the two high school basketball games where I was the analyst for WBBY-FM in 1976.

Rick Middleton, former Ohio State linebacker who was drafted in the first round by the New Orleans Saints in 1974 and also played for the San Diego Chargers, joined me for three high school football games in Delaware County–he had played for Delaware Hayes High School–for WINF-FM in 2011. A versatile player, in 1971, he caught one of the Buckeyes' two touchdown passes on the year as a tight end.

Chris Miles was my broadcast partner for my very first baseball game, in 2012 between New Albany and Delaware Hayes High School, carried on the Gameday Broadcasting Sports Network.

Greg Mitchell called a Dublin Jerome High School basketball game with me on the Gameday Broadcasting Sports Network.

Zack Molle was a student at Olentangy High School in 2010 when he joined me to call the Olentangy vs. Westerville South football game for WINF-FM. He also joined me for an interview that basketball season.

Andy Powell, former Walnut Ridge and Beechcroft High School football coach. Andy had the misfortune of being with me at Grove City Christian High School in 2014 when our broadcast of the Columbus Academy football game for the Gameday Broadcasting Sports Network died in the third quarter. Andy is also on the Ohio State football official stats crew with me and granted me an interview on another occasion, talking about his coaching experiences.

Scott Reeves, former Ohio State basketball player, joined me for some Ohio Wesleyan basketball games. Scott probably continues to get as much face time on video highlights as any former player, since he appears prominently bouncing off the bench to celebrate Jim Jackson's basket to force overtime in the 1991 win over Indiana.

Scott Rex joined me for an Ohio Wesleyan basketball game. Scott's role on the Ohio State football official stats crew is to identify every player involved in a play, the type of play, the yard line, and more. When an Ohio State basketball game is on TV, Scott can be seen at the scorer's desk, as he is also involved in those official statistics. He also has the distinction of being the person with whom I have recorded an interview the most often—five times as of this writing—talking about his role for the official stats and about the Central Catholic League football teams that he has seen while doing the stats for 820 AM radio. He was a backup quarterback at Otterbein College, and is quite proud of the time that he completed a pass for a two-point conversion on a busted play against Marietta College in 2001 in one of his rare appearances; he has a video to prove it.

Jim Sanders has been my analyst for Dublin Jerome High School basketball games on the Gameday Broadcasting Sports Network, and says that it was much more enjoyable after his first year, when he was calling games while his son Derek was playing. I was able to interview Derek for a short time at halftime of a Jerome basketball game, two years after he graduated.

Jon Sewell has called Dublin Jerome High School basketball games with me for the Gameday Broadcasting Sports Network, thanks to Aaron Cassady sending him my way.

Blake Sherry is one of the leaders of the local Hank Gowdy chapter of the Society for American Baseball Research (SABR) organization, and has broadcast Ohio Wesleyan baseball and softball games with me. A bonus for me in joining SABR is that it gave me access to several chapter members who are well-versed in baseball and willing to broadcast games with me. One of my icebreaker questions for a first-time analyst is what their favorite baseball movie is. Blake says that *Field of Dreams* is not only his favorite baseball movie, but also gets his vote as the best movie of all time!

Mick Shimp played basketball for Ohio Wesleyan and has joined me to call some OWU games. I called Gahanna Lincoln High School games for WCVO-FM when he (known as Micky at the time) played for the Gahanna Lincoln Lions. He was an excellent ball handler, and Steve Geiger tells me that when they were teammates at OWU, Mick was as good a point guard as you will ever see. I recall one of his Gahanna Lincoln games in which his team was up by about six points with about 40 seconds remaining, where I said "This game is over, they cannot get the ball out of Micky Shimp's hands!" I was also able to interview Mick as an assistant coach for Olentangy High School in 2021.

Chris Solwecki joined me for an Ohio Wesleyan softball doubleheader. Also, I was Chris's analyst when he called a Gahanna Lincoln vs. Olentangy Liberty High School football playoff game, with our position on the roof at Liberty on a chilly November night. In that game, Chris used the word "accoutrements", of which I remind him each time that I see him.

Bob Vincent was a play-by-play broadcaster for Warner QUBE in the 1970s, and I was his analyst for some high school basketball games and his statistician for others. Bob at one time was a disc jockey for WDLR radio in Delaware, Ohio.

Rob Walker. Every time that I see Rob on a WOSU-TV fundraiser, I am reminded of the time that he joined me to call the Grandview Heights vs. New Albany high school basketball game–each of us did two quarters of play-by-play–in the 1981-1982 season for WCVO-FM. At halftime, Rob interviewed Larry Larson, the athletic director and football coach at Grandview Heights who had also been the basketball coach the previous season, and he interviewed Grandview Heights' basketball coach Jim Duffy, who recorded his first Bobcat win, after the game.

Bill Walters--I call Bill "Mr. Dependable", because I can always count on him. He has probably joined me for the biggest variety of sports--high school basketball, high school football, high school baseball, men's basketball, women's basketball, college baseball, and college softball. I refer to him as the biggest Cleveland Browns fan in Central Ohio, and he would give weekly reports on the Browns at halftime of our Dublin Jerome High School football games. On one weekend, Bill went to the Ohio State vs.

Rutgers football game in New Jersey, a night game, and drove to Cleveland after the game to make it in time the next day to see the Browns game, getting a few hours of sleep on the way..

Eric Welch. Room does not permit to describe everything about Eric, a Professor of Sport & Exercise Studies at Columbus State Community College, former baseball coach at many levels, Columbus Clippers broadcaster, and high school sportscaster. My favorite Eric Welch story: at a Columbus State basketball game, he was to insert the CD for the National Anthem, only to accidentally play the Rolling Stones' "If You Start Me Up". Eric has joined me to call high school football and baseball games for the Gameday Broadcasting Sports Network, and Ohio Wesleyan football and basketball games. Eric was also the color announcer when I worked the stats for a women's football game televised on Columbus Sports Network in 2007, played at Dublin Coffman High School.

Andrew Williamson, a member of Ohio Wesleyan's cross country and track teams, joined me for an Ohio Wesleyan baseball game when he was a freshman.

Ben Wolf joined me for some New Albany High School baseball games on the Gameday Broadcasting Sports Network and for Ohio Wesleyan basketball games.

Court Zeppernick, who has the Big Ten Network and local TV sports work on his resume, joined me for a Dublin Jerome High School basketball game for the Gameday Broadcasting Sports Network.

From WCVO-FM: Steve Biffle, Paul Gierman, Paul Leithart, Dan McLaughlin, Mike Rector, and Dan Wegner.

CHAPTER 10

MISHAPS, TECHNICAL DIFFICULTIES, AND THE LIGHTER SIDE

ANY BROADCASTER WILL TELL YOU that we need to expect the unexpected. Thankfully, some of these glitches were not of my doing!

On two occasions for high school football games, through a miscommunication, my broadcast partner did not show up. While many broadcasters have gone solo, at least they were prepared for it, but these were nightmares for me. During one of the games, a high school representative in the press box recognized my plight and bailed me out by grabbing a headset and chatting with me at halftime. During the other game, I was floundering through the broadcast, then was caught off-guard when I heard a voice in my headset describing the last play--our engineer decided to become a color announcer on the spot, for which I was grateful!

In the 1980s, I was on my way to the WCVO-FM studio on Reynoldsburg-New Albany Road in northeast Franklin County to pick up the equipment for the Gahanna at Reynoldsburg high school football game, only to have my car die on Morse Road near Hamilton Road. I was able to pull into a neighborhood, ask someone if I could use their house phone, get the car towed to a service station, borrow a car from a family member, and make it to the studio to get the equipment and then to

Reynoldsburg, with the game in progress. Paul Leithart was able to do the play-by-play to that point by calling on a phone to the studio, though he said that his arm was going numb from holding the phone.

In 2022, as Chris Intihar and I were calling a high school basketball game, we suddenly could not hear ourselves in our headsets. I saw that the thin power cord to our amplifier had become frayed, causing the problem. But, if I held it just right, the sound was fine. We survived the game, and the next day, a $6.00 splitter from a local music store gave us a long-term solution.

A lesson learned is to never assume that the football field for a high school is actually located at the high school. I experienced this for a Thursday night telecast by driving around the city of Chillicothe, eventually asking for directions. This has also happened at a different facility to a broadcast partner of mine, who shall remain nameless.

In 2021, I arrived at the brand-new Licking Heights High School to call the Dublin Jerome basketball game … or so I thought. I found the gym (actually, *a gym*), but there were only a few fans to be seen. Upon asking, I learned that I was at the middle school building; luckily, the high school was only about a half mile to the west.

At one high school football game in the 1980s, there was a nest—it may have had hornets or wasps, I'm not an entomologist—outside the auxiliary press box that was our location to call the game for WCVO-FM. During the game, we kept our eyes on three teams--the two on the field and the team of insects.

In 1983, the biggest Ohio State game of the year was the road trip to Oklahoma, which the Buckeyes won, 24-14. It was originally set to be my first-ever flight with the WOSU-TV crew to work at a road game, but the producers had to back off on that a few days before the game. I was totally fine with that on game day, as I was recovering in the Emergency Department of Riverside Methodist Hospital from a kidney stone that started attacking on Friday night, which could have been in mid-flight.

In 1986, I worked the stats for the three girls' basketball state championship games in Akron, televised by WCMH-TV in Columbus. The station arranged for a free hotel room for me, but when I checked in, the front desk had no reservation in my name. I asked them to look under "WCMH-TV" and the producer's name, but no luck, so I booked a room on my own. After settling in, I received a call from the front desk that the producer had arrived and settled the matter. Ohio State was playing at Ohio University that night in the first round of the National Invitation Tournament--the Buckeyes would win the NIT that year--and I had to call home to get the score. My mother gave me the good news, adding that the graphic on the TV screen noted that it was OSU Coach Eldon Miller's 400th career win.

During the Ohio State vs. Purdue football game of 1988, broadcast by WOSU-TV, analyst Paul Warfield had the best line of the year. Twins John and Mike Sullivan of the Buckeyes collaborated for a sack on defense, and Paul said, "Purdue has the Silver Twins, and the Buckeyes have the Sullivan brothers."

In 2010, Steve Geiger and I called the Big Walnut vs. Uniontown Lake high school football game in the third round of the playoffs for WINF-FM, played at the relatively new Jack Miller Stadium at Ashland University. I take pride in arriving at a game early, but this time, I was a bit late. Compounding this, trying to get my pass at the check-in gate, they had no record of me or WINF-FM. After much haggling, we determined that they had both my name and WINF-FM misspelled, so all was well. Needless to say, this was our first venue that year that had an elevator to its press box, a fact lost on Steve Geiger, who needed to catch his breath after climbing up the stadium steps. In addition, I had arranged for *Columbus Dispatch* reporter Steve Blackledge to join us for an interview at halftime. I had prepared a list of interview questions, which I handed to Steve Geiger to lead off with while I visited the restroom. When I returned, I took over the interview and asked Steve Blackledge a question. He responded, "Yeah, Steve Geiger just asked that question, and ..." Lesson learned!

I once threw Bill Walters a curve by having him read a list of other high school football games scheduled for that night. The only problem was that the list was in my shorthand–such as AC for Amanda-Clearcreek and BC for Bloom-Carroll–which obviously would not be clear to anyone else. At a high school basketball game about 15 years later, I had in my notes the fact that a player would be playing at ODU. Luckily, my broadcast partner asked in advance if ODU stood for Old Dominion University; in reality, it was Ohio Dominican University. You would think that a lesson had been learned!

At a high school basketball game in 2011 for WINF-FM, I had to search for an outlet to plug in the cell phone that we used for the broadcast. In the nick of time, Steve Geiger found a power cord that was used for the advertising mechanism and had an extra outlet, and all was well.

After working a high school football game at Bishop Hartley for 820 AM, our crew was the last group of attendees to leave the stadium, which took us several minutes trying to find an exit that was not locked!

Weather seemed to be a frequent problem when calling Columbus Academy High School football games for the Gameday Broadcasting Sports Network:

- One year at London High School in Madison County, threatening weather caused a 50-minute delay to the start of the game, which ended in a downpour. The next week, referring to my broadcast partner, I said in the pre-game segment, "We have Eric Welch on our broadcast for two reasons--for his vast knowledge of football, and the fact that he has an umbrella the size of Rhode Island."
- At another game, this one also in Madison County at Madison Plains High School, high winds knocked out power to the press box and the scoreboard for part of the game.

- Another was a home game against a very good North Union team. Since the game was also being televised on a Thursday night, Steve Geiger and I were set up on the roof. Naturally, rain started to fall in the fourth quarter, and we had to shut down our broadcast. Call it a coincidence, but Academy was ahead 24-10 at the time, only to lose in overtime.

On another occasion in Madison County, we had a televised Thursday night game at Jonathan Alder High School interrupted by weather at halftime, and it was unable to resume that night, so we televised only the first half of a game. While calling a game in the 1980s for WCVO-FM on a road game, we had a torrential downpour, and even though the windows of the press box seemed water-tight, rain was still coming in and seeping near our equipment, which we rescued in time.

In 2014, Eric Welch joined me on the Gameday Broadcasting Sports Network to call the semifinal high school baseball championship game between Gahanna Lincoln and North Royalton at Huntington Park, home of the Columbus Clippers. Testing the equipment, we could not hear anything in our headsets. I was going crazy, while Eric as usual was very calm, saying "Take it easy, walk through the steps." I even called the company owner Aaron Cassady, without luck; he was on a beach in Virginia. Ten minutes before the first pitch, I figured out what I had done wrong in plugging in the headsets, and we got on the air as if nothing had happened. I'll never make that mistake again; a different one, yes, but not that one.

… as in: At least twice, I forgot to plug the computer into the power strip, luckily seeing the "low battery" message in time. I have since learned to check the number of required plugs plugged into my power strip.

… as in: It might be a good idea to listen to the entirety of a recorded interview. Luckily, I had sent a recorded interview to my broadcast partner a few days before our game. He listened to all of it, and informed me that at the end, it had included some of the post-interview chit-chat that I had with my guest!

… as in: For the interviews where I use my digital recorder that plugs into the mixer with a cable, it might be a good idea to test the recording before going live. At one high school basketball game, I played an interview at halftime that turned out to be all garbled. This was when I had informed our listeners during the first half that my interview would be with Craig Krenzel, the quarterback on the 2002 Ohio State National Championship team. Luckily, I had a spare cable, swapped it, and the recording sounded perfect. Later, I learned that the issue was not inserting the cable just right, but the lesson learned was to test the recording before going live.

In the first high school football game of the 2014 season, our broadcast of the Columbus Academy at Grove City Christian game on the Gameday Broadcasting Sports Network died in the third quarter. The next day, after watching the Ohio State vs. Navy game, which was played in Baltimore, I tested the equipment, upon which smoke started coming out of the mixer. Thankfully, I was able to order and receive a new mixer in time for the next game.

In 2015, my third year of calling Columbus Academy High School football games for the Gameday Broadcasting Sports Network, the Academy Vikings had Robin Miller as their new coach. I always recorded my pre-game interview with the Academy coach on the field during the warm-up. In Coach Miller's first game, I turned on my recorder, and when I reached for my list of questions, they were nowhere to be found. Luckily, I got through the interview using my memory, finally seeing the notes on the ground after it was over.

In 2016, Milan Jordan and I wrapped up the Gahanna Lincoln at Pickerington Central high school football game. When shutting down the computer, I saw the message "Do you want to install Windows updates now?" Lesson learned: say no, since the updates took an hour to install.

Fortunately for me, a Pickerington Central staff member stuck around to let me finish before shutting down the press box.

More computer problems: in 2017, I was calling the Dublin Jerome at Dublin Scioto high school football game. The brand-new computer seemingly refused to boot up, finally doing so after seven minutes. The next week, I had an IT staff member at my work office look at it, and he determined that it was due to an anti-virus software that I had installed. After he uninstalled it, assuring me that the built-in Windows Defender was sufficient, the problem was solved!

Near the end of one high school football game where I was the play-by-play broadcaster, I handed my broadcast partner his pay for the game. He said "Thank you", which came across on the air and must have mystified our listeners. Lesson learned!

I worked the stats for Randy Rhinehart at a high school football play-off game. The third quarter ended after a team ran a play on second down, so the next play should have been a third down play. For some reason, when the fourth quarter started, the down marker showed fourth down, and the team with the ball punted. I passed Randy a note saying that it should be third down, but he was unsure whether to mention it on the air. The next day, I watched the replay. As soon as the fourth quarter began, my phone rang, with Randy calling to say "You were right!"

At one high school basketball championship game where I was working the stats, play resumed after a timeout with one team having six players on the court. D.C. Koehl, the long-time Ohio State Sports Information staffer who was in charge of the official stats, yelled to the officials, pointing it out. At another high school basketball championship game, play resumed after a timeout with a team having only four players on the court, so I guess that it all evens out.

At another high school basketball game, we had the challenge of identifying the players, because their numbers were only on the back of their jerseys.

I once was the timeout coordinator for a televised high school football playoff game, with my duty to be on the field and tell the referee when TV was ready to resume play. For the opening kickoff, the TV staff told me to stick by the referee at mid-field, so I gave him that heads-up. However, another official said to come with him to the end zone, which I did. Bad choice on my part--I lost communication with the referee, and the kickoff took place before the production staff was ready. I got yelled at by the director, rightfully so.

In two different basketball games at the same venue when I worked the stats, a player for the visiting team missed a free throw, but the scoreboard operator counted it as good! I tried to point it out to the athletic director, to no avail.

At a high school football game, the officials on two occasions allowed a kick returner to return the kickoff out of the end zone, which is not allowed in high school football.

After one championship game, our television sideline reporter interviewed the winning coach, with a long introduction such as "Congratulations .... This must be a big thrill for you ... You must be very proud of your team ..." We expected a long response from the coach, but all he said was "Thank you". I could hear the production staff in my headset break into laughter.

I HAVE HAD MY SHARE OF BRAIN FREEZES:

- For a 1978 high school basketball game on Warner QUBE, we had a live on-camera segment before the game to set the stage. I was talking about a player for Independence named Tom Brunet, but I blanked on his first name, so I called him "Mr. Brunet".
- When a penalty took place on a football broadcast, I said "That's 15 yards for Unsportsmanlike ... Contact?"

- After finishing a segment on high school basketball in the WCVO-FM studio, the engineer said that he would love to see the player whom I had described as having a "40 foot vertical leap."
- One factor in baseball games that we always pay attention to is the wind. During one Ohio Wesleyan game, Steve Leppert observed that there was no wind and said "That flag is still", and I said to myself: *That flag is still what? Still flapping? Still straight out? Is he going to finish his point?*
- At another Ohio Wesleyan baseball game, a runner trying to score was called out at home plate on a close call. My broadcast partner asked me "Did he look out to you?" Confused, I asked him to repeat the question. If he had said "Did he look to be out to you?" or "Did he appear to be out to you?", my brain may have thawed sooner. I thought that he was asking me if the runner was looking at me in the broadcast booth and thus "looking out to me"!
- In 2021, Ohio Wesleyan's shortstop on the softball team was Carly Schafer ... except that I mistakenly called her Carly Simon in a game. After Seth Duckworth set me straight, I tried to recover by saying that "Nobody Does it Better", and referring to her in the on deck circle with "Anticipation".

This was not me, but it could have been: a radio play-by-play broadcaster at a high school football game informed: "First and goal from the one-yard line ... short gain ... now it's second and less than goal."

I had a broadcast partner at a high school football game once who said that a team should not "*alleviate* from its game plan." I thought that it was a slip of his tongue, but a little later, he said, "*alleviate*" again. I let it go.

I had a high school basketball game where a team substituted in five players. My broadcast partner said that the team had "five fresh legs" on the court. I didn't ask him which five legs he was referring to.

Before each game, I connect with a team representative to get pronunciations. At one game, the roster listed the player's first name as "Aj". I asked "How do you pronounce that, is it 'Aj'? I was told *No, it should be "A. J."* One year, I called a player by the wrong first name all season, because that's how the program had it.

A common response at a high school basketball game, when I ask an assistant coach before the game how to pronounce a name, is: "I don't know, we just call him [nickname], let me ask him. *Hey [nickname]! How do you pronounce your name?*"

Oftentimes, fans at high school football games confuse us on the broadcast staff for the public address announcer, and will come up to our open window while a broadcast is progress and inform us "You are mispronouncing my son's name!" or "You are not giving my son credit for tackles!", or ask us "Has anyone turned in a set of keys?"

Some fans think that since I am wearing a shirt that has the home team's logo, I have control over game-day management, as in the time that I happened to be on the court at halftime and a fan from the visiting team pointed out to me that the visiting team had no basketballs to warm up with.

Public address announcers are often entertaining, such as the one at a high school football game who said "about" to describe each play, as in "Gain of about 4, ball is on about the 27-yard line ... Gain of about 2, ball is on about the 29-yard line." Another would grumble when a play went against his team, before turning on his microphone and describing the play in an unbiased, charming voice. My brother Mark was at a high school football game where the clock on the scoreboard was not working. At one point, the public address announcer informed that there was "considerably less than three minutes left in the game."

At one high school basketball game, I asked a woman who was obviously associated with the high school if the athletic director, whom I did not know, was in the gym. She pointed across the gym and said "That's him, standing next to Coach Smith (not his real name)." Later, I noticed that her badge showed that her last name was Smith. I was amused that she referred to her husband as "Coach Smith".

One challenge for us at a football game is the rare stadium that has the press box on the east side instead of the west, which means that in many early season games, we are looking into the sun. Another high school had the press box so low that it seemed to be at ground level, before remodeling made its new press box a great place to see a game.

Before one basketball game where I was working the stats, the graphics operator asked me "Can you keep track of points in the paint?" I replied "Only if Sherwin-Williams is a sponsor." Amazingly, I kept the gig.

After I interviewed Neal Billman–who had coached football at my Jones Junior High School, Upper Arlington High School, and Gahanna Lincoln High School–at halftime of a football game in 1990, I said on the air that the last time that I had seen Coach Billman, he told me to get a haircut and tuck my shirt in. Bill Walters responded that Coach Billman had told me the same after the interview!

In one of the years where I worked the stats for televised high school basketball games at the Greater Columbus Convention Center for the Coaxial National Hoops Classic, I told the broadcasters to avoid saying "He shot that from downtown!", because all shots in the game were from downtown.

At a game when my broadcast partner informed on the air that play was stopped due to a player not wearing his mouthguard, I said "The preceding announcement was brought to you by the American Dental Association", which produced polite laughter.

During a Dublin Jerome High School basketball game broadcast, Chris Intihar mentioned that the theme for the Jerome student section must be military appreciation, since many students were dressed in camouflage gear. I asked him that since they were in camouflage, how could he see them?

I had an Ohio Wesleyan basketball game where OWU scored late to cut the deficit to six points. Steve Geiger said that it was a two-possession game. I said something like "Wait a minute. The other team will have the ball and the Bishops need to get a stop, then the Bishops need to score, then the Bishops need to get a stop, then the Bishops need to score. Doesn't that make it a four-possession game?" Steve said that I was just confusing the fans. What's that saying--don't confuse me with logic?

With apologies to Robert Louis Stevenson, I once heard a player in an interview describing his team's inconsistency as a "Heckle and Jeckle" season.

I mentioned previously the Columbus Academy football game at Madison Plains High School where high winds knocked out power to the press box and the scoreboard for part of the game. At the next week's game, I threatened to recap that game by singing the lyrics from the musical *Oklahoma*: "Oklahoma, where the wind comes sweepin' down the plain."

During one high school baseball game that Aaron Cassady and I called for the Gameday Broadcasting Sports Network at Gahanna Lincoln's facility, a few miles from the high school and near a woody area, Aaron paused and noted that some riders on horseback had moseyed by near the left field fence. I asked him if the Stallions of Columbus St. Francis DeSales High School were supposed to play.

Another animal story: In 2021, when Chris Intihar and I called a Dublin Jerome High School football playoff game at Springfield High School, Chris observed that some deer had entered the baseball field that is behind the stadium and were grazing on the grass. Luckily, the football field had artificial turf.

It's fun to observe what's going on outside a football stadium while the game is in progress--such as the traffic on US Route 23 when calling a football game from Selby Stadium, a baseball game from Littick Field, and a softball game from Margaret Sagan Field on Ohio Wesleyan's campus; the traffic on Interstate 77 beyond Canton's Tom Benson Hall of Fame Stadium for football; the traffic on Interstate 71 behind the stadium at Grove City Christian High School; and the trains to the west of Worthington Kilbourne High School's football stadium.

I worked the stats for a game at Upper Arlington High School where the play-by-play broadcaster asked me if I knew how to pronounce the street that is the north border of the high school--Zollinger Road. Since the house that I grew up in while attending Upper Arlington High School was a few blocks away on Zollinger Road, it was my easiest task of the night!

At one Columbus Clippers game at Cooper Stadium, we had a visit from the Philly Phanatic, the mascot of the Philadelphia Phillies. Randy Rhinehart has a more vivid memory of this than I do; he writes: "The Phanatic game was when we were broadcasting from the first base overhang, and you didn't know he was there. He hit you with silly string, and you pushed him with two arms in the stomach and knocked him against the wall. Brute!"

In the Columbus Blue Jackets' first year of 2000-2001, I had an assignment to record player interviews after the pre-season game against the Pittsburgh Penguins. Having not followed the National Hockey League, at the conclusion of joining other reporters and sticking my microphone near a Penguins player in the locker room, I asked someone "Was that Mario Lemieux?" He looked at me as if I had two heads. I give myself credit for at least being aware that Mario Lemieux played for the Penguins.

In the Too Much Information department: in the interview after a race, I asked the winner what his training routine was, and he said "Sporadic ... My girlfriend just broke up with me, so I'll definitely get back into more training time."

In my first year of calling Ohio Wesleyan games, we had players from visiting teams named Paul Simon and Bob Dillon. Perhaps that offer in 1991 to be a disc jockey had come back to haunt me! Years later, my tongue is still raw from having to bite it during those games.

CHAPTER 11

RECAP

THE "LAST REGULAR SEASON GAME SYNDROME"–several occasions where the last regular season game had a dramatic conclusion:

- Of the 22 Ohio State vs. Michigan football games that I worked the stats, 10 were decided by five points or less: 1983, 1986, 1987, 1988, 1990 (a field goal by Michigan on the last play), 1996 (an interception by Michigan on the last play), 2002 (an interception by Ohio State on the last play), 2006, 2012, and 2016 (two overtimes).
- Olentangy Liberty beat undefeated Westerville South in boys basketball, 66-64 in 2011.
- Ohio Wesleyan beat undefeated DePauw in women's basketball, 65-64 in 2014, breaking DePauw's 77-game regular season winning streak.
- Ohio Wesleyan lost to DePauw in men's basketball on a three-point field goal with one second remaining to give DePauw a 64-63 win in 2014.

- In 2016, Pickerington North beat Gahanna Lincoln in football, 28-21 in overtime.
- In 2019, the Ohio Wesleyan vs. Denison men's basketball game had Denison winning, 95-94 in overtime.
- In 2019, Dublin Jerome lost to Hilliard Darby, 57-55 in boys basketball.
- Dublin Jerome beat Hilliard Darby in boys basketball, 61-60 in overtime in 2022.

The two high school basketball games that I called for WBBY-FM in 1976 had scores of 48-47 (in overtime) and 63-59. The first three high school basketball games that I called in my next gig, for Warner QUBE in 1977, had scores of 58-57, 50-48, and 59-57. That's five games decided by a total of ten points.

BY THE NUMBERS

- 1: Football Bowl Subdivision head coach for whom I attended one of his press conferences and who would become a United States Senator--Tommy Tuberville of Auburn, senator from the state of Alabama. The press conference was after the Sugar Bowl game of the 2004 season, which his team won.
- 2: Football Championship Subdivision teams for which I have worked at least one game--Youngstown State and Florida A&M
- 2: father/son coaches for whom I have called some of their high school basketball games. They are John W. Feasel and John Feasel, and Ed and Anthony Calo.
- 2: brother/sister pairs for whom I worked a game in which they played: Ronnie and Amber Stokes in the

Jump25.com 5th Annual Ohio College All-Star Classic, and Aaron and Cait Craft of Findlay Liberty-Benton

- 2: football teams whose games I worked the stats and finished with an 0-10 record–the Columbus Thunderbolts of the Arena Football League in its only season in Columbus in 1991 and Ohio Dominican University in its inaugural season of 2004

- 3: coaches for whom I worked the stats and who won college national championships--Fred Taylor for Ohio State men's basketball, Pete Hanson for Ohio State men's volleyball, and Tara VanDerveer for Stanford women's basketball

- 3: broadcast partners for whom I had called some of their basketball games for WCVO-FM when they played in high school. They are John Feasel, who played at Groveport Madison, Mick Shimp, who played at Gahanna Lincoln, and Doug Flowers, who played at New Albany. Mick became John's assistant at Olentangy High School, and both of them have joined me for Ohio Wesleyan games. Doug Flowers joined me for New Albany games.

- 4: sportscasters for whom I have worked the stats in at least one game and who appear in the cast of movies. Bob Costas, Joe Theismann, and John Gordon appeared on-camera, and The Internet Movie Database for the 1997 movie "Flubber" has "Pat Hughes ... Basketball Announcer (voice) (uncredited)".

- 4: the most Ohio State games that I worked in a Football Bowl Subdivision stadium other than Ohio Stadium. I worked those four games in Michigan Stadium, in 1983, 1985, 1987 (Earle Bruce's last game as coach), and 1989.

- 4: different broadcast outfits for whom I worked the stats for an Ohio State football game between 1980 and 1981–Warner QUBE, ESPN, WOSU-TV, and Metrosports
- 4: high schools where Brian Cross was the football coach and I worked one of his games–Eastmoor, Grove City, Olentangy Orange, and Bishop Ready
- 5: major college quarterbacks for whom I worked the stats--Greg Frey, Cornelius Greene, Jim Karsatos, Mike Pagel, and Joe Theismann
- 5: different basketball interactions with John Feasel. I broadcast one of his high school games when he played for Groveport Madison, I broadcast one of his girls high school games when he coached for Olentangy, I have broadcast some of his boys high school games in his current role at Olentangy, he has called Ohio Wesleyan men's games with me, and has called Ohio Wesleyan women's games with me.
- 5: The Capital University basketball team has had five coaches since 1968, and I have interacted with all five– Dave Grube (stats), Vince Chickerella (stats), Dave Cecutti (stats and broadcast partner), Scott Weakley (interview), and Damon Goodwin (a post-game interview when I called a Capital game and a pre-game interview when Capital played Ohio Wesleyan).
- 6: members of the 2010-2011 Ohio State men's basketball team for whom I worked the stats in one of their high school games–Jared Sullinger, J.D. Weatherspoon, Jon Diebler, David Lighty, Aaron Craft, and Jordan Sibert. All of them played in a tournament game that I worked at the Jerome Schottenstein Center.

- 8: the most games that I worked in one day. This was for scorekeeping 75-minute softball games.
- 9: the most Ohio State football games that I worked the stats in a season, in 1983 and 1984
- 9: consecutive years that I worked the stats for the Ohio State vs. Michigan game (1982 through 1990), the longest streak against any Ohio State opponent
- 9: winners of the Paul Walker Award presented by the Ohio High School Basketball Coaches Association whose games I worked: Greg Nossaman of Olentangy Liberty, Dave Butcher of Pickerington Central, Bob Miller of Thomas Worthington, Paul Wayne of Holgate, Jack Van Reeth of Millersburg West Holmes, Joe Petrocelli of Archbishop Alter, Harold "Doc" Daugherty of Euclid, Gene Milliard of Bexley, and Herb Russell of Grove City. David Sheldon, the Colonel Crawford boys coach and Ohio High School Basketball Coaches Association President informed that "The Paul Walker award is presented annually by the OHSBCA to an active coaching member of the association who has made significant contributions to high school basketball. The award is named in honor of the late Paul Walker, the longtime coach of Middletown High School. At the time of his retirement, he had the most wins as a boys' basketball coach in Ohio High School Basketball History."
- 11: states in which I have worked at least one game--Illinois, Indiana, Iowa, Kentucky, Louisiana, Michigan, New Jersey, North Carolina, Ohio, Pennsylvania, and Tennessee
- 15: stadiums in which I have worked at least one game involving a Football Bowl Subdivision team, including

eight in the Big Ten--Ohio State, Michigan, Michigan State, Purdue, Indiana, Northwestern, Illinois, and Iowa. The others are at Middle Tennessee State, Miami (Ohio), Akron, Ohio University, Toledo, Bowling Green, and the Superdome in New Orleans.

- 21: NCAA Division III universities in Ohio for which I have worked at least one game; I have worked a game for all 21.
- 23: high schools not in Ohio for which I have worked at least one game, including a team from Freeport, Bahamas
- 27: Ohio counties (out of 88) in which I have worked at least one game
- 51: NCAA Division III universities for which I have worked at least one game
- 73: Football Bowl Subdivision teams for which I have worked at least one game
- 105: the most number of games that I worked in a calendar year, in 2007
- 188: consecutive Ohio State home football games for which I worked the stats, from 1993 through 2019, before the pandemic reduced our staff for the 2020 season
- 312: high schools in Ohio for which I have worked at least one game

CHAPTER

EPILOGUE

AS OF MAY OF 2022,
I have now worked 2,113 games …
and counting.

PHOTO MEMORIES

Page 1 of my log of the over 2,001 games that I have worked, starting in 1975. Without the luxury of a personal computer, this was my tool of choice

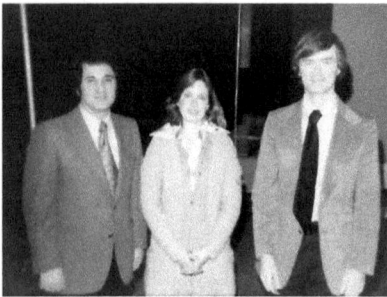

Red Jamison and me, doing our pre-game segment before the Grove City at Upper Arlington boys basketball game for Warner QUBE in 1978. My sports coat would have made Bob Knight envious

Bob Vincent, Mary Armentrout, and me, before the Upper Arlington at Grove City boys basketball game for Warner QUBE in 1978. Monday Night Football was not the only production with a three-announcer team.

John Gordon, Fred Taylor, and me at an Ohio Wesleyan basketball game for Warner QUBE in the 1980s. Thirty years later, Ohio Wesleyan would be my second home, as a play-by-play broadcaster

Me (pencil in hand), Bob Costas, and Fred Taylor at one of the two Ohio State men's basketball games that I worked for NBC in the 1980s. Two of the three of us are in a hall of fame.

Me, Jim Henderson, and Paul Warfield at Don Scott Field before one of our flights to an Ohio State football road game for WOSU-TV.

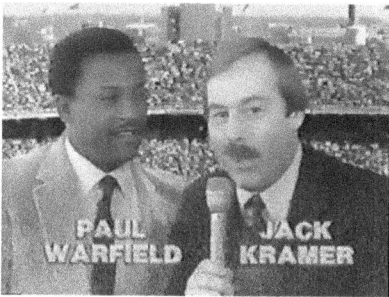

Paul and Jack doing their pre-game segment before an Ohio State game on WOSU-TV. I did the stats from 1981 through 1990

Steve Geiger and me at an Ohio Wesleyan football game. We have also called the men's and women's basketball games since the 2013-2014 school year.

Dave Purpura and photographer Shane Flanigan of ThisWeek Community News gave Chris Intihar and me some publicity during the pandemic.

While a game on ESPN has a satellite system, this is the corresponding setup for one of my high school basketball broadcasts, when space was limited.

www.ingramcontent.com/pod-product-compliance
Lightning Source LLC
Chambersburg PA
CBHW060300100426
42742CB00011B/1813